Kevin A Shepard

S0-BSZ-118

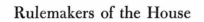
Rulemakers of the House

Rulemakers of the House

SPARK M. MATSUNAGA
AND
PING CHEN

UNIVERSITY OF ILLINOIS PRESS

Urbana   Chicago   London

© 1976 by the Board of Trustees of the University of Illinois
Manufactured in the United States of America

LIBRARY OF CONGRESS CATALOGING IN PUBLICATION DATA

Matsunaga, Spark M.
　Rulemakers of the House.

　Bibliography: p.
　Includes index.
　1. United States. Congress. House. Committee on
Rules. I. Chen, Yung Ping, joint author.
II. Title.
JK1430.R842M37　　328.73'07'65　　76-18985
ISBN 0-252-00626-7

To
THE HONORABLE JOHN W. MCCORMACK,
former Speaker of the United States
House of Representatives

A good, great man, who lived
by a code which he himself best
expressed: "If I were given a
choice, I would rather be known
as a good man than a great man."

Contents

Foreword

Spark M. Matsunaga is one of the most highly respected and truly effective members of the Congress, and we are indebted to him for undertaking the added task of distilling his experience in *Rulemakers of the House*. He is remarkably successful in this short work in defining the role of the House Rules Committee. As a member of that committee for the past ten years, he combines a theoretical approach with the excitement of its practical operations.

During the twenty-year period which this book covers, the Rules Committee underwent many basic changes, as its control shifted three times from one chairman to another. With his co-author, Dr. Ping Chen, Congressman Matsunaga guides the reader through the intricacies of the day-to-day actions and the interplay of opposing views during this fascinating period in the history of the House Rules Committee.

Rulemakers of the House promises to become one of the standard works in its field, and I commend it to all students of the legislative process, both within and outside the Congress.

CARL ALBERT
Speaker of the House

Preface

The Rules Committee is neither a regular standing committee of the House of Representatives (as are the legislative committees) nor a leadership organ (as is the whip organization); nevertheless, it has the organic structure of a legislative committee and carries out leadership functions. It is the rulemaker of the House.

As members of one of only three exclusive committees of the House, the Rules Committee members consider themselves entitled to at least the same legislative and personal goal satisfactions as their fellow legislators. These satisfactions can be achieved, it would seem, only when the Rules Committee plays the independent role of a decision maker. However, the very purpose of the Rules Committee makes it dependent on the leadership, because it is charged with relieving the leadership of its major tasks of 1) screening the numerous bills reported by the various House committees and 2) formulating a legislative program by setting priorities and rules for their consideration by the House. The committee is, thus, clearly operating under the leadership's authority, and the leadership necessarily demands a cooperative Rules Committee.

The authors set out to demonstrate that the historical role of the Rules Committee is one of searching for a balance between its own goals and those of the House leadership. Whenever the two sets of goals were balanced, harmony and stability existed between the leadership and the committee. However, because each has always attempted to gain an advantage, the harmony and stability which result from balanced sets of expectations have been short-lived. In

other words, the tension which exists between the goals of the
leadership (loyalty) and those of the committee (independence)
means that the optimal status of the committee, that of semi-independence, has been only temporary. As a result, the normal state
of the leadership–Rules Committee relationship is one of change.

The authors define the two sets of goals in Chapter 1. In Chapter
2, they discuss the means the committee has at its disposal to achieve
its goals. Chapter 3 spells out the sanctions which the House may
impose on the committee. The problem of membership recruitment
is the subject of Chapter 4. The goals of individual members and
their record of success in satisfying their goals are discussed in Chapter 5. In Chapter 6, the chairman's role is examined; the committee's image as independent, semi-independent, and subordinate in
relation to the leadership (during the chairmanships of Howard W.
Smith, William M. Colmer, and Ray J. Madden) is also discussed.
Finally, in Chapter 7 the authors attempt to assess the committee's
voting behavior and decisions by examining the past twenty years
of committee roll-call votes. Again in the context of the three chairmanships studied, the committee's success in meeting both the
leadership's demands for loyalty and its own goal of attaining independence is measured.

Studying the twenty-year period 1957 through 1976 enabled the
authors to examine the full range of the committee's relation to the
leadership during its independent (Chairman Howard Smith),
semi-independent (Chairman William Colmer), and subordinate
(Chairman Ray Madden) phases.

The senior author has been a participant-observer of the committee since 1967. In that year he was assigned to the committee to
replace the involuntarily retired Howard Smith. Matsunaga has
also had the good fortune of being able to observe the committee
from the vantage point of the leadership since his appointment as
a deputy majority whip in 1973. It goes without saying that he has
gained a noteworthy insight into the leadership-committee relationship, since he is a member of both parties to it. Moreover, one of
the book's sources, Congressman Thomas P. "Tip" O'Neill, Jr.
(D-Mass.), in his dual capacity as both the majority whip and a

senior member of the committee in the 92nd Congress, has proven to be a most knowledgeable aid to the authors on the subject of the leadership-committee relationship.

The experience of examining materials such as the committee minutes and roll-call votes, materials which are restricted to members,[1] has been rewarding. The limitations of this phase of the research, however, were as follows:

1. Until the 92nd Congress adopted the practice of making roll-call votes a matter of public record, the Rules Committee had made decisions primarily through voice votes and show of hands. Since the roll-call vote was the exception rather than the rule, the voting record, other than for roll calls, remains only as trustworthy as the memory of the participants.[2] Prior to the enactment of the 1970 Legislative Reorganization Act, the roll-call votes in the committee were confidential, although it was always possible for newsmen to attempt to poll the individual members to find out how they voted.

2. Until the 93rd Congress began the practice of keeping verbatim minutes for the Rules Committee proceedings, the committee's hearing minutes were mere outlines and its executive session minutes were in fact summaries.[3]

The authors interviewed fifty-nine members of the House during a period of four years (1970-1974; see Appendix A-1) with marked emphasis on the leadership and the committee itself. They were kindly granted interviews by both on an annual basis. They were also privileged to speak at length to the three chairmen of the Rules Committee covered in this book. The authors also found it helpful to have had the opportunity to interview chairmen and ranking members of other committees and Rules staff members.

Both structured and unstructured methods were employed (for sample questions, see Appendix A-2), and because of the trust his colleagues placed in Matsunaga, the authors almost invariably were able to use a cassette recorder to assure accuracy and conserve time. For this reason the selected quotes in this volume are directly attributed to those interviewed. Consequently, the reader who is seriously interested in the work of the Congress is permitted to judge for himself the merit and significance of these direct quotations.

This work, it is hoped, will contribute to the understanding of the Rules Committee, whose members are truly "the Rulemakers of the House."

The writing of a book can never be successfully accomplished without the counsel and assistance of those who, for friendship or other reasons, offer such counsel and assistance. While there are many to whom we are grateful, we wish especially to thank Barry S. Rundquist, assistant professor of political science, University of Illinois, and Jerome B. Long, associate professor of philosophy, Eastern Illinois University, for their critical view of the entire manuscript.

We wish also to thank the Council on Faculty Research of Eastern Illinois University for making a grant available to us to do the necessary research for this volume.

To Gene Sumner, Diana Nichols, Sue Smith, Mohammed Zabarah, Harold Cumbo, Su-hui Tung, and Julie Hall, who all assisted us as individuals during the five-year period of our struggle, we express our special appreciation.

Karen Steele, now a member of Congressman Paul Simon's staff, deserves special mention for having volunteered her researching and proofreading services to us over a four-year period. Other volunteer assistants in this area were Virginia Ing, Dolly Apo, Cherry Matano, Gwen Fukagawa, Grace Miyasaki, and Gladys Karr. To them we are grateful.

To the Rules Committee staff members, and former staff members Mary Spencer Forrest and Robert Hynes, who lent us their fullest cooperation, we say "thank you."

And finally, to Speaker Carl Albert, former Speaker John McCormack, Majority Leader Tip O'Neill, Majority Whip John McFall, Rules Committee Chairman Ray Madden, former Chairmen Howard Smith and William Colmer, Congressmen John Anderson, Richard Bolling, Dave Martin, Claude Pepper, James Quillen, and B. F. Sisk, and former Congressman William Anderson, without whose interviews the substance of this volume would not have been available, we owe our deepest gratitude. We thank them one and all.

NOTES

1. U.S. Congress, House, Committee on Rules, *Rules of Procedure,* 5 (d).

2. The Rules Committee employs voice, show of hands, and roll call as the three main methods of voting, as do all other committees. While any member can demand a roll-call vote, the majority of votes are cast without recording the individual members' votes. It is a general rule for members not to ask for roll-call votes unless the motion in question is controversial. As Congressman John Anderson (R-Ill.) has put it, "I just like to see a record vote on everything. I don't see any reason why we should hide behind voice votes. . . . I'll be very honest and say that I have hesitated on many occasions to request a record vote knowing that other members of the committee could be offended and put on the spot." Interview, March 12, 1971.

3. Beginning with the 93rd Congress, the Rules Committee, as most of the committees of the House, has been conducting business in open sessions. According to present practice, it would take a recorded vote to get the committee to go into closed session.

Rulemakers of the House

1

The Role of the Rulemakers

HOUSE AND LEADERSHIP EXPECTATIONS

ARM OF THE LEADERSHIP

John W. McCormack, former Speaker of the United States House of Representatives, described his conception of the House Rules Committee in this way, "The Rules Committee is the political arm of the Speaker in enabling the House to consider and enact legislation reported by other committees of the House."[1] Carl Albert expressed similar views: "The Rules Committee is the Speaker's committee, not merely a traffic-cop or staff function. It is the manifestation of division of labor."[2]

The leaders of the majority party consider the Rules Committee an instrument of the majority leadership, but of course the minority leadership also expects its members of the committee to be loyal to it. President Gerald Ford, while House minority leader, voiced this expectation: "Our minority members of the Rules Committee have shown a high degree of cooperation with me and the other leaders. If the Republicans were in the majority in the House, our ten members on the committee would be expected to follow the same practice and pattern of cooperating with the leadership."[3]

In a structured interview, the authors asked thirty-four House Democrats and seventeen House Republicans, "Should the Rules Committee be an arm of the leadership?" Twenty-four Democrats (70.5%) and nine Republicans (53%) replied affirmatively. Four out of nine Southern Democrats (44.5%) professed adherence to the "arm of the leadership" theory (see Appendixes A-1 and A-2, pp. 180, 182).

Another index of the Rules Committee's role as an arm of the leadership is seen in the close working relationship between the other committee leaders (chairmen or ranking minority members) and the Rules Committee. The view typical of Democratic chairmen was expressed by George Mahon (D-Tex.), chairman of the House Appropriations Committee: "Of course somebody has to set the schedule and the Speaker and the leaders are responsible for this so the guiding hand of the Rules Committee is very important. Before a member goes on Rules, he more or less assures the majority party, or the minority party, whichever he belongs to, that he will, within the bounds of reason, cooperate with the leadership."[4]

Senior Republicans of the House on the whole agreed with their Democratic counterparts in recognizing the leadership's closeness to, and influence over, the Rules Committee. The late Congressman John Saylor (R-Pa.), while ranking minority member of the Interior Committee remarked: "It [the Rules Committee] is the Speaker's own committee. Because the Speaker must represent his party and his political philosophy, the members of that committee more than any other committee of the Congress must subvert their own personal feelings in their approach to legislation."[5] A senior Republican has also alluded to this point: "I would say that the members of the Rules Committee, to the extent possible, should go along with the House leadership on their side. Loyalty to party leadership is going to be mighty important even to the Republicans."[6]

There appears to be little doubt that both the House leadership and members on both sides of the aisle, with only differing degrees of emphasis, expect the Rules Committee to serve as the instrument of the leadership.

Expected Partisanship

Although loyalty to the party is not necessarily equivalent to loyalty to the House leaders, the respective leaders still like to think that they are their parties' true voices in the House. Making this clear, Speaker McCormack said, "The Rules Committee is expected to cooperate with the Speaker whenever the committee has difficulty in ascertaining the spirit of the party platform."[7] McCormack obviously saw being the final arbiter of questions pertaining to the Democratic Party program as one of the roles of the Speaker.

While party loyalty could mean a dozen different things to a dozen different people, all House leaders queried in structured interviews conducted by the authors in 1971-1972, and a majority of the Democrats and some of the Republicans, expected the members of the Rules Committee to be loyal to their respective parties in some general way. Speaker Albert, Majority Leader Thomas "Tip" O'Neill, Jr. (D-Mass.), former Minority Leader Gerald R. Ford, and former Minority Whip Leslie Arends (R-Ill.) all agreed that "loyalty to party platform" is one of the obligations the Rules Committee should fulfill. In addition, twenty-three Democrats (67.8% of the total interviewed) and five Republicans (29.4% of the total interviewed) also concurred with the statement, "the Rules Committee should be loyal to the party platform."

On the subject of partisanship, O'Neill commented, "I believe the members of the Rules Committee should adhere to the philosophy of their party."[8] The comments of Chairman George Mahon and those of the late Frank Bow (R-Ohio), then ranking minority member of the Appropriations Committee, are probably indicative of what their colleagues expect of the members of the Rules Committee. Mahon said, "I think the party platform should be given consideration, but not to the same extent as the wishes of the leadership";[9] and Bow commented: "I'm on the Committee on Committees on the Republican side and we've had occasion several times to pick a member for the Rules Committee. What I have tried to do is to get a good party man who will go down the line with the Republican Party."[10]

INDIFFERENCE TO PRESIDENTIAL WISHES

The House leadership and membership do not expect the Rules Committee to heed the wishes of the incumbent President even if he happens to be the chief of the Rules Committee member's own party. Carl Albert, questioned in an interview while he was majority leader in 1970, did not name the presidency as one of the institutions to which the Rules Committee should owe its allegiance.

Nor did Gerald Ford, questioned in 1971 while he was minority leader and a Republican was President, mention the President as someone to whom the Rules Committee should be loyal. Out of five Democratic leaders above the majority whip level interviewed by the authors during the period of 1970-73, only the late Hale Boggs (D-La.), while majority leader, suggested that the President deserved some loyalty from the Rules Committee.

Thirty-four Democratic congressmen responded to the same interview question, and only six of them (17.7%) thought that the Rules Committee ought to heed the President's wishes, and then only after those of the House leadership and the party power structure. The Republicans, similarly, do not expect the Rules membership to be very loyal to the President even when a Republican is in the White House. Only three (17%) of the seventeen Republicans who responded to this question wanted the Rules Committee to owe some degree of allegiance to the White House.

The authors' study seems to indicate that the House members, and particularly the leadership, expect the committee to make a proper contribution to the stability of the House–Rules Committee relationship. It may be, however, that "proper contribution" means that the committee must subordinate itself to the leadership of the majority party internally and remain independent from all pressures, even presidential, externally. The general concept appears to be that the Rules Committee must remain responsive to the will of the House, as vested in and exercised by the leadership of the majority party.

COMMITTEE EXPECTATIONS

Fulfillment of House Expectations

Richard Fenno, in emphasizing the importance of the Appropriations Committee's striving to satisfy the expectations of the House, wrote: "From the perspective of the Appropriations Committee, its relationship with the parent chamber can be stated, most abstractly, as one which centers on the problems of adaption to the environment. Given the kinds of sanctions which the House can and has exercised over the Appropriations Committee, the Committee cannot survive unless its behavior satisfies House expectations as to what that behavior should be."[11]

The same type of relationship exists between the Rules Committee and the House. However, the House would be inclined to demand even more explicit accommodations to its expectations from the Rules Committee than from its Appropriations Committee because the Rules Committee is generally regarded as an instrument of the House leadership, to be used, as necessary, even for partisan policy prosecution. The Rules Committee can survive only so long as it conscientiously attempts to satisfy House expectations.

Acceptance of this proposition means a definite diminution of the independence and power of the Rules Committee, but members of the committee themselves openly subscribe to it. Congressman Richard Bolling of Missouri, a long-standing Democratic leader of the committee, viewed the situation this way: "In my judgment, the Rules Committee should exercise the power on behalf of the leadership to forward bills, stop bills, give bills an advantage or give them disadvantages. In other words, it's an arm of the leadership to forward the proposals of the party. I believe this very strongly. As a matter of fact, I would actually favor returning to the situation where the Speaker was the chairman of the committee."[12]

Ray Madden (D-Ind.), interviewed in 1970 when he was the ranking majority member of the committee, saw an unmistakable obligation of a Rules Committee member to the House leadership: "The Rules Committee should be the policy committee of the party that is in power. A member of the committee who belongs to the party in power should go along with the leadership."[13] Even former Chairman William Colmer (D-Miss.), who was never known to be subordinate to the leadership's wishes in all his thirty-one years of service on the committee, recognized the necessity of having the committee cooperate with the leadership. He stated, "The members of the Rules Committee should cooperate with the leadership without violating their own principles."[14]

Thus it seems quite clear that the Democratic members of the Rules Committee perceive their role as one of agreeing with the leadership, if not being subservient to it, in the attainment of House majority wishes or the party platform. Republican members of the committee harbor a similar partisan loyalty. John B. Anderson (R-Ill.) a senior member of the committee (who relinquished his ranking minority seat to retain his chairmanship of the Republican conference in the 93rd and 94th Congresses) voiced the prevailing sentiment among his party colleagues:

> I think that in the interests of harmony and party loyalty there is a conscious effort on the part of those Republicans who serve on the Rules Committee to try to harmonize their views with the Policy Committee where that is possible; I think it's necessary in our democratic process and under our representative form of government that we do have a degree of loyalty to a party. Without that, if everybody feels absolutely unfettered and free to go his own way without any compunction, it seems to me that you have the kind of fragmentation that makes it difficult for a party to function very usefully and effectively.[15]

CONVERGENCE OF LEADERSHIP AND COMMITTEE EXPECTATIONS

In pointing out the inevitability of tension in the relationship between the Appropriations Committee and the House, Fenno wrote: "Tensions are inherent in the Committee-House relationship. Short of a total convergence of system and subsystem, these tensions cannot be eliminated. But they can be controlled so that the relationship remains reasonably stable."[16]

A similar tension exists in the Rules Committee–House leadership relationship. A major point of difference is that, theoretically at least, it is not impossible to converge the goals of the House leadership and those of the committee. If reduction of tension were the objective, convergence could be accomplished in at least two ways: 1) By abolishing the Rules Committee and having the Speaker's or the majority leader's staff perform the committee's functions; and 2) By including the leadership as members of the Rules Committee.

In suggesting that the Rules Committee be relieved of its scheduling functions, James Robinson, author of a descriptive work on the committee, wrote as follows:

And in the U.S. House of Representatives, these [scheduling] functions could be performed by someone other than the Rules Committee. Why not the majority party leadership? As of now the leadership shares these responsibilities: after the Rules Committee grants a rule the Speaker and Majority Leader decide when to call it up, and when the rule is adopted the leadership determines when to debate the bill. Why not, then, leave it to the Speaker to recognize the Majority Leader to offer a privileged motion that the House consider a bill reported by a committee, under certain conditions governing time and amendments?[17]

Robinson failed to mention the necessary increase of responsibility on the part of the leadership staff should his proposed scheme be implemented. In effect, *Speaker–majority leader* scheduling would mean *staff* scheduling. The Speaker or majority leader by himself cannot possibly study the vast number of bills reported out of the legislative committees. The question "Can this [scheduling] function be carried out just as effectively by the staff members of the Speaker or majority leader?" was posed to leaders on both sides of the aisle, as well as to Rules Committee members. The answer was an emphatic "no" even from those who held the strong conviction that the Rules Committee ought to be the obedient servant of the majority leadership. Congressman Richard Bolling explained his negative response: "I don't think that you can do that. I think that you have to have the people exercise the power and have the responsibility who are elected by the people. After all, the members are elected and the leadership is elected, that is the way representative government works. I don't think that you can delegate a function of power held by people who hold elective offices to the staff."[18] Carl Albert, interviewed when he was the majority leader in 1970, was quite emphatic when he said: "I wouldn't want to have the staff take over. The members are constitutionally elected and possess the good judgment to render this responsibility."[19]

There are many good reasons why the staff of the leadership cannot perform the leadership scheduling functions. A few of these reasons may be noted:

1. A staff without the confidence of the members would be in no position to assess intelligently the mood of the House, a vital

process in setting priorities for bills to be considered by the House.

2. The staff, lacking access to the communication channels open to the members of the House, would be unable to make proper decisions on the requirements of specific rules.

3. The staff, being only hired help and not elected members of the House, would have neither the power nor the prestige to protect the leadership or legislative committees from undue internal or external pressures.

Whatever the reason may be, it is highly improbable that convergence will be accomplished through replacement of the Rules Committee by leadership staff.

A second alternative method of converging the goals of the House leadership and the Rules Committee to lessen tensions is to designate the Speaker and majority leader as members of the committee. The proposal is not without precedent for history reveals that the Speaker was, in fact, a member of the Rules Committee from 1858 until 1910. In 1910, Speaker Joseph G. Cannon (R-Ill.) was removed from the committee as a result of the so-called revolution led by Congressman George Norris (R-Nebr.). The Legislative Reorganization Act of 1946 made the Speaker eligible to "rejoin" the committee, but Speakers Joseph Martin, Sam Rayburn, and John McCormack all chose not to claim membership.[20] Speaker Carl Albert has also declined to exercise his right to membership on the committee.

In the historical context of Speaker Cannon's abuse of power, it is understandable why the later Speakers declined to participate directly in the committee's affairs. It is perhaps yet too soon for a Speaker to risk identification with possible "Czarism" and with Cannon's way of making the Rules Committee his own instrument of political power. This is especially true if the Speaker can receive reasonable cooperation from the committee by using other sanctions and means.

By accident rather than design, certain Democratic Party leaders have been members of the Rules Committee in recent years. Tip O'Neill served on the committee while he was majority whip. Spark M. Matsunaga (D-Hawaii), a member of the committee, is currently a deputy Democratic whip. In contrast, the ranking Republican on the committee has always been a member of the Republican leadership. However, the recent history of the House would seem to indicate that this arrangement merely suggests better committee-leadership liaison rather than leadership control.

TENDENCY TOWARD COMMITTEE INDEPENDENCE

It can be theorized without serious objections that an institution ceases to exist as such whenever it becomes completely ruled by environmental pressures. Whether the Rules Committee members recognize this theory or not, while they publicly acknowledge the subservient role of the committee to House and leadership expectations, they also attempt to exert their independence as individual members, as well as a committee, from environmental constraints.

Individual members of the Rules Committee, while expressing a willingness to adapt themselves to the expectations of the leadership or of the party, invariably qualify their willingness with some form of escape clause. They do this so that they can show a genuinely independent attitude, if necessary because of philosophical convictions, constituency pressures, or national interests.

Tip O'Neill, while still a member of the committee, gave an example of the independent spirit of its members when he said, "No one should be bound by any commitments that would transcend his own philosophy and feelings on any issue."[21] And Congressman B. F. Sisk (D-Calif.), who displayed increasing independence in the 93rd Congress, commented in 1973: "On the one hand, I do agree that the committee should be cooperative with the leadership. On the other hand, I don't necessarily feel that we have sold our souls to the leadership and are totally dictated to by the leadership. We can work closely with the leadership without necessarily surrendering our independence of action and our right to vote for the things we believe in, according to our own conscience."[22]

District pressure also frequently determines a member's voting behavior in the House. This was found to be true of the members of the Rules Committee, despite its being ostensibly an arm of the leadership. A Democratic Rules Committee member was not expected to render loyalty to the leadership or to the party at the expense of his constituency interests. On the principle that "a defeated loyalist is no loyalist" it was understood that the loyal member had to be permitted a certain flexibility in voting in the committee, especially when clear constituency pressure was present. Reelection of the member is paramount to the member and necessary for the party to remain in the majority to retain control of the House.

Ray Madden spoke of the importance of rating one's constituency higher than the leadership when he remarked, "I would vote against the leadership if my constituency is positively against a specific bill."[23] Former Representative William Anderson (D-Tenn.), a McCormack appointee, made the point concerning survival at the polls very effectively when he remarked: "In Tennessee and within my district in particular, I would say that the constituents were more than nine to one strongly opposed to the gun control bill (H.R. 17735-90th). At the same time, Speaker McCormack was dedicated to moving this bill through the House. He was initially pretty upset that I decided not to go along with him, but understood that my constituents do have to come first; otherwise I doubt that I would be here now."[24]

If committee members of the Democratic majority have expectations of independence, certainly the Republicans, who have fewer obligations to assist their leadership in its legislative programs because of their minority status, would have a more independent attitude. How, it may be asked, do the Republicans invest this attitude with respectability? John B. Anderson (a recognized leader of the liberal Republican faction in the House) refers to the national interest as his justification for independence: "[In the Rules Committee's work] you have that tug and conflict between party loyalty and what you think is in the best interest of the country. I have to say that if it's between those two standards, i.e., the party loyalty and the overall public interest, I think the former has to give way."[25] James Quillen (R-Tenn.), while not known for his disagreement with the Republican leadership, nevertheless buttresses independence by citing the convictions proper to each member as an individual: "I don't think that the members of the Rules Committee would let loyalty to their party and leadership go beyond their convictions. I think first of all they must speak for themselves."[26]

Thus, the Republicans, because of their minority position and lack of responsibility for the legislative program, except for a brief time in the period studied, had less difficulty than the Democrats with conflicts between their leaders' wishes and constituency demands or philosophical considerations.

Whatever its real motivation may be — philosophy, constituent demand, public interest, etc. — whenever this individual independence is exercised, as it is from time to time, Rules Committee members contribute, purposely or incidentally, to the attainment of committee independence.

Rules Committee members can also gain a degree of independence for the committee by identifying themselves with the leadership, not as obedient servants but as decision-making partners. The committee's image as the *independent* arm of the leadership can, of course, aid its search for independence. Thus, it is of paramount importance to the members that the committee be recognized as a "leadership committee." How dear to the committee members, then, must have been the words of Speaker Carl Albert when he spelled out this very quality in a speech at the portrait-unveiling ceremony honoring Chairman Madden on October 25, 1973: "This group [the Rules Committee] more than any other group must have national field leadership quality unimpaired by the particular slant which it has toward the importance of a particular field of legislation. This committee is geared as it has never been geared before, in my opinion, to the main thrust of the two great political parties which make up the government instrument of our nation. It is the legislative committee leader of the House."[27]

Walter Kravitz, a senior specialist in American government at the Library of Congress, defined the committee's role in a similar way when he wrote the following: "In short, the Committee on Rules is to a large degree the governing committee of the House. To it the House has largely delegated the power to regulate procedure vested in the House itself by the Constitution. Furthermore, by virtue of its influence in determining the order and the content of floor business, the committee may also function as a 'steering' committee, steering the House in whatever directions the exigencies of the hour appear to demand."[28]

Although it is doubtful that Albert and Kravitz had the committee's independence expectations in mind when they used these words, it is hardly contestable that the committee would end its search for independence if it were to become fully identified as a decision-making partner of the leadership. It would then have its independent attitudes and actions legitimized. In this connection, a former minority counsel of the committee, Robert Hynes, provides the interested observer of the Rules Committee with the following insight: "If at one time or another they [committee members] find themselves on different sides of an issue, they can invoke the leadership's authority, either to move forward with something or to hold something back. Naturally their main argument is 'well, let's do what the leadership wants.' The fact of the matter is, it *just happens also to be what they want.*"[29] (italics added)

The President of the United States, in full recognition of the role of the Rules Committee in the legislative process, has from time to time attempted to influence its members by direct contact. President Lyndon B. Johnson frequently telephoned individual members for support of specific measures pending committee action. President Richard M. Nixon attended private lunches with the committee and presented gifts to its individual members. To what extent such presidential overtures were successful in influencing the actions of the committee is not known. However, enough concern has been expressed in this area to warrant serious study.

Robinson has argued that a centralized leadership in the House would help Congress gain more independence from the presidency.[30] House leaders and members may have some such centralization thesis in mind when they speak of expecting the Rules Committee to be independent from the White House. However, although Rules Committee members would also like to have independent status vis-à-vis the presidency, they are not necessarily thinking in terms of enhancing their loyalty to the House leadership.

Democrat William Anderson of Tennessee, while a member of the committee, stated: "You know, I am very much a believer in the principle of the loyal opposition. I don't think that the members of the Rules Committee should go along with the President just for the sake of going along."[31] Former member Clem R. Mc-

function, whereas five (three Democrats and two Republicans) ranked the traffic-cop, rule-setting function as first. It appears that in the eyes of the members of the Rules Committee, the two functions are equally rated.

The function of the Rules Committee is perhaps best understood as being a constituent body. In other words, the committee attempts to satisfy the House and leadership expectations, as well as its own goal expectations, through its role as the constituent body of the House in the same way a constitutional convention serves in each and every state. It can write any new rule and amend any old rule, subject, of course, to the approval of the House. Former Congressman Durward Hall (R-Mo.) described the constituent power of the committee in this way: "Our Committee on Rules can do anything regardless of precedents, or the rule of the House, as long as the House will support it."[6]

On this point, William Mailliard, ambassador to the Organization of American States and former Republican representative from California, commented, "The Rules Committee cannot usurp power. Anything the Rules Committee recommends has to be approved by a vote in the House as they don't have any power except what the House gives to them."[7] But although its actions are subject to House approval, the committee does initiate all the "fundamental laws" for the House in the same manner a constituent assembly does for a nation. The House or the nation, as the case may be, merely ratifies the proposals. The difference between the power to propose and the power to ratify should be quite obvious.

To enable the Rules Committee to satisfy the leadership's demands and its (the committee's) own goal expectations, the House has granted the committee a vehicle called the rule-making or constituent power. It is by using this power that the committee accomplishes its aims. A discussion of the various aspects of the committee's constituent power follows.

LEGISLATIVE POWERS — PRE–HOUSE PASSAGE

SUBSTANTIVE CONTROL OF LEGISLATION

The Rules Committee determines the priorities to be assigned to each one of the various measures referred to it for House floor consideration. In performing this function, the committee acts quite independently, except that it normally yields to the wishes of the House leadership in matters of national priority or partisan interest. In these matters, to be sure, the committee does serve as an arm of the leadership. Nevertheless it has demonstrated, time and again, a fierce independence, and it can and does, not infrequently, frustrate the desires of the leadership. Such independence was prevalent during Howard Smith's chairmanship. Since the enlargement of the committee, however, and especially since the assumption of the chairmanship by William Colmer, the committee has in fact functioned as an arm of the House leadership in exercising its priority-setting power. It has not completely lost its autonomous spirit, however. In the 91st Congress, for example, the committee upheld Chairman Colmer's stubborn refusal to take any action on the Equal Employment Opportunity Act (H.R. 17555-91st), despite repeated pleadings from the Speaker and majority leader to schedule the nationally significant measure for committee action. In the 90th Congress, too, the expressed wishes of the House leadership for a rule on the Common Situs Picketing Act (H.R. 100-90th) were completely ignored.

The power to time or schedule the release of bills for floor action provides the committee with great control over legislation. Upon the formal or informal request of the leadership, the committee may expedite or delay its action on any bill. The effect of this timing could be to kill a bill or to insure its passage, depending upon the mood of the House. Of course, the committee could choose to withhold and kill a bill in committee regardless of the wishes of the leadership or the mood of the House, as it did in the case of the Equal Employment Opportunity Act referred to earlier.

"Traffic-Cop" Function

The complexity of the House rules governing debate on the floor affords the Rules Committee great latitude in setting the rules of debate on a bill, thus permitting it to influence the fate of the bill. In this respect, the Rules Committee, with its power to grant or refuse a rule, serves as a veritable legislative "traffic cop." It determines not only when and how a bill shall be debated, but also how long the debate shall continue, and it may even kill the bill by refusing to grant it a rule. Even though this power represents a leadership function in the sense that it directly affects the legislative program, the leadership has been quite willing, except on rare occasions, to delegate it to the committee.

In setting the rules for debate, the Rules Committee has the following options open to it:

1. The committee may grant an "open rule" for the consideration of a bill on the House floor. Under this rule any member may offer amendments to the bill under consideration, provided such amendments are germane to the subject matter of the bill itself. This is the usual rule granted, since it provides the widest latitude for the House to work its will. It best satisfies the demand for maximum participation by the House membership in the democratic legislative process, despite the fact that it is most time-consuming and that it at times frustrates the original sponsors of the bill by permitting amendments which alter the original bill beyond recognition.

2. The committee may go to the other extreme and grant a bill a "closed rule." Under this rule no amendments (except those offered by the chairman or ranking minority member of the committee with original jurisdiction) will be allowed, and the House membership will be permitted only to vote the bill up or down in its entirety (as reported out by the legislative committee). The Committee on Ways and Means has traditionally taken all of its tax measures to the floor under a closed rule. The reason for this is that tax laws are so technical and complicated that it would be foolish and even dangerous to attempt to write a tax measure on the floor. A single innocent-looking amendment, proponents of the closed rule say, could adversely affect the entire tax structure. It would only be to seek a closed rule or a waiver of points of order that the Committee on Ways and Means would appear before the Rules Committee, for Ways and Means is privileged to report its bills directly to the House floor under an open rule if it so chooses.

Other legislative committees on rare occasions request and obtain a closed rule on extremely involved and technical measures to avoid crippling amendments which may doom the bill to certain failure. The Sugar Act amendments bill of 1971 (H.R. 8866-92nd) with its enlarged South African sugar quota, for example, was granted a closed rule, for it obviously would have run into extreme difficulty if it had been granted an open rule.[8] Although the request for a closed rule is rarely denied where it is deemed proper, members of the committee are becoming increasingly reluctant to grant such requests because they are more and more persuaded that the House should be as free to work its will as the Senate, which is not bound by any such rule.

Since 1973 there has been more willingness on the part of the Committee on Ways and Means to forego requesting a closed rule on every measure. Congressman Herman Schneebeli (R-Pa.), ranking minority member of that committee, has offered this explanation:

> Traditionally, the committee got a closed rule on almost all legislation it proposed. Then there came a conviction that we didn't need a closed rule on everything, just on big, broad bills where self-serving amendments which were not for the good of the country might cause harm to the whole bill. For instance, we're going in today to the Rules Committee to ask for a rule on the debt ceiling bill which I think always in the past has been a closed rule. Well, we're asking for an open rule this time because we want the Rules Committee to realize that we're being very careful and conscientious in trying to observe the wishes of the House, and we're going to try to reserve our requests for a closed rule to that legislation which specifically needs it.[9]

3. As a compromise between the harsh, undemocratic closed rule and the time-consuming, democratic open rule, the Rules Committee may grant a bill a "modified closed rule." Under this rule, only specified sections of the bill will be open to amendments or only certain specified amendments to the bill will be allowed.

In discussing a rule for the income (surcharge) tax bill (H.R. 12290-91st), the senior author proposed a rule which would permit any member of the Ways and Means Committee to offer amendments only to increase revenues. Madden proposed a rule to permit the acceptance of the Vanik amendment (H.R. 13270-91st) to the bill. In the 92nd Congress, the committee granted a modified closed rule to permit a separate vote on the family assistance plan, Title II of the Social Security Act amendments (H.R. 1-92nd).

Various procedural possibilities (ways of handling a bill on the floor) may also be outlined in a modified closed rule.

4. To permit the House membership to make a choice between conflicting proposals, one of which may be subject to a point of order on grounds of nongermaneness, the Rules Committee may permit an amendment in the nature of a substitute. The substitute may be, and usually is, in the form of an entirely different bill, which will be permitted as an amendment to the bill being reported out. For example, Matsunaga, in an effort to remove the specter of American concentration camps, introduced H.R. 234-92nd, which called for the repeal of the Emergency Detention Act of 1950. This bill was referred to and subsequently reported out of the House Judiciary Committee in 1971. The Internal Security Committee, claiming jurisdiction over the subject matter, reported a bill (H.R. 820-92nd) introduced by its own chairman, Richard Ichord (D-Mo.), to amend the Detention Act in a mild way but not to repeal it. The Rules Committee granted a rule (H.Res. 483-92nd) for the House to consider H.R. 234 first and making it in order to consider H.R. 820 as an amendment in the nature of a substitute for H.R. 234. The House adopted the rule and then rejected the Ichord bill and passed the Matsunaga bill.

5. The Rules Committee has the power to grant a waiver on any point of order which may be raised on the House floor against a bill, or any provisions thereof, for the reason that its consideration would be in violation of the House rules. The effect of this action is to permit the floor consideration of a bill with all its provisions which might otherwise be rejected, in whole or in part, on a point of order under the rules of the House. For example, an appropriations bill, privileged otherwise, would be subject to a point of order if reported to the floor containing legislative provisions or before the corresponding authorization bill had been approved by both the House and the Senate. A rule waiving the point of order may be granted by the Rules Committee to permit the bill's consideration by the House. In essence, this device enables the committee and the House to circumvent certain rules of the House by proposing the necessary exemptions to these rules on a temporary basis.

DISCHARGING A LEGISLATIVE COMMITTEE

Since the Rules Committee can propose procedural rules, it can discharge and has discharged legislative committees through the vehicle of a resolution, without having to resort to the official discharge procedure which requires 218 signatures. It simply needs to provide for the consideration of a certain bill in the proposed rule. Mindful of the House's reluctance to circumvent its traditional ways of handling business through the committee system, the Rules Committee has been, throughout its history, extremely cautious in evoking this power. From 1944 to 1974, the committee sent only four bills to the floor for House consideration which were not first acted upon favorably by their respective jurisdictional legislative committees. Although none of these bills had support from the leadership, they all received decisive majorities for passage: the striking labor draft bill (H.R. 5262-79th) from Education and Labor (258-114), the excess profits tax extension (H.R. 5899-83rd) from Ways and Means (325-27), the federal courts in reapportionment bill (the Tuck bill, H.R. 11926-88th) from Judiciary (218-175), and the settlement of the west coast dock strike bill (H.J. Res. 1025-92nd) from Education and Labor (214-139).

When the Interstate and Foreign Commerce Committee refused to report out a bill (H.R. 7189-93rd) which he had introduced, Matsunaga succeeded in obtaining a rule from the Rules Committee permitting him to take his bill directly to the floor and to offer it as an amendment to a bill on which the Commerce Committee had acted favorably. That rule, however, was rejected by the House in December, 1974.

The circumstances which compel the Rules Committee to exercise this extraordinary power and practically usurp the power of a legislative committee are varied but are invariably based on what the Rules Committee considers to be an unwarranted refusal of the legislative committee to act on a measure referred to it. The discharge power has been used to extract bills designed to meet regional emergencies, as in the case of the bill providing for the settlement of the 1971-72 west coast dock strike by compulsory arbitration (H.J. Res. 1025-92nd), which was extracted from the Education and Labor Committee. Constituency interests could also compel a leadership Democrat to vote to extract from a legislative committee legislation which is not even supported by the leadership. Matsunaga, who had the highest leadership agreement score (91%) (see Chap. 7) of any member of the Rules Committee in the 92nd Congress, actively supported a resolution to discharge the Education and Labor Committee from further consideration of the dock strike resolution because Hawaii is almost completely dependent on ocean transportation and because its economy would have suffered irreparable damages from a prolonged west coast dock strike. Indicating strong reluctance to report any "strike-breaking" bill, the Education and Labor Committee had failed to act on both the west coast dock strike bill (H.J. Res. 1025-92nd) and Matsunaga's own bill (H.J. Res. 1054-92nd), which provided for two successive 30-day moratoriums on strikes while collective bargaining continued and for a "final offer selection device" to settle the remaining issues. Despite the leadership opposition to such a move, Matsunaga voted with the majority of the committee to discharge the Education and Labor Committee from further consideration of both bills.

At times the mere threat of the Rules Committee's discharging a legislative committee from considering a specific bill is sufficient to prompt it to report the bill. For example, in 1967, Chairman Emanuel Celler (D-N.Y.) of the Judiciary Committee, a confirmed liberal, was reluctant to report the anti-riot bill (H.R. 421-90th). Because of the prevalence of riots and unrest throughout the country, and under pressure from the conservative members of the House, Chairman Colmer and the Republicans on the Rules Committee were prepared to act. Colmer served notice that the Rules Committee would hold its own hearings on the bill, and this was enough to prompt Celler and his committee to report the Judiciary version to the Rules Committee for action.

LEGISLATIVE POWERS — POST–HOUSE PASSAGE

REVIVING HOUSE BILLS DEFEATED IN THE SENATE

The normal way for the House to revive a House-passed bill that has been defeated in the Senate is to reintroduce it and run it through the House legislative gauntlet again. In 1971, the House passed the Foreign Assistance Act amendments bill (H.R. 9910-92nd), which was subsequently defeated in the Senate. In its place, the Senate passed two of its own bills, one on foreign military assistance (S. 2819-92nd) and one on foreign economic aid (S. 2820-92nd), which did not include certain provisions of the House-passed bill. The Rules Committee, upon the request of the chairman and the senior Republican of the Foreign Affairs Committee, proposed a rule to resurrect the dead H.R. 9910 by substituting for each of the two Senate bills the text of the dead House bill, thus enabling the House to go into conference with the Senate. Essentially, what the Rules Committee did in this unique move was to save time for everyone concerned by using its almost unlimited rule-making power.

GRANTING AND AVOIDING CONFERENCES

Until 1965 the House rules required either unanimous consent of the House or majority consent to a rule obtained from the Rules Committee before a bill could be sent to conference with the Senate. In other words, unless there was unanimous consent of the House, the Rules Committee could literally prevent bills from going to conference by refusing to grant a rule. For instance, in 1960 the committee independently voted seven to five to refuse to grant a conference rule for the School Construction Assistance Act (H.R. 10128-86th). (The bill represented the first time the House had approved a general school construction bill.) After that, in January, 1965, the House, as a part of its effort to curtail the Rules Committee's independent attitude, adopted a rule permitting "the Speaker, at his discretion, to recognize a Member to offer a motion that would permit the sending of a bill to conference by majority vote. The action had first to be approved by the committee with jurisdiction over the bill."[10]

By exercising its power on the other side of the conference coin, namely the power to *avoid* a conference, the Rules Committee can facilitate the enactment of bills by the House. The Rules Committee can write a rule agreeing with the Senate amendments on a House-passed bill, thus rendering the convening of a conference unnecessary and expediting the legislative process. A classic example was the enactment of the law extending the right to vote to eighteen-year-old citizens, which was first considered by the House as a Senate amendment to the House-passed Voting Rights Act extension bill (H.R. 4249-91st). The House leadership was concerned that it might not get the bill passed at all if it went to conference. To resolve the dilemma, Matsunaga introduced House Resolution 914 to authorize the House to take the bill from the Speaker's table and agree to the Senate amendments. In urging support of Matsunaga's resolution, Congressman Richard Bolling (D-Mo.) made the following observation in a committee executive session: "There is a strong possibility that unless we accept the Senate bill we will never have an opportunity to take further action on the matter. I urge that we support Matsunaga's resolution since a conference would not work."[11] The Matsunaga resolution was favorably reported out by the Rules Committee and was overwhelmingly adopted by the House.

WAIVING POINTS OF ORDER ON NONGERMANE CONFERENCE REPORTS

The Rules Committee is called upon from time to time by the leadership and committee chairmen to save the fate of a bill after it has gone through conference. Although agreed to by the conferees, the bill would be subject to a point of order if it contained any matter extraneous to both the House and Senate bills considered by the conferees. The conference report on the military draft extension bill (H.R. 6531-92nd) is a good example. It set forth an agreement in areas which were clearly beyond the jurisdiction and authority of a conference committee. It even reported an explicit change in a provision on which there had been no disagreement whatsoever between the House and the Senate versions of the bill as passed by the respective bodies. The conference report contained violations of the Legislative Reorganization Act of 1970 and was clearly subject to points of order which could have been raised against the bill on the floor. In order to save the package, the leadership and then Chairman Edward Hébert (D-La.) of the Armed Services Committee sought a rule providing for the general waiver of all points of order against the bill as agreed to by the conferees. The Rules Committee granted the request by reporting out a resolution (H.Res. 578-92nd) which the House subsequently adopted.

IMPARTIAL ARBITER

In its apparent quest for prestige and a recognized independent leadership role, the Rules Committee has on occasion set itself up as the judge and protector of the House. It has done this by attempting to arbitrate disputes between House committees and to protect both the House leadership and its membership from unwarranted pressure.

ARBITRATING COMMITTEE JURISDICTIONAL DISPUTES

The jurisdiction of each standing committee is spelled out in House Rule XI. As specific as the provisions appear to be, the various committees of the House find themselves locked in jurisdictional disputes from time to time, disputes which the Rules Committee has been asked to arbitrate. In a classic case, in 1958, both the Agriculture Committee and the Interstate and Foreign Commerce Committee had reported a packers and stockyards bill (Agriculture, H.R. 9020-86th, and Commerce, H.R. 11234-86th). Chairman Howard Smith suggested to those concerned that Chairman Oren Harris (D-Ark.) of the Commerce Committee would find H.R. 9020 agreeable if the Agriculture Committee would accept four amendments from the Commerce Committee. The Rules Committee then authorized Smith to use his good offices to arrange an agreement between the two committees. After Smith reported to the Rules Committee that the Agriculture Committee had accepted the four amendments in question, the Rules Committee granted a rule to H.R. 9020, the Agriculture Committee bill.

In 1971, the Rules Committee tried an unprecedented method to settle a jurisdictional conflict involving three committees: Education and Labor, Agriculture, and Interior and Insular Affairs. The

Education and Labor Committee had reported the Higher Education Act amendments bill (H.R. 7248-92nd), which contained provisions relating to agricultural colleges and experiment stations, matters within the jurisdiction of the Agriculture Committee. Matters falling within the jurisdiction of the Interior Committee were also included. As a consequence, the chairmen of both the Agriculture and Interior committees appeared before the Rules Committee to oppose the jurisdictional infringement by the Education and Labor Committee. Since the House rules offered no remedy for a situation in which a comprehensive bill is reported out by one committee, the Rules Committee specified in its proposed rule that points of order could be raised on the floor against the disputed provisions, thus permitting the chairman of the Committee of the Whole House to be the final judge of the jurisdictional dispute.[12] The Rules Committee, in its attempt to be fair to all three committees, specifically allowed the Agriculture and Interior committees to raise points of order on the floor against an Education and Labor Committee bill, a unique action on the part of the Rules Committee since it is normally in the business of granting waivers of points of order rather than permitting them to be raised.

In 1974, the report of the House Select Committee on Committees, chaired by Richard Bolling and Dave Martin of the Rules Committee, recommended that the Rules Committee be designated as a kind of court of appeals whenever two or more legislative committees claim jurisdiction over the same bill. The recommendation was rejected by the House, even though in practice the chairmen and other members of legislative committees have regularly appeared before the Rules Committee whenever dissatisfied with the Speaker's decision on referral of bills. Adoption of the Bolling-Martin proposal would have formalized and strengthened the Rules Committee's function as an impartial arbiter of disputes between committees.[13]

SERVING AS HEAT SHIELD FOR THE LEADERSHIP AND MEMBERSHIP

In exercising its "traffic-cop" and timing powers, the Rules Committee frequently serves to protect both the leadership and individual members of the House, who are often pressured by sectional, factional, or constituent interests to push certain bills which are ill-conceived or which lack congressional support. The Rules Committee's reluctance to act expeditiously or refusal to act at all on such bills frequently saves the leadership or the congressman concerned from a considerable amount of embarrassment. Conversely, the ill-timed release of a bill can prove disastrous to a congressman seeking reelection in a close race. By timing the exercise of its traffic-cop power the Rules Committee on occasion can, intentionally or unintentionally, even influence the outcome of an election.

The committee's "heat-shield" function has usually been referred to as the "whipping-boy" function because the committee frequently takes the blame for the leadership and the rest of the House. Peabody quoted one of the best descriptions of this function by a Republican Rules Committee member:

> There are some bills that just shouldn't get to the floor, and the members know it. I had this congressman come to me and say, "You've got to keep that bill from coming on to the floor. I've got a primary coming up, and it's going to be close, and which ever way I vote on that bill, I'm dead." So I told him that I would do him a favor, and I sat on the bill, and what happened? A week later, I get this letter from one of his constituents, a lady, and she has written to all of the members of the Rules Committee. She says, "Why haven't you let such and such a bill out of your committee? I know that you're holding it up because I have the proof right here," and she encloses a letter from her congressman, this fellow that I'm taking the pressure off, saying that he favors her bill and is most sympathetic to it, but he can't get the Rules Committee to let the bill out on the floor so he can vote on it.[14]

It is generally agreed that the Rules Committee on its own initiative, or on that of others, does serve from time to time as a cushion between the House leadership and members and the extra-House pressure.

Appropriations Committee Chairman George Mahon commented: "The Rules Committee performs very useful functions in protecting the leadership and the members of Congress generally by killing extremely controversial and divisive bills."[15] The late Representative John Saylor, once ranking minority member of

Interior, spoke in the same vein: "Very frankly, in the years that I have been here I have watched the Rules Committee taking abuse, being criticized for killing bills. But when you investigate you will determine that the Speaker or the leadership on whichever side is in control of the Congress has asked the committee not to report out that bill, or to hold it up for any reason whatever."[16]

House Majority Leader Tip O'Neill, a former member of the Rules Committee, described the heat-shield role of the committee as follows: "Many, many times in the Rules Committee in the nineteen years that I served on it, legislation would come before it that was basically bad. If the committee reported it, certain members just wouldn't be able to stand the heat. They would say, 'well, you have good stable men on the Rules Committee. Let the Rules Committee handle it.' The Rules Committee does the Congress a complete favor by pigeon-holing bad bills and keeping them there. It takes the heat for the rest of the Congress, there is no question about that."[17]

Rules Committee member B. F. Sisk (D-Calif.) perceived the protector's role of the committee in a similar vein: "Because of pressures, you want to try to protect your leadership, so the Rules Committee takes the heat. We have done this many times. I know when I went on the committee back in 1961, I was told, 'Now you are being selected because you come from a fairly safe district, you can take unpopular positions, you can take the heat and get away with it politically.' "[18]

OTHER RULES COMMITTEE POWERS

The Rules Committee is vested with a number of other powers which, if exercised, would only indirectly affect the outcome of pending legislation. These powers may be deemed administrative rather than legislative.

APPROVING THE CREATION OF SELECT COMMITTEES

Under House rules, resolutions to create special or select committees must be cleared by the Rules Committee before the House can consider them. These select committees are technically temporary in nature, since they go out of existence automatically at the end of each Congress. To continue their life into another Congress, another approval of the Rules Committee would be required. Historically, the Rules Committee has not favored the creation or continuance of select committees. (For instance, during the 94th Congress it refused to continue the life of the Select Committee on Crime, even though its chairman, Claude Pepper, was an influential member of the Rules Committee.) This stance is evidently based on the feeling that any subject matter which proponents claim needs the extra special attention of a select committee can be taken up by one of the House standing committees. While serving as chairman of the Rules Committee, Colmer expressed a personal dislike for the proliferation of select committees as a matter of principle. Congressman Trent Lott (R-Miss.), while administrative assistant to Colmer, expressed Colmer's views: "The chairman [Colmer] is against the creation of select committees because he thinks that it is a waste of public money."[19]

Although Congressman David Pryor (D-Ark.), now the governor of Arkansas, gained national publicity by calling for the creation of a select committee on aging, primarily to investigate nursing homes for the aged (H. Res. 118-92nd), he was completely frustrated by the refusal of the chairman of the Rules Committee to even schedule a hearing on his resolution. It was only by circumventing the Rules Committee that Congressman C. W. Young (R-Fla.) successfully led a move to create the permanent Select Committee on Aging in the 94th Congress. Young's success was achieved by offering an amendment establishing the select committee to the general House reform resolution (H.Res. 988-93rd) on October 2, 1974. It was not until Congressman Sonny Montgomery (D-Miss.) had obtained the Speaker's support and 288 cosponsors to his resolution calling for the creation of a select committee to investigate the missing-in-action of the Vietnam War that he finally succeeded (in September, 1975) in getting favorable Rules Committee action.

The conclusion that a proposed select committee will not be approved by the Committee on Rules, except with strong endorsement from the leadership or the House membership in general, is unavoidable. It is clearly evident that no standing committee is going to agree to the establishment of a select committee if it means a reduction of its own jurisdiction.

CONTROLLING COMMITTEE TRAVEL

Upon the insistence of the leadership, the Rules Committee was vested with the authority to regulate committee travel. Congressman Bolling described the origin of this power to control travel in a floor speech: "A number of years ago, in the speakership of Mr. Rayburn, when Mr. Martin was the minority leader, a few individual Members of the House were guilty of both excesses and indiscretions in such a way that it brought the House itself into bad repute because of things said and done overseas. Then, the Speaker and the minority leader requested the Committee on Rules to squeeze down on the committees of the House, to try to cut back on travel authorizations."[20] As a consequence, at the beginning of each Congress the Rules Committee entertained resolutions which granted committees either blanket authority or limited authority to travel to foreign lands and within the United States. In each instance in which a committee wished to go beyond the travel authority set forth by the Rules Committee, it had to request the latter's permission. Certain committees were exempted from the scrutiny of the Rules Committee in their travels, e.g., Appropriations and Ways and Means (see Table 2.1, p. 146).

At the beginning of the 93rd Congress, the leadership and the Rules Committee agreed that the legislative committees as a whole were mature enough to control the travels of their own members without being supervised by the Rules Committee. Thus, with a few exceptions, the committees were granted blanket travel authority by resolutions adopted by the House in February, 1973. Congressman Bolling expressed the position of the Rules majority as follows: "In other words, the responsibility [of authorizing travel], I repeat, rests on the committees and on the leaders of the committees and on the members of the committees. I am sure at this stage of history it will work, because I am convinced that there is not a committee chairman or a committee ranking minority member who wants to allow a situation to develop which will bring the House itself into disrepute."[21]

The Rules Committee's policy of granting all standing committees blanket travel authority was confirmed by the House on October 8, 1974, when it adopted the House reform resolution (H.Res. 988-93rd) that included such authority for all its committees.[22]

PROPOSING GENERAL RULES GOVERNING THE HOUSE

The Rules Committee not only serves as judge or arbiter for the leadership in granting rules on bills reported to it by legislative committees; it also initiates or kills bills designed to reform or re-organize House procedure or structure. A good example of the committee's negative use of this prerogative was its refusal to clear the abortive Monroney-Madden reorganization bill (H.R. 2544, S. 355-90th), even though it was the product of the joint efforts of Senator Mike Monroney (D-Okla.) and a Rules Committee member, Ray Madden (D-Ind.). It was by exercising this prerogative positively that the committee proposed the Legislative Reorganization Act of 1970. This long-overdue and highly lauded measure was primarily the work of the Rules Committee's Subcommittee on Reorganization headed by B. F. Sisk. In urging House approval of the measure, Sisk reported that he and his colleagues on the Rules Committee had labored for months to work out an acceptable piece of legislation. It was adopted by both houses.

As if in recognition of this prerogative of the Rules Committee, when the House on January 31, 1973, adopted a resolution (H.Res. 132-93rd) to create the Select Committee on Committees to study and review the committee structure and jurisdiction of the House, both its chairman (Richard Bolling) and vice-chairman (Dave Martin) were selected from the Rules Committee. The impression that the Rules Committee does have and does exercise the prerogative of initiating House reforms is obviously an accurate one.

NOTES

 1. Interview, March 10, 1971.
 2. Interview, July 16, 1973.

3. Personal recollection.

4. Robert Peabody, "The Enlarged Rules Committee," in Robert Peabody and Nelson Polsby, eds., *New Perspectives on the House of Representatives* (Chicago: Rand McNally & Co., 1963), pp. 134-35.

5. R. L. Pratt, "The Taming of the Shrew: Myth and Politics in the House Committee on Rules" (B.A. thesis, Wesleyan University, 1969), p. 71.

6. *Congressional Record,* Daily Edition, November 18, 1971, p. H11241.

7. Interview, May 7, 1972.

8. Opponents of the South African quota would have liked to have had an opportunity to delete the South African provision under an open rule on the floor.

9. Interview, June 12, 1973.

10. *Congressional Quarterly Almanac* (Washington, D.C.: Congressional Quarterly, 1965), p. 587.

11. Interview, June 4, 1970.

12. When a bill containing matters belonging properly to the jurisdiction of two committees is referred to one of the two committees, and that committee acts upon the bill and reports it out to the floor of the House, the present House rules provide that jurisdiction was properly exercised over all matters in the bill by the committee to which the bill was referred.

13. U.S. Congress, House, *Report to Accompany H. Res. 988-1974,* 93rd Cong., 2nd sess., 1974.

14. Quoted in "Enlarged Rules Committee," pp. 143-44.

15. Interview, March 6, 1972.

16. Interview, March 7, 1972.

17. Interview, December 1, 1970.

18. Interview, July 17, 1973.

19. Interview, March 11, 1971.

20. *Congressional Record,* Daily Edition, February 28, 1973, p. H1211.

21. *Ibid.*

22. U.S. Congress, House, *Rules,* 92nd Cong., XI, 1(b).

3

House and Leadership Sanctions

Because the House leadership imposes a heavier demand on the Rules Committee than on any other committee in the House, the Rules Committee frequently tends to exert its independence. The leadership and the House have, therefore, reserved unto themselves certain extraordinary sanctions to be used against the Rules Committee whenever the expectations of the House have been repeatedly frustrated.

RECORD OF EXTRAORDINARY SANCTIONS

James Robinson cites three historical controversies involving the Rules Committee: 1) the revolt against Speaker Cannon; 2) the enlargement of the committee; and 3) the 21-day rule.[1] All three reflect the record of the continual struggle between the House and the committee over the failure on the part of the latter to satisfy the expectations of the former. It is interesting to note the kinds of sanctions the House is prepared to use to insure that its expectations are substantially met.

The current House structure favors informal and traditional sanctions and the leadership or the House membership will seldom resort to extraordinary sanctions.[2] It appears that extraordinary sanctions are resorted to only when 1) a majority of the House members agree that the will of the House is being frustrated by committee action; and 2) the readily available sanctions and informal folkways of the House have failed to provide necessary relief from the tension produced by the consistent failure of the committee to satisfy House expectations. In three of the four cases to be discussed below both of these conditions existed.

THE REVOLT AGAINST SPEAKER CANNON

This was a situation in which the total convergence of the goals of the Speaker, Joseph G. Cannon (R-Ill.), and the Rules Committee existed. In fact, Speaker Cannon was in effect a one-man Rules Committee who assumed the entire responsibility of setting the agenda of the House. There was no clash between the expectations of the House leadership and those of the Rules Committee, which consisted of five members, including the Speaker. The revolt of 1910, led by George Norris (R-Nebr.), took place because of the extreme tension created by the failure of the Rules Committee, led by Cannon, to accommodate the demands of the House majority (composed of members on both sides of the aisle). As the Robinson analysis informs us, "His czarism became an intra-party as well as an inter-party issue, and indeed, were it not for a split in Republican ranks, the overthrow of Cannon would not have been possible in 1910."[3] The end result of this House revolt was the creation of a new and enlarged Rules Committee of ten members who were more responsive to the House majority and the negation of the total convergence of the House leadership and the Rules Committee by prohibiting the Speaker from serving on the committee.[4]

ENLARGEMENT OF THE RULES COMMITTEE

The membership of the Rules Committee was increased to eleven in 1911, then to twelve in 1917, and, except for a brief period in the 1930s when there were fourteen, remained at twelve. However, it became apparent toward the end of 1960 that the tie vote of the liberal and conservative members of the Rules Committee would continue to thwart Democratic liberal legislative proposals in the 87th Congress as it had in the 86th Congress. As Bolling observed in his book, "The consequence of this line-up was that the committee members split six to six on most major issues. It was a straight liberal-conservative split, with Smith and Colmer, Democrats, joining the four Republicans to create a deadlock."[5]

It became obvious to the leadership that some extraordinary measure had to be taken by the House to end the semipermanent autonomy of the Rules Committee, with its bipartisan conservative coalition. After considering a number of alternative sanctions (including the enlargement of the committee, re-adoption of the 21-day rule, widening the Democratic-Republican two-to-one ratio on the committee, and purging Congressman William Colmer), Speaker Sam Rayburn and his strategists decided to enlarge the committee from twelve to fifteen members. For all practical purposes this meant a new lineup of eight liberals and seven conservatives. As is well known, the House majority led by Speaker Rayburn did succeed in temporarily implementing this scheme of reorganization in 1961, and subsequently in 1963 it was made permanent.[6]

THE 21-DAY RULE

There have been three serious attempts to adopt the 21-day rule as a sanction against the Rules Committee. Two such attempts were successful (81st and 89th Congresses), but in each case the restrictive rule was rejected in the succeeding Congress. The most recent move to re-adopt this rule was approved by the Democratic Caucus but rejected by the House in January, 1971 (92nd Congress).

In essence, the 21-day rule enables the legislative committee chairmen to bypass the Rules Committee by seeking direct recognition from the Speaker for the purpose of calling up their bills on the House floor, in case the Rules Committee fails to report those bills favorably after a period of twenty-one calendar days or, as in the 1971 proposal, thirty-one days.

The first 21-day rule, adopted in 1949, in theory, at least, made it mandatory for the Speaker to recognize the committee chairmen. Rayburn's anxiety over possible chairmen dominance in scheduling led him to render only lukewarm support for its adoption. In any event he, the House majority (formed mainly by the members of the majority party), and Rules Chairman Adolph Sabath (D-Ill.) joined efforts in the battle against the bipartisan conservative majority of the Rules membership. Walter Kravitz observed, "As a result of repeated complaints of the 'obstructive tactics' and the 'undemocratic and arbitrary dictatorship' of the Rules Committee, the House amended its rules at the beginning of the 81st Congress by adopting the so-called '21-day rule.' "[7]

It is interesting to note that this was also a case of an administration- and leadership-oriented Rules chairman, who was not a member of the committee's majority coalition, supporting a proposal to curb the committee's independence in favor of leadership dominance.[8]

The 21-day rule of the 89th Congress was readily distinguishable from the earlier versions because it made unmistakably clear the fact that the Speaker had the *discretion* to recognize the representative of the legislative committee. Thus the final power to call up a bill rested in the hands of the Speaker. Understandably, Speaker Mc-Cormack strongly supported this resolution, with emphasis on the rule's potential to satisfy the House membership's expectations: "I think the 21-day rule is a rule that is for the benefit of the individual members of the House without regard to party affiliation in giving them the opportunity of passing upon legislation that has been reported out of a standing committee."[9]

The enlargement of the committee in 1961 succeeded in breaking the six to six vote (even though the newly formed majority of eight during the 87th Congress was not reliable when it came to civil rights issues), but not in curtailing the personal prerogatives of Chairman Smith. As the authors will later attempt to show, Smith could still block legislation favored by the leadership, principally by his power to call meetings and set the agenda of the Rules Committee. By adopting the 21-day rule the House effectively curtailed the autonomy of the Rules Committee and the power of its chairman, to satisfy the expectations of the House and those of the Speaker.

The seating of a new chairman in the 90th Congress, the numerous complaints against the abuse of the 21-day rule in the 89th Congress, and the addition of more Republicans to the House membership caused the House majority to vote, in 1967, to rescind this extraordinary sanction and to decide instead to rely on more traditional ways of dealing with the Rules Committee. Former

Ranking Minority Member Dave Martin (R-Nebr.) described the alleged abuse in this way: "I am opposed to the 21-day rule. There has been too much abuse of it. Perkins, chairman of the Education and Labor Committee, for example, regularly submitted requests for a rule to the Rules Committee while at the same time asking the Speaker to invoke the 21-day rule."[10]

The performance of the Rules Committee and its chairman in the 90th and 91st Congresses seems to have satisfied the expectations of the House majority and those of the Speaker. In fact, Carl Albert, questioned about the 21-day rule in an open-ended interview on August 10, 1970, while he was still majority leader, replied, "There is no need for reform in the light of the present composition of the Rules Committee." Majority Leader Tip O'Neill commented on August 11, 1970, three months before the attempt was made to adopt the 21-day rule, and before his selection as the majority whip: "Apparently the Democratic party will control the House in the 92nd Congress and all the Democrats on the Rules Committee will be returned to office. With Chairman Colmer continuing to be responsible to the leadership as in the past, I see no need for the 21-day rule. I supported it in the 89th Congress when Judge Smith was chairman of the Rules Committee." Richard Bolling suggested on August 14, 1970, that the 21-day rule is "somewhat useful in absence of leadership's firm control of the committee. However, there will be no need for re-adoption of this rule in the 92nd Congress."

Despite his earlier lack of interest in the re-adoption, Speaker Albert was quoted, both in an NBC "Meet the Press" interview and by Bolling as saying, in January, 1971, that he favored the adoption of the 21-day rule.[11] At the beginning of the 92nd Congress, Speaker Albert and fellow liberal Democrats succeeded in adopting a 31-day rule in the Democratic Caucus, only to have it defeated on the House floor. The rule would have given the Speaker the same discretion the 1965-66 rule had given him. The previous question on the proposed rule was defeated by a substantial margin (133-254). In fact, only 20% of the Rules Committee members (Madden, Bolling, and O'Neill) supported the Speaker-endorsed rule, as compared to 41.7% in 1949 and 46.7% in 1965 (see Table 3.1, p. 147). By this action the House once again demonstrated that it is very reluctant to impose extraordinary sanctions on any committee or change its traditional informal ways, unless the committee has completely failed to perform to the satisfaction of House expectations. The suggestion of the need for a mere additional check on the Rules Committee or an extra safeguard for the leadership would not, in the view of the majority of the House, justify extraordinary restraints.

DEMOCRATIC CAUCUS SANCTIONS

Since its revival in the 93rd Congress, the Democratic Caucus has taken an increasing interest in the operations of the Rules Committee. It has become involved with giving voting instructions to the committee members, confirming the committee chairman, and giving the Speaker the power to reappoint Democratic members of the committee, three aspects which are discussed below:

1. Giving voting instructions to the Rules Democratic membership. The Democratic Caucus by a voice vote on May 15, 1974, instructed the Rules Committee to permit the floor consideration of both the William Green (D-Pa.) amendment (a call for the repeal of the oil depletion allowance) and the Charles Vanik (D-Ohio) amendment (a move to convert the existing tax credit into a simple business deduction). Rules was to include these permissions in the rule for the oil and energy tax bill (H.R. 14462-93rd). Clearly these instructions to the Rules Committee meant that the caucus was attempting to force floor votes on amendments to a Ways and Means bill for the first time since the 1973 closed-rule change.

Compliance with these caucus instructions would have been difficult for the Rules Democrats from the three oil-producing states, Long of Louisiana, McSpadden of Oklahoma, and Young of Texas. However, they were spared this difficulty since the chairman of the Ways and Means Committee, Wilbur Mills, not only declined to seek any rule from the Rules Committee but also failed to take the entire bill to the floor.

Again in the 93rd Congress, House Democrats, on July 23, 1974, by a voice vote adopted a resolution directing the Rules Committee to send both the Bolling reform bill (H.Res. 988-93rd) and the

Hansen reform bill (H.Res. 1248-93rd) to the floor under an open rule. The Rules Committee, by a voice vote on September 25, complied with those directives of the caucus, and subsequently the House adopted the Hansen substitute as the basic reform plan by a 203-165 vote on October 8.

The Democrats acquired an overwhelming majority of almost two-to-one over the Republicans in the 94th Congress. Thereupon, their caucus, ignoring the leadership's opposition, voted 152-99 to instruct the Rules Democrats to report H.Res. 259 (February 25, 1975). This rule permitted a floor vote for amendments dealing with the oil depletion allowance amendments, that is, to pending emergency tax-cutting legislation (H.R. 2166-94th). On February 26, in the face of Republican opposition, the eleven Democrats on Rules including the dissenting John Young (D-Tex.) adopted H.Res. 259 by a voice vote. Subsequently, on February 27, the House majority adopted the oil depletion rule by a vote of 242-162.

Given the above examples of caucus instructions, one can easily provide answers to some questions pertaining to the committee's status of independence or subordination in relation to the caucus. First, if these caucus instructions had not been given to the Rules Committee, would it have voted for something like them anyway? Certainly such a vote should be considered as unlikely, since the three oil-state Democrats would not have wanted to create a vehicle through which the oil depletion allowance could be abolished. Moreover, the majority of the Rules members would have favored instructions produced by a select committee chaired by its own ranking members (H.Res. 988-93rd) rather than those of a caucus committee (H.Res. 1248-93rd). Thus it is safe to assume that the caucus, when it acted on these three occasions, to some extent at least, doubted whether the Rules Committee would report out a rule that it, the caucus, favored.

Second, would the leadership have been able to use its influence to get the same results from Rules? This question was never really put to a test since Speaker Albert, as a representative of an oil-producing state, and as one having little to do with the Hansen Committee's appointment, was not enthusiastic about any of the three caucus instructions. And, in fact, the Speaker was not alone among the leadership in his lack of enthusiasm. Majority Leader

O'Neill joined Chairman Al Ullman (D-Ore.) of the Ways and Means Committee in speaking in the caucus against the proposed rule (H.Res. 259-94th), which would have allowed a vote on the oil depletion allowance issue at the same time as the tax-cutting legislation was being considered on the floor. The fact remains that the caucus contemplated the unusual step of instructions to the Rules Democrats only when it learned that the usual leadership-Rules mechanism was not sympathetically reacting to what the caucus held to be legislation of vital importance. From this extraordinary caucus action, one can conclude that the position of the Democratic leadership is not always the same as that of the Democratic majority in the House, nor, of course, of the entire House membership majority.

2. Confirmation of the Rules Committee chairman. One of the new rules adopted by the Democratic Caucus in 1974 provided for the caucus's approval of the nominee for Rules's chairmanship at the beginning of each Congress.[12] This rule gives the majority of House Democrats a veto power over a disloyal chairman's seniority-oriented reselection at two-year intervals. It should increase the degree of subordination to the leadership of the chairman of Rules, if there is a convergence of policy orientation of the Democratic leadership with the majority of the Democratic party.

3. Giving the Speaker the power to reappoint committee Democrats. Since December, 1974, the Speaker has had the power to reappoint all the committee Democrats at the beginning of each Congress (see p. 54). Taken together with the caucus's own power to approve the Rules chairman, this newest Speaker's prerogative exhibits the caucus's clear desire to reduce the committee's independence without bypassing it all together.

The authors submit that the caucus's employment of instructions constitutes a drastic sanction against the committee by the House Democratic majority but not necessarily on behalf of either the leadership or the House majority in general. The frequent use of this practice would naturally damage Rules's desire for independence and indeed would soon render its existence meaningless. On the other hand, the caucus's decisions both to approve the nomination of Rules's chairman and to have the Speaker nominate all Democrats to the committee at two-year intervals will enable the Democratic Party and its leadership to periodically examine the Rules Committee's general performance without attempting overtly and explicitly to assume the committee's decision-making role.

Of the four extraordinary sanctions the 21-day rule appears to be most objectionable to committee members for the simple reason that only this alternative directly threatens to undermine the committee's very existence and to reduce both the members' prestige in the House and their opportunity to serve their constituents. Even with the additional 10-day grace period, the rule would permit the Speaker to bypass the Rules Committee completely by the mere passage of time. Matsunaga, although priding himself as a loyal Democrat, argued before the Democratic Caucus that the adoption of the 31-day rule would reduce the Rules Committee to impotency so that no member who valued any degree of independence and prestige would want to serve on the committee.

As a matter of course, one would expect the majority of the Rules Committee members (the dominant coalition or majority party) to reject such a proposal. However, a minority of the committee could be expected to support the rule because they generally cannot identify themselves with the committee posture and feel more comfortable in league with noncommittee forces, such as the leadership, House majority, etc. (see Table 3.1, p. 147). Sometimes members of the dominant group of the committee also find themselves justifying their support of the 21-day rule by identifying themselves more closely with the House leadership than with the committee.

SANCTIONS ON RULES COMMITTEE'S BLOCKING POWER

As James Robinson has observed, there is more than one way to circumvent the Rules Committee in the legislative process.[13] In certain prescribed instances, as in the case of private and District of Columbia legislation, bills regularly go to the floor without any Rules Committee action. Certain public bills, which are qualified or which enjoy the support of a substantial majority of the House membership, may bypass the Rules Committee for floor consideration in the following instances:

1. Under the provisions of the Legislative Reorganization Act of 1970, certain bills or resolutions from the House Administration Committee and the Committee on Standards of Official Conduct are privileged to receive immediate floor consideration at any time. In addition, Rule XI, clause 22, of the House rules specifically provides that certain bills covering certain specified subject matter from the Appropriations Committee, Interior and Insular Affairs Committee, Public Works Committee, Veterans' Affairs Committee, and Ways and Means Committee are privileged to receive floor consideration three calendar days after their reports are made available to all members (see Table 3.2, p. 148). These privileged bills, however, lose their privilege and must be granted a rule by the Rules Committee for floor consideration if they require waivers of points of order or a rule other than an open rule.

2. Certain noncontroversial bills, although not privileged, are routinely placed on the Consent Calendar by the leadership, with the concurrence of the minority leadership, at the request of the legislative committee chairmen. Bills listed on this calendar must receive unanimous approval of the House for passage, and they are normally disposed of on the first and third Mondays of each month. Objection on the floor from any one member to any measure placed on this calendar means its defeat. However, in recent years over 200 noncontroversial bills have been passed by the House via the Consent Calendar during each congressional session. In a number of instances, bills with respect to which unanimous consent was considered impossible at the time they were reported out by their legislative committees (and thus promptly referred to the Rules Committee) were later passed by way of the Consent Calendar. It appears that the leadership has astutely taken advantage of the fact that placement of a bill on the Consent Calendar has the psychological effect on members of assuming it to be noncontroversial and unobjectionable.

3. Under Rule XXVII, clause 1, of the House rules, on the first and third Mondays of each month the Speaker may entertain a

motion to suspend the House rules for floor consideration of any bill without its having to be cleared by the Rules Committee. Upon the strong insistence of Speaker Albert, the first and third Tuesdays of each month were added to the Suspension Calendar days in the 94th Congress. The rules may also be suspended any time during the last six days of any session. To suspend the rules and pass a bill, a two-thirds majority vote with a quorum present is required, and no amendment to the bill is permitted. While most of the bills on the Suspension Calendar are so scheduled because of their noncontroversial nature, there have been instances when the suspension procedure was employed to free bills held up by the Rules Committee. Some of these bills have had national attention leading to public condemnation of the Rules Committee, such as H.R. 2266 (92nd) involving the highly controversial school busing issue. Because of its inability to obtain expeditious action on this measure from the Rules Committee, the leadership chose the suspension route, which meant that no amendment, including the anti-busing amendment, could be offered. As a consequence, the leadership was subjected to considerable criticism.[14]

As is true for the Consent Calendar, the Suspension Calendar is under the absolute control of the House leadership. No bill may be considered under the suspension of the rules without the approval of the leadership, which normally insists on the concurrence of the legislative committee chairman and its subcommittee chairman.

The curious student of the legislative process might observe that although it takes only a two-thirds majority vote for passage of a bill under suspension of the rules, as compared to a unanimous vote under the Consent Calendar, far fewer measures are disposed of under the Suspension Calendar than under the Consent Calendar. Perhaps less well known and even more amazing is the fact that more bills are passed by unanimous consent than by a divided vote, so one can conclude that there is more unanimity of thought on many matters in Congress than one is at first glance led to believe.

4. Should the sponsor of a bill fail to muster unanimity or a two-thirds vote, he can still have his bill considered on the floor without approval of the Rules Committee. This he can do by way of a discharge petition, following the procedure prescribed in Rule

XXVII, clause 4, of the House rules. Generally, the petitioner must file a written motion to discharge the Rules Committee or any other standing committee from further consideration of his bill or resolution, if it has been referred to the committee at least thirty days prior to the filing of this motion. The written motion will then be laid on the clerk's desk for other petitioners to sign. When a majority (218) of the total House membership have signed the petition, it is entered in the House Journal, printed with the signatures thereto in the *Congressional Record,* and placed on the Discharge Calendar. On the second and fourth Mondays of each month, except during the last six days of any session, after the discharge motion has been on the calendar for seven or more days, any signer of the petition may call up the motion for consideration by the House. The motion is then debated for a maximum time of twenty minutes and immediately put to a vote. If the motion to discharge a standing committee prevails, it shall then be in order for the House to consider the bill or resolution which is the subject of the discharge motion, under the regular procedures of the House.

The discharge petition is rarely resorted to, and when used, it is generally directed to a standing committee other than the Rules Committee. Since 1965 only two such petitions have been successful, and both were aimed at the House Judiciary Committee. Of these two only one, the equal rights for women amendment (H.J. Res. 264-91st), was passed by the House. The other, the prayer amendment (H.J. Res. 191-92nd), was rejected by the House.

Discharge petitions may be filed against the Rules Committee if it has failed to act on any resolution which has been referred to it for seven or more days prior to such filing. However, since the 75th Congress (1936), no more than four measures have been successfully discharged from the Rules Committee in any one Congress (see Table 3.3, p. 149). The use of the discharge petition against the Rules Committee has become less frequent in recent years, with three filed in the 91st, two each filed in the 90th and 92nd, and one each filed in the 93rd and 94th Congresses. This trend suggests that the Rules Committee has become increasingly cooperative with the majority and has not blocked any measure truly desired by a majority of the House.

5. Another procedure which may be employed to circumvent the Rules Committee, but which has not been attempted since 1962, is the little-understood "Calendar Wednesday." By using this procedure, legislative committees, with the consent of the leadership, may call up "unprivileged" bills for immediate floor consideration every Wednesday on a committee-by-committee basis. Though in theory this method presents itself as a way to bypass the Rules Committee, in practice, due to the lack of adequate time to entertain all committee requests on an equitable basis and the improbability of House action, the use of the Calendar Wednesday has, since the 88th Congress, been automatically and completely dispensed with at the request of the leadership.

During the twenty-seven-year period commencing January 3, 1949, the Calendar Wednesday procedure was used only four times in attempts to have the House consider bills blocked in the Rules Committee. Of these attempts only two were successful: namely, in the cases of the Fair Employment Practices Commission Act (H.R. 4453-81st) and the Area Redevelopment Act (S. 722-86th).[15]

The most recent attempt to utilize the Calendar Wednesday was made on June 8, 1973. Former Congressman H. R. Gross (R-Iowa), in an effort to expedite House consideration of the Postal Service authorization bill (H.R. 2990-93rd), action on which was being deferred by the Rules Committee, objected to the unanimous consent request to dispense with the Calendar Wednesday. As a consequence, a two-thirds majority vote had to be obtained by the leadership to dispense with the Calendar Wednesday of June 11, 1973.

6. Prior to the Reorganization Act of 1970, the Rules Committee could be completely circumvented by the attachment of a bill (held up in that committee or in any other House committee) as a rider to a House-passed measure in the Senate. The amendment could then be accepted by the House without any action on the part of the Rules Committee. Frequently, the Senate rider amendment would be completely unrelated to the subject matter of the amended House bill. A classic example is the case of the Congressional Reapportionment Act of 1969, which was enacted into law as a Senate

amendment to a House-approved private bill (H.R. 2275-90th) granting permanent residence in the United States to a refugee physician from Cuba. The Reorganization Act of 1970 made all such nongermane Senate amendments subject to a point of order when being considered in the House.[16] The Rules Committee, however, is still authorized to grant a waiver of any such point of order.

LIMITATIONS ON RULES COMMITTEE'S POWER TO ADVANCE LEGISLATION

Observers of the legislative process seldom note that there is more than one possibility of a piece of legislation being killed before it can be voted upon on the floor, even after the Rules Committee has given it a green light to proceed. Consequently, the Rules Committee is frequently unjustly blamed for a bill's failure to reach the floor after it has been reported out by another committee. The little-known fact is that after a bill has been granted a rule it can still be blocked in one of the following ways:

1. The House leadership can and frequently does delay scheduling for floor action a Rules Committee–passed resolution providing a rule for the consideration of a bill. For example, the interstate taxation bill (H.R. 2158-90th) was given a rule by the Rules Committee on July 25, 1967, but was not called up for floor action by the leadership until May, 1968, almost a year later, because the majority whip's poll showed a lack of membership support. The resolution providing a rule for House consideration of the federal surplus property use for parks bill (H.R. 18275-91st) was permanently laid on the Speaker's table for the same reason. In fact, the leadership has withheld the scheduling of a number of Rules Committee resolutions in every Congress.

2. A legislative committee acting through its chairman can withdraw a measure from the House floor any time up until the time it is actually being voted upon, regardless of whether it has been granted a rule or not. The most interesting recent example of the use of this form of blockage can be found in the floor fight on the trade bill of 1970 (H.R. 18970-91st). Chairman Wilbur Mills of the

Ways and Means Committee actually threatened, by the use of this power, to take the bill back to his committee if the House failed to approve a closed rule. His threat brought the desired result.

3. Finally, the House can, and sometimes does, refuse to adopt a rules resolution reported by the Rules Committee. In 1967, for example, the House refused to adopt a proposed open rule for the consideration of the rat extermination bill (H.R. 11000-90th) and, thus, killed the bill, although the rule was voted out by an overwhelming majority of the Rules Committee. The frequency of House disapproval of the Rules Committee's decisions was at a minimum during the period 1951 to 1973, and the committee suffered no more than three defeats in each Congress. But, at the beginning of the 93rd Congress, something unusual happened. Ten rules proposed by the Rules Committee were rejected by the House in the first nine months of the first session alone, more than the total of all the rules defeated in the previous four Congresses. The cause of this phenomenon will be analyzed in Chapter 7 (see Table 3.4, p. 151).

NOTES

1. James A. Robinson, *House Rules Committee* (Indianapolis: Bobbs-Merrill Co., 1963), pp. 60-80.

2. For an excellent discussion on the House informal norms see Leroy Rieselbach, *Congressional Politics* (New York: McGraw-Hill Book Co., 1973), pp. 140-46.

3. *House Rules Committee*, p. 60.

4. For an authoritative account of the 1910 revolt see Kenneth W. Hechler, *Insurgency: Personalities and Politics of the Taft Era* (1940; reprint ed., New York: Russell & Russell Publishers, 1964).

5. Richard Bolling, *House Out of Order* (New York: E. P. Dutton & Co., 1965), p. 204.

6. For authoritative studies of the enlargement movement, see Bolling, *House Out of Order*, pp. 203-20; and Milton Cummings and Robert Peabody, "The Decision to Enlarge the Committee on Rules: An Analysis of the 1961 Vote," in Robert Peabody and Nelson Polsby, eds., *New Perspectives on the House of Representatives* (Chicago: Rand McNally & Co., 1963), pp. 167-94.

7. Walter Kravitz, "A Short History of the Development of the House Committee on Rules" (mimeo) (Washington, D.C.: Legislative Reference Service, Library of Congress, 1969), p. 9.

8. For Speaker Rayburn's position in the campaign for the adoption of the 21-day rule, the abortive attempt to repeal it in 1950, and the subsequent

repeal of the rule in 1951 see Bolling, *House Out of Order,* pp. 202-3; and Robinson, *House Rules Committee,* pp. 63-71.

9. *Congressional Record,* January 4, 1965, p. 23.

10. Interview, August 5, 1970. For more detailed discussion of the 1965-66 21-day rule see Kravitz, "Short History of Committee on Rules," p. 11; and R. L. Pratt, "The Taming of the Shrew: Myth and Politics in the House Committee on Rules" (B.A. thesis, Wesleyan University, 1969), pp. 40-50.

11. "Meet the Press" (Washington, D.C.: Merkle Press Inc., 1971), p. 4; and *Congressional Record,* Daily Edition, January 22, 1971, p. H60.

12. U.S. Congress, House, *Preamble and Rules Adopted by the Democratic Caucus,* February 2, 1975, p. 2.

13. *House Rules Committee,* pp. 1-9.

14. "The House Rules Committee refused on October 14, 1971, to provide a rule for consideration of H.R. 2266.... The bill was then placed on the Suspension Calendar usually reserved for measures of a non-controversial nature. Bills placed on this calendar are considered under suspension of the rules ... and a two-thirds vote is required to pass them. H.R. 2266 failed to win even a simple majority, largely due to the procedure under which it was brought to the floor. John N. Erlenborn (R-Ill.) said he voted for the bill in committee but would vote against suspending the rules to pass it. John M. Ashbrook (R-Ohio), who voted against bringing the bill out of the subcommittee, said that it was totally inappropriate to consider, under suspension of the rules, any bill authorizing $1.5 billion." *Congressional Quarterly Weekly Report,* November 6, 1971, p. 2276.

15. For details of the 1950 experience see Legislative Reference Service, Library of Congress, Service Report on Calendar Wednesday, March 31, 1967. For details of the 1960 experience, see Clem Miller, *Member of the House: Letters of a Congressman,* John W. Baker, ed. (New York: Charles Scribner's Sons, 1962), p. 42-43; and John Bibby and Roger Davidson, *On Capital Hill: Studies in the Legislative Process* (New York: Holt, Rinehart and Winston, 1967), pp. 211-13.

16. U.S. Congress, House, *Rules,* 92nd Cong. XX, 1.

4

Recruitment

LEADERSHIP EXPECTATIONS

DEMOCRATIC LEADERSHIP

"The Democratic Committee on Committees looks to the Speaker to recommend the filling of a Democratic vacancy in the Rules Committee. Even if the members of the Democratic Committee on Committees do not agree with the Speaker, they will elect the man to the Rules Committee that the Speaker recommends." These words, spoken by former Speaker of the House John W. McCormack at the ceremonial unveiling of Chairman Madden's portrait on October 25, 1973, describe the relationship between the Speaker and the Democratic Committee on Committees which existed in the McCormack era. Speaker Carl Albert appears to enjoy the same relationship. Rep. Gillis Long (D-La.) quoted Albert as having said, "I really have not made any decision on what my recommendations for the Rules Committee are going to be. I don't name the members, but the Democratic Ways and Means Committee usually follows my recommendation."[1]

Thus, in spite of the fact that the Democratic members of the Committee on Committees had always had the official responsibility of filling the Democratic vacancies on the Rules Committee until 1975, the Speaker, on behalf of the incumbent majority, had been personally making the selection for this committee to insure that its members would be responsive to the integrative norms of the House. As Tip O'Neill, then majority whip and a member of Rules, related in 1971: "The Rules Committee is in effect the Speaker's cabinet.

In the event that a vacancy occurs, the Speaker probably would say to Hale [Rep. Boggs (D-La.), the late majority leader] and me, 'I have in mind so-and-so for the job. What do you fellows think of him?' And that is it!'"[2] Normally the Democratic leadership's choice would automatically receive the approval of the Democratic Committee on Committees and the Democratic Caucus. In fact, according to the late Speaker Sam Rayburn, not since the 73rd Congress (1933-34) has a rebellion against the Speaker's wish in this regard succeeded.[3]

When Speaker Albert had his first opportunity to fill Rules Committee vacancies in 1973, he was in a position to nominate three candidates in a package proposal. As his close ally on the Rules Committee, Richard Bolling, observed: "It was a special situation. There were three vacancies after it was decided that the new majority leader was going to leave the committee, and it's enormously difficult to fill three vacancies with the people the Speaker feels would be loyal to him and helpful to the majority of the Democrats. It was a very bitter, somewhat hidden battle, and it was necessary in order to put things together, to put it together the way it was. Actually the three people went on as a trio. They didn't go on as separate individuals."[4]

Apparently Speaker Albert was able to make some meaningful decisions in choosing specific candidates to satisfy leadership expectations. He chose liberal Congressman Morgan Murphy (D-Ill.) of Chicago (backed by Mayor Daley and the Illinois Democratic delegation) over Rep. James Stanton (D-Ohio) (nominated by the Ohio delegation) to fill the seat vacated by another Northern liberal, O'Neill. Albert also selected Congressman Gillis Long (D-La.). Long, a freshman member who had served one term in the 88th Congress and who was a liberal in the Hale Boggs tradition, was chosen by Albert despite the opposition of a large number of conservative Southern Democrats, who thought that the Colmer seat should have gone to one of them, possibly Sonny Montgomery (D-Miss.). The Speaker also made the precedent-setting move of appointing freshman Congressman Clem McSpadden, a fellow Oklahoman and close personal friend, to replace William Anderson of Tennessee (another border state), who was defeated.

In practice, the Democratic leadership has involved itself in the recruiting process of all three exclusive committees — Ways and Means, Appropriations, and Rules. However, in the first two, the Speaker-led leadership has had only strong or predominant *influence;* whereas in the case of Rules, the leadership has always had the final say. Thus a study of the record reveals that, as far as one can tell, while the Speaker's choices for both Ways and Means and Appropriations have over the years suffered occasional defeats at the hands of the Committee on Committees or the Democratic Caucus, the leadership's choices for Rules have not been rejected since 1933.[5]

On December 2, 1974, the Democratic Caucus voted 106-65 to give the Speaker the power to appoint (not nominate) all the Democratic members of the Rules Committee at the beginning of each Congress (eleven members in the 94th Congress, 1975-76). This action of the governing body of House Democrats merely formalized the appointive power of the Speaker, which he had long exercised. By caucus action the Speaker also acquired the power to replace Democratic members on the Rules Committee who do not perform satisfactorily during each two-year term.

REPUBLICAN LEADERSHIP

In contrast with the Democrats, the Republicans allow far more non-leadership participation in the Rules Committee selection process. The Committee on Committees, principally through its executive committee which is dominated by the delegations of the large and politically powerful states and chaired by the minority leader (or Speaker, as the case may be), normally makes the decision, with the concurrence of the senior Republican on the Rules Committee, to fill Republican vacancies on Rules. The Republican leader's preference, though influential, has not necessarily been decisive. For example, Sen. Hugh Scott (R-Pa.), a former member of the House Rules Committee, has said that he cannot recall former Speaker Joseph Martin (R-Mass.) playing any decisive role in securing his appointment to Rules in 1953 during the Eisenhower Congress.[6] Congressman John Anderson, the second-ranking Republican on Rules, related his experience by saying: "I do not recall having any prior conversation with Charles Halleck (R-Ind.), the minority leader, regarding my appointment. I think it is generally true that members of the leadership do have considerable interest in whomever is picked. I don't know that I would go quite so far as to say that everyone who aspires to a seat on that committee has always had the suggestion that they serve emanate from the leadership."[7]

The Republicans can permit themselves more non-leadership participation in their Rules Committee membership selection process primarily for at least two reasons:

1. As Manley and Fenno suggested in their studies of the Ways and Means Committee and Appropriations Committee, the Republican membership has been remarkably homogeneous in its political and economic philosophies. By the same token, the executive committee of the Republican Committee on Committees has been dominated by conservative party regulars almost to a man.[8] One must consider this homogeneity to understand why it is easier for the Republican leadership to accept more participation by other established institutions within the House structure than it is for the Democrats.

2. The fact that the Republicans have managed to control the House only twice since 1931 (80th and 83rd Congresses) has essentially reduced the need for their leadership's close supervision of their Rules members for the purpose of planning their legislative program. John Anderson explained this phenomenon by saying, with respect to the Democratic leadership's point of view: "When you look at the committee and the function it serves, you'll see that from the Democratic Speaker's standpoint, it's a little different. He is more desirous of having down-the-line obedience."[9]

The minority status of the Republican Party has weakened the Republican leadership's claim for their party's complete identity with the Rules Committee. However, the homogeneous character of the House Republican establishment has cancelled out the disadvantage of not being able to exert complete dominance over the membership recruitment process. The end result is that only members philosophically acceptable to the Republican leadership are appointed to the Rules Committee from the Republican ranks.

To say that the Republican leader does not have absolute power to appoint Rules Committee members is not to say that he does not participate actively in the recruiting process. Because he must depend upon responsiveness from the Republican Rules Committee members, he attempts to appoint loyal and dependable members to the committee. In relating his experience in connection with the appointment of Congressman Del Clawson (R-Calif.) to the committee in 1973, Dave Martin, then ranking minority member, stated, "It was satisfactory with Gerry Ford, the minority leader. I suppose in a way he was the one who gave final approval to the appointment of Mr. Clawson."[10]

EXPECTED QUALIFICATIONS

Both Democratic and Republican leadership expectations have been evident in the assignment of members to the Rules Committee. It is almost the unwritten law that prospective committee members must "pass" both intangible and tangible tests at the time of their selection.

Intangible Qualifications

Any weighing of the committee's probable effectiveness with and without the prospective member inevitably involves evaluating some of his intangible qualifications as a person and a congressman. For instance, Matsunaga's selection in 1967 was of special interest because there was some speculation that he was selected to appease those who were insisting that a nonwhite be placed on the "all-white power committee." (That was long before Andrew Young (D-Ga.), a black congressman, was appointed to the committee by Speaker Albert in 1975.) However, when queried later, former Speaker John McCormack denied that racial considerations had played any part in the selection of Matsunaga.

Leaders of both parties spoke of "exceptional ability," "personal integrity," "enthusiasm to serve," and "independent judgment" as qualifications for selection. Since these qualifications cannot be quantified and measured easily, they can only be interpreted as being equal to the personal acceptability of the congressman to the men who constitute the majority and minority leadership, and, in the case of the Republicans, the Committee on Committees and the senior member on Rules.

Tangible Qualifications

Electoral security. Masters, Fenno, and Manley have all theorized that one of the qualifications for membership on the three exclusive House committees is coming from a "safe district," i.e., the prospective member must come from a district in which he can be expected to win re-election.[11] This qualification appears to be especially applicable to membership on the Rules Committee, the theory being that since the Committee on Rules is an arm of the leadership (whereas the other two prestigious committees are not), a member of the Rules Committee must be strong enough in his own district so that he need not yield to each and every home constituent demand while trying to support the programs designed by the leadership or the party.

Since 1953, no member of the Democratic Party with a popular vote percentage of less than 56.7% in his district immediately before committee assignment has been appointed to the Rules Committee. By the same token, no Republican with a popular vote percentage of less than 53.5% has been appointed to the committee. Indeed, if Hugh Scott with his credentials as Eisenhower campaign manager and Republican National Chairman were excluded, the lowest Republican average would have been the 57.2% of William Avery (R-Kan.) (see Table 4.1, p. 153). This safe-district margin of Rules Committee members compares favorably with similar margins on the other two exclusive committees. Fenno observed that 26.9%, or more than one-fourth, of the Appropriations Committee members on both sides of the aisle had a popular vote average of less than 55%.[12] Also, Manley found that of the twenty-eight Democrats first elected to the Committee on Ways and Means since 1947, only four failed to receive more than 55% of the vote in the election immediately preceding their assignment to Ways and Means; and of the twenty-four Republicans appointed to the committee since 1947, five did not break the 55% mark.[13]

Ironically, although named as a major qualification by both party leaderships, the electoral safety factor can also contribute to independence, unreliability, and even rebellion on the part of individual members. Colmer and Delaney among the Democrats and Republican Anderson may be cited as examples of this, sometimes on crucial partisan issues.

Although the leadership's nod was needed for a Democrat to be initially elected to the Rules Committee, until January, 1975, he needed no such approval *to remain* a member of the committee. Upon his reelection to the House, his membership on the committee was automatically continued. By action of the Democratic Caucus of the 94th Congress, the Speaker now has the power to appoint anew the whole Democratic membership at the beginning of every Congress. This new policy may control member independence and unreliability. The Republican leader, on the other hand, cannot dismiss a Rules Committee member, and a member's popularity at home may continue to breed independence from the leadership.

The selection process seems to indicate that the Rules Committee member, once appointed, will remain loyal to his leader and party, subject only to occasional deviations based on his personal political judgment and principles. However, political views as expressed in party platforms, and as espoused by individuals, do change over the years, and the House leadership has occasionally had to cope with renegades. Colmer, for example, was appointed to the Rules Committee as a New Dealer during Franklin D. Roosevelt's administration, but over the years he became an out-and-out conservative and sided with the Republicans more than with the Democrats. Colmer used to admit to the unbeliever, "It is true that I was a New Dealer. In fact, I even traveled to Ohio to speak for FDR's reelection at one time."[14] Delaney, a liberal-turned-conservative, cast the crucial vote to kill the federal aid to schools bill in 1962 against the wishes of his party and its leaders. On the Republican side, Representative Anderson, for one, admitted that he is much more liberal today than he was at the time of his appointment to the

Rules Committee. "I am more liberal than I was and have voted against the wishes of the majority of my party," he explained to the authors. "However, being a member of the minority, my loyalty to my leadership should not be measured merely by votes on individual issues on which the party has taken a position."[15]

Another variable which is important to the recruitment of safe members to all exclusive committees is the requirement that a prospective member experience a minimum probation period of one term before appointment. According to Fenno, "by enforcing a House apprenticeship, the selectors helped to bring about the selection of Committee members with safe election margins. The putative 'one-termer' is automatically eliminated from consideration, and the man whose electoral circumstances will not allow him to adopt the House as an important reference group can be spotted."[16] While a House minority leader, Gerald Ford spoke in support of this view by stating, "A person doesn't get on the Rules Committee without serving a period of time in the House."[17] Between 1947 and 1975 no freshman Democrat was ever assigned to the Ways and Means Committee, and only four out of twenty-four Republicans appointed to Ways and Means were freshmen.[18]

Due primarily to the comparatively larger size of the Appropriations Committee, 15% (18) of all its members appointed since 1947 have been freshmen.[19] In comparison, as shown in Table 4.2 (p. 154), no freshman congressman from either party, except Clem McSpadden, was given a Rules Committee seat from 1953 to 1975. In fact, up until 1973, except for John O'Connor in 1923, no freshman, at the beginning of his first session, has ever received a Rules Committee assignment.[20]

McSpadden came to Congress in 1973 with an unusual set of credentials. Majority Leader O'Neill described McSpadden's House debut: "McSpadden is the Speaker's own personal choice. He served twenty years in the state senate and is a tremendously powerful man in his own home state. He has been very close to Speaker Albert through the years. With the appointment of McSpadden, the Speaker has gained a trustworthy ally on the Rules Committee and at the same time set a precedent. Anyone in a position of leadership, like the Speaker, likes to set precedents because people will forever

refer to them as history-making."[21] Speaker Albert did break the
accepted House tradition of not nominating freshman members to
the Rules Committee, but he did not neglect to observe the purpose
for which this tradition was established, i.e., to require the apprenticeship period needed to gauge the member's electoral security,
dependability, and loyalty to the leadership's satisfaction. In the
case of McSpadden, Speaker Albert simply did not need the probation period to satisfy his expectations.

Loyalty to party leadership. An expectation strongly emphasized
by the leaders of both parties is "loyalty to the party leadership"
(see Appendix A-2). However, there are significant differences between a congressman's loyalty to his party and his loyalty to the
House leadership. On the one hand, party loyalty requires him to
support the planks laid down in his party's platform, his party's
caucus decision, or even proposals spelled out in White House mes-
sages if he happens to wear the same party label as the President.
On the other hand, loyalty to the House leadership involves a personal relationship not necessarily tied to party ideology. For all practical purposes, the House leadership's concept of loyalty is of this
type. This is especially true when loyalty is discussed in relation to
selection of members for the Rules Committee. The Rules Committee would cease to function as a leadership committee if the
element of personal loyalty were completely disregarded.

How then should the leadership measure a prospective member's
loyalty? A tangible basis on which party loyalty can be measured is
the *Congressional Quarterly's* party unity/disunity score. The party
whip's vote tabulation records and other types of statistical surveys
can also be used. These measurements, of course, can only indicate
a member's past voting pattern, not how he intends to vote after he
is named to the committee. Nevertheless, the past voting record of
a member appears to be a major consideration in the eyes of the
leadership.

From 1953 to 1975, none of the committee Democrats, except
McSpadden, had less than a 70 party unity score or more than a
12.5 party disunity score (on a scale of 100) at the time of their
selection.[22] Although the Republicans were less rigid on the loyalty
variable in two cases (Hugh Scott had a unity score of 60 and dis-

unity score of 18, and William Avery had a unity score of 63 and disunity score of 27.5), their overall minimum party unity score stood at 71 and maximum disunity score at 12.5 (see Table 4.1, p. 153).

As suggested earlier, the Democratic leadership, by its initial insistence on party loyalty, has been able to exercise a degree of control over the Rules Committee members. This assumption can be further substantiated by the fact that the Rules Committee evidences a higher minimum party unity score for Democratic appointments than the two other exclusive committees. Immediately preceding their assignment, seven of thirty Democrats appointed to the Ways and Means Committee since 1951 had had a party unity score of less than 70.[23] In the same period of time, more than half (twelve out of seventeen) of the Democratic appointees to the Appropriations Committee had not made the 70 mark.

In contrast, since 1951 no Republican with a unity score of less than 60 (the minimum for Rules appointment) has been appointed to either of the two money committees except Joseph McDade (R-Pa.). His score was 59 when he took his committee seat in 1965. It is rather apparent that the Republican leadership has not been demanding a higher standard of party loyalty for Rules Committee appointments than for appointments to the money committees.

In an attempt to develop a system for determining eligibility for membership on the Rules Committee, the authors devised a scheme of measuring the so-called tangible qualifications. While the authors are fully aware of the limitations of any scheme which omits the intangibles which are necessarily considered in the selection process, they believe they may have hit upon a method which could be applied in the preliminary phase of selection.

The scheme simply calls for comparing the minimum popular vote percentage and the *Congressional Quarterly* party unity and disunity scores which have been "required" since 1953 by each party (see Table 4.1) to an individual's own popular vote percentage and unity scores. When the device is used to determine the eligibility for Rules Committee membership of members of the 93rd Congress (minus the freshmen members who are by tradition not assigned to Rules), a total of fifty Democrats and ninety-five Republicans emerge as being "qualified" in this initial phase of selection (see Table 4.3, p. 155). In keeping with the policy that no state may be assigned more than one seat on Rules, qualified members of both parties coming from states already represented on the committee were also eliminated. In addition, since it has been hypothesized that congressmen already serving on an exclusive committee or enjoying great seniority on any other standing committee (belonging to the top ¼ of their party's hierarchy on a committee) are not likely to accept a Rules appointment (see p. 73), these senior House members were also excluded from consideration. By a process of elimination the authors finally came up with two lists of prospective candidates for Rules Committee vacancies. When presented with the Democratic list, one Democratic leader commented, "What do you know? It so happens that the leadership does have its eyes on one of your finalists for possible future service on the Rules Committee."

Curiously, of the members of the 93rd Congress's Rules Committee, only four Democrats (Madden, Matsunaga, Murphy, and Long) survived the test, as did four Republicans. The remaining six Democrats and one Republican (Anderson) failed to meet the minimum party unity score and consequently would not have been considered for Rules Committee service in 1973. The exceedingly low Democratic survival rate (40%) and correspondingly high disqualification rate (60%) strongly indicate an institutionalization process which demands a member's increasing loyalty to the committee and point to the difficult task which the Democratic leadership faces in expecting the selected members to maintain their loyalty to it continuously (see Table 4.3).

HOUSE INSTITUTIONAL EXPECTATIONS

While the satisfaction of leadership expectations in the recruitment process serves House integrative aims, other institutional expectations, if fulfilled, serve as environmental restraints on leadership influence. The two sets of expectations, therefore, can and will work at cross purposes from time to time. In other words, the fulfillment of leadership expectations may mean the frustration of institutional expectations and vice versa.

REGIONAL AND STATE EXPECTATIONS

The regional and state delegations expect the committee makers to appoint candidates to Rules vacancies from among the members of the delegations. In the past, certain norms have been followed in making these appointments.

First, no state has ever had more than one member from each party on the Rules Committee. In the 92nd Congress, California and Tennessee had two members each and in the 93rd and 94th California and Illinois have had two members each, but in both instances the members belonged to opposite political parties.

This one state–one member principle is designed to assure a fair geographical distribution of membership, in accordance with the state delegation expectations, in view of the small size of the Rules Committee. So far the Democratic leadership, even in its zealous search for highly responsive members for the committee, has not yet found it necessary to break this restraint. In contrast, the considerably larger Appropriations Committee has always allotted more than one seat each to some large state delegations. The Ways and Means Committee has also occasionally had two members from the same state with the same party affiliation, and Illinois, New York, and Texas now have two Democratic members each.[24]

Second, both parties have given serious consideration to maintaining a geographic balance so that no region of the country would have an advantage over the others on the Rules Committee. The West, however, has traditionally been at a disadvantage in obtaining seat assignments. In 1945, there was only one Rules member from the area west of the Mississippi River and none from that area west of the Missouri River.[25] In the 90th, 91st, and 92nd Congresses, the regional distribution in the committee showed three Democrats from the South, two from the East, two from the West, one from the Midwest, and two from the border states; there were three Republicans from the Midwest, one from the West, and one from a border state.[26]

Both parties observed regional principles in the 1973 membership change (the first in three Congresses) with the exception of the substitution of Murphy (D-Ill.) from the Midwest for the seat vacated by the easterner, O'Neill. At the beginning of the 94th

Congress, the East's representation was increased by one with the addition of William Moakley (D-Mass.). The replacement of the retiring Dave Martin (R-Nebr.) by Trent Lott (R-Miss.) marked the first time that a member from the Deep South had served on the Republican side.

Although regional demands have placed some limitations on the leadership's choice, the limitations have not been too stringent. For instance, in 1955 Speaker Rayburn nominated members from Missouri, Arkansas, and Massachusetts to fill the slots vacated by members from Illinois, Georgia, and Washington respectively. Speaker John McCormack appointed Matsunaga of Hawaii to succeed Judge Smith of Virginia in 1967. This certainly was a choice which did not reflect regional expectations. The Republican Committee on Committees, under the leadership of Martin, Halleck, and Ford, has also had a record of filling Rules Committee seats by nominating congressmen who were not from the same regions to which their successors belonged.

Third, big-state delegations from both parties normally want to claim a vacant seat on the Rules Committee if possible. Morgan Murphy (D-Ill.) described the activities of his delegation in helping him to get on the committee in this way:

> The Illinois delegation met in caucus and it was suggested that there was an opening on the Rules Committee, and that Illinois had not had a position on the prestigious committee for twenty-two years, since Congressman Sabath was its chairman. My fellow Democratic members from Illinois made a concerted effort on my behalf with the Speaker and that effort was led by Congressman Melvin Price, the dean of our delegation, Frank Annunzio, and Dan Rostenkowski, who is on the Ways and Means Committee. They and other influential Illinoisans persuaded the Speaker to select me.[27]

In speaking of the Illinois Republican delegation's role in getting him assigned to the Rules Committee in 1964, John Anderson said, "In my own case, the minority whip, Leslie Arends, who comes from Illinois and by seniority is the dean of the Illinois delegation, had a hand. I had his help when I sought this position, and to that extent he was an initiating factor."[28] Hugh Scott, relating the experience of his original appointment in 1953, stated:

> The strong support of the Pennsylvania delegation had been chiefly responsible for my assignment to the Rules Committee in the Republican-controlled 83rd Congress. Then the Democrats held control in the 84th Congress and I was dropped from Rules and given an assignment on Judiciary. In the 85th Congress, however, there was a vacancy for the fourth Republican seat on Rules and the Pennsylvania delegation again pushed me to take the seat. The Republican conservatives fought to have a Californian on the committee — to no avail. I got the seat by about five votes difference in the Committee on Committees. The fact that former Pennsylvania Congressmen Harry Ransley and Robert Rich served on Rules had helped my delegation's claims.[29]

On the "same-state rule," Republican John Anderson had the following to say: "Leo Allen, one of my predecessors, had been on the committee and was a former chairman of the committee. There had been an Illinois seat, so to speak. I got on the committee because my immediate predecessor, Elmer Hoffman, resigned from Rules to go back to Illinois to run for the Secretary of State."[30]

While there is no written rule or even established tradition, there is a marked tendency for a large-state delegation which loses a member on the committee by resignation, retirement, or defeat at the polls to claim the vacant seat for another of its members.[31] Often these claims are successful. For example, on the Republican side, John Anderson (Ill.) succeeded Elmer Hoffman (Ill.) in 1960, Delbert Latta (Ohio) replaced Clarence Brown (Ohio) in 1965, and Del Clawson (Calif.) followed H. Allen Smith (Calif.) in 1973. On the Democratic side, James Delaney (N.Y.) replaced John Delaney (N.Y.) in 1949 and John Young (Tex.) succeeded Homer Thornberry (Tex.) in 1964.[32]

These illustrations of adherence to the same-state variable are not intended necessarily to provide norms for the selection process. They are offered to show the role the state delegations may have played. One should bear in mind that while the state variable can be decisive to the Republicans, it can be merely influential to the

Democrats because of the predominant role played by the Democratic leadership, which allows less room for maneuvering by state delegations. Since 1941 the Democrats have filled vacancies on Rules following the same-state principle only 14.3% of the time (three of twenty-one cases), whereas in the same period and with fewer seats to distribute, the Republicans have filled their vacancies using the same-state "rule" 35.2% of the time (six of thirteen cases). The following support the contention that Democratic Speakers do not usually yield to the state delegations' attempts to satisfy their expectations to the point of frustrating the leadership's demands: Speaker Rayburn invoked the same-state "rule" only twice in his twelve opportunities to make appointments (not including enlargement appointments); John McCormack invoked the "rule" only once in four appointments; and Speaker Albert did not countenance the "rule" at all in his five new appointments.

EXPECTATIONS OF CHAIRMAN AND RANKING MINORITY MEMBER

The question to what extent, if any, the incumbent Rules Committee chairman's and the ranking minority member's expectations can be satisfied in filling the vacancies may also be raised. Although the normative structure of the House does not preclude leadership–committee chairman consultation of this kind, the Democrats have not so consulted since the addition of four Rules members in 1955. This happened for the Democrats because of the differences of political philosophy between the Democratic leadership and Chairmen Smith of Virginia and Colmer of Mississippi.

Speaker McCormack, for instance, in reply to the question as to whether or not former Chairman Colmer of the Rules Committee had any hand in Matsunaga's selection, said, "Absolutely not! The Rules Committee is an arm of the leadership, and the Speaker must have complete freedom to select those members on whose personal loyalty he can reasonably depend."[33] When O'Neill was asked in 1971 whether or not the current leadership would consult Representative Colmer in case of a Democratic vacancy, he replied, "No, absolutely no, we are now concerned with the task of getting the Rules Committee completely back to the leadership's fold."[34]

The Democratic leaders have thus made it clear that they will not allow their own expectations to be frustrated by those of the committee chairman regarding Rules appointments. On the other hand, a cooperative chairman who has the same expectations as those of the leaders can and will be consulted by them. With regard to the case of Chairman Madden, Majority Leader O'Neill relates, "Before the appointments took place in 1973, Madden was informed of what was going to happen and asked if he had any objections. He was told of the background, caliber, consistency, and dependability of each of the three men and he had no objections."[35] Madden himself corroborated the above, "Yes, Speaker Albert mentioned the new members to me before the official appointment. I told him Murphy, Long, and McSpadden were all satisfactory to me."[36] Similarly, John Manley concluded that Chairman Mills of the Ways and Means Committee had been consulted by the party leaders on Ways and Means' Democratic assignments since Mills was the chairman of the Democratic Committee on Committees and considered a party regular himself.[37] By the same token, Chairman George Mahon of the Appropriations Committee has been exerting some influence over Democratic selections because he has been living up to House and leadership expectations. However, according to Richard Fenno, his predecessor, former Chairman Clarence Cannon (D-Mo.), was seldom consulted about Democratic choices for Appropriations vacancies by either the leadership or the Democratic Committee on Committees members because he became unacceptable to the House and leadership in 1962. In fact, in 1962 five new Democratic members were added to that committee by the leadership without Cannon's knowledge.[38]

There appears to be a direct relationship between the Democratic leadership's willingness to consult and an individual committee chairman's demonstrated behavior toward the leadership. The Republican leadership, on the other hand, appears to make it a practice to consult the senior member on the committee. Although conditions governing the selection process change, this has been the case at least for the years since 1964. John Anderson reported that "Congressman Clarence Brown (R-Ohio), the ranking minority member of the committee, approved my more conservative voting record and nomination to the committee in 1964."[39] Speaking of his own appointment, Dave Martin, then ranking minority member, said, "Mr. Brown was for me and the minority leader, Halleck, was against me. Brown's wishes prevailed in the Committee on Committees."[40]

Martin's appointment seems to suggest that the ranking minority member of the Rules Committee in 1964 was able to overrule the wishes even of the minority leader. Then, in 1972, H. Allen Smith, the outgoing senior Republican, appears to have picked his successor on the committee. Martin recalled:

> Well, actually I was consulted about the Clawson appointment. We had this situation: Allen Smith from California, who was the ranking member, announced early in 1972 that he would retire. He wanted to hold his seat for California. He visited with me about it because it was anticipated that I would very probably be the ranking Republican in the new Congress since John Anderson would not be eligible by remaining as Republican Conference Chairman. Allen Smith is really the one that sort of handpicked Del Clawson.[41]

Manley also recognized the active involvement of the senior Republican member on Ways and Means in the recruitment process. In describing the role of Congressman John Byrnes (R-Wis.), the immediate past ranking minority member, Manley stated, "He is notified of potential nominees before the final decision is made by the Republican Committee on Committees. This courtesy notification symbolizes that the ranking Republican does check the flow of members to the Committee."[42] When asked whether he has an informal veto power over the Republican committee recruitment process, Congressman Byrnes stated: "I suppose if I had a real strong feeling against the choice of the Committee on Committees, I would have a veto. But that doesn't really happen in practice. For the most part, the objectives of the committee would be the same as mine. There is no nice formula for the selection process. It is just a matter internally discussed between the ranking member and members of the executive committee of the Committee on Committees."[43] Congressman Herman Schneebeli, the current ranking Republican member, added, "I have only a negative role, a veto power. I don't even know whether my veto would always be upheld.

At least they would give me the courtesy of saying 'Would you object to so and so?' "[44]

In the case of the Appropriations Committee the same general guideline for Republican membership selection also holds true. The Republican leader, being the chairman of the Committee on Committees, obviously has a definite, but not necessarily decisive, influence over the choice of prospective Appropriations Committee members. Fenno observed the important role played by the senior Republican on the committee with this remark, "The Republicans have given (at least up until John Taber's retirement in 1962) great influence to their senior man on the Appropriations Committee itself."[45] Taber's successor, Congressman Frank Bow, ranking minority member until 1973 (since deceased), also commented: "The Committee on Committees could, of course, approve anyone without my clearance. But they don't. Normally, I approved. In fact, Ohio and I used to have the largest number of votes of any state on the Committee on Committees."[46]

Representative Elford Cederberg (R-Mich.), the incumbent ranking minority member, although also on the Committee on Committees, did not go as far as his predecessor in his remarks: "The statement that the ranking minority member has veto power is not quite correct. However, he does have an input into the Committee on Committees. It is fair to say that if the ranking Republican has stated that the prospective appointee is absolutely unsuitable to him, the Committee on Committees would probably respect that. It is not a veto power. It is a courtesy."[47] Apparently the senior Republican on Rules has had a record of more active involvement in the recruitment process than his counterparts on the other two exclusive committees.

CANDIDATE EXPECTATIONS AND NONEXPECTATIONS

While the final decision to appoint rests with the committee makers, the final decision to serve rests with the potential committee member. For this reason it is important to examine the recruitment process from the candidate's perspective.

Lester G. Seligman spoke of three different patterns a candidate could follow to gain a committee seat. They are self-starting, inner-circle recruitment, and cooptation.[48] All three patterns characterize recruitment to the Rules Committee.

Self-starting

Rohde and Shepsle are not quite accurate when they assert that the Rules candidate almost never initiates his own appointment process.[49] Because of the prestige attached to a Rules appointment, and the small number of vacancies that usually occur on that committee, a member without an "inside track" would probably not hope for or initiate the "impossible." However, this consideration has not prevented some from trying and even succeeding. On the Democratic side, William Colmer was an admitted self-starter. As he recalls, "Frankly, I wanted to go on the committee. My friend of the same conservative philosophy, who was on the Ways and Means, had more to do than anyone else. He spoke to Speaker Rayburn and I spoke to the Speaker myself in 1940."[50]

A more recent example is the case of Gillis Long, who admitted: "Actually I sought the assignment. I, as a nonconsecutive second-termer, was not in a position by seniority and historical precedent to expect too much. But frankly, I went out after it and aggressively sought the seat."[51] John Anderson is the Republican case in point. He relates, "As you know, Elmer Hoffman resigned to run for Illinois Secretary of State in 1964 and left the state without representation on Rules. I actively sought to succeed him by discussing the matter with the Committee on Committees."[52]

Inner-Circle Recruitment

Both parties have recruited members of the Rules Committee through the inner-circle method. One should, however, recognize the vagueness of the demarcation between the self-starting and inner-circle patterns. On the one hand, a member's initiative could quickly develop into a concerted action on the part of his delegation together with that of his other supporters; on the other hand, the activities and encouragement of an inner circle of friends could also interest the member enough to start his own campaign for appointment. Both methods lack the element of surprise for the member, which is normally prevalent in cooptation.

Democrat Morgan Murphy made it very clear that he got on the committee with the Illinois state delegation's initiative and support, and Republican Del Clawson is another who suggested inner-circle recruitment when he related the story of his appointment: "Last year when Allen Smith made the announcement that he would retire, some members of the California delegation came to ask me to take his seat. They felt that California with its political clout in the House Republican party should be able to retain its seat on Rules. Then during the campaign, William Mailliard, chairman of the delegation, came to me again asking for my decision."[53]

Cooptation

The Democratic segment of the Rules Committee is noted for its high rate of cooptation in recruitment because of the leadership's commitment to finding highly responsive men. The record is quite full of surprised members tapped for Rules service. Tip O'Neill has told this story of his appointment in 1955: "I [had] applied for Public Works and was sitting in the dining room one morning [when] Mr. Walters came over to me and said, 'I was down at the Speaker's apartment. I understand that you are going on the Rules Committee.' That was amazing. I [had] never applied for it and nobody had even asked me about it."[54]

B. F. Sisk was called by Speaker Rayburn one afternoon in 1961 and asked to go on Rules. When Sisk asked for some time to consider the offer, he was given until 8:00 the next morning to make a decision. Congressman Claude Pepper (D-Fla.) stated his experience in the following reminiscence: "Speaker McCormack called me up on the telephone in my home in Miami and told me that I should tell nobody but my wife that he was going to recommend me for the Rules Committee."[55]

The senior author himself, having served only two terms in the

Congress, and being from the youngest and one of the smallest states in the Union, was not seeking a Rules Committee position. He had had the good fortune of stepping into a subcommittee chairmanship on the Committee on Agriculture in his second term, and he was anticipating his second subcommittee chairmanship, as a relatively senior member of the Post Office and Civil Service Committee. Matsunaga was taken by complete surprise, therefore, when Speaker McCormack, accompanied by Majority Leader Albert and Majority Whip Boggs, approached him on the day of the pre-session Democratic caucus and said, "Spark, we want you to serve on the Rules Committee."

Matsunaga's response was, "Who, me?"

"Yes, you," the Speaker continued, "and we won't take 'no' for an answer."

Matsunaga was flattered and delighted with the leadership's choice, but jokingly replied, "You mean I haven't got a choice?" However, he followed his question with an immediate affirmative, "I will serve."

Similarly, William Anderson (D-Tenn.) and Clem McSpadden (D-Okla.), appointed to the Rules Committee in 1967 and 1973 respectively, were also caught by complete surprise when told of the intentions of the Speaker. McSpadden, being a freshman who had definitely not thought of the "impossible," told of his experience in the following words: "I asked to be on the Interior Committee, on which my predecessor served, and [which] is vital to my constituency interest. The Speaker looked at me and said, 'How would you like to serve on the Rules Committee?' and I guess it was ten seconds before I could say anything. I asked him if he was serious. It would be like a poor kid getting three bicycles and four electric trains for Christmas, having never owned a toy."[56]

The authors could not discover a single definite case of Republican cooptation from all the incumbents interviewed. On their side of the aisle the element of surprise was completely lacking. There appears to be some correlation between the fact that the Republican leadership demands less responsiveness from its Rules Committee members and the fact that the Republican recruitment process has lacked cooptation, at least in recent years.

CANDIDATE NONEXPECTATIONS

While members with aspirations to serve on the Rules Committee could be satisfied in the previously mentioned ways, a few have actually refused to serve on the committee, purely for their own personal considerations. Thus, for various reasons the best-qualified members may not wish to serve on the Rules Committee. The chairman and ranking minority member of any other standing committee, for example, would obviously be out of the picture. So would the chairmen and ranking minority members of important subcommittees of other major House committees. James O'Hara (D-Mich.), for example, chose to remain as a senior member on the Education and Labor Committee and to wait for the opportunity to become a major subcommittee chairman instead of accepting the invitation of Speaker McCormack to fill the vacancy left by Howard Smith's defeat in 1967. On the other hand, Edith Green (D-Ore.) gave up her ranking majority position on the Education and Labor Committee to take a near-the-bottom seat on Appropriations in 1973. Her decision must, however, be considered the exception rather than the rule.

Incumbent members of the other two exclusive committees may be expected to refuse to serve on another equally important committee if it means moving down to the bottom of the seniority ladder. Since 1937, only Hamer Budge (R-Idaho) and Del Clawson (R-Calif.) have accepted transfers from the Appropriations Committee to the Rules Committee, in 1959 and 1973 respectively.[57] Clawson gave up thirteenth position out of twenty Republicans on the Appropriations Committee to accept fifth position on the Rules Committee.

A member serving on a committee which is extremely important to his constituency may decline a Rules Committee assignment, if it means surrendering his seat on the former committee. Examples would include refusals on the part of farm district members on the Agricultural Committee, western congressmen on the Interior Committee, etc.

Under House rules, membership on the Rules Committee excludes membership on any other standing committee. However, waivers had been allowed in exceptional circumstances until 1975. For example, Representative B. F. Sisk, a farm district congressman serving on the Rules Committee, was allowed by the leadership to serve on the Agriculture Committee. This permission was given because no other California Democrat would accept a seat on the Agriculture Committee, and because the California Democratic delegation believed its agricultural state should not go unrepresented. In fact, when the vacancy on Agriculture occurred in 1969, no other Democrat in the entire House wanted to fill it. More recently, because of the imminent extension of the Sugar Act, which was expiring on December 31, 1971, Matsunaga was able to acquire an additional assignment to the Agriculture Committee in the 92nd and 93rd Congresses. Relying on the Sisk case as a precedent, Matsunaga sought the second committee assignment to protect his sugar-producing constituency interests in Hawaii. Both of these cases are classic exceptions to the rule. A third member of the Rules Committee, Claude Pepper, was permitted to serve on the Internal Security Committee because no other liberal acceptable to the leadership would accept the assignment.

Regardless of the manner of nomination (self-starting, inner-circle recruitment, or cooptation), the refusal or acceptance of a Rules appointment is a decision which must ultimately be made by the member himself on the basis of his assessment of the degree of importance of serving on the Rules Committee compared with the opportunity for more rapid seniority and responsibility advancement elsewhere in the House. As Table 4.4 (p. 157) shows, all the Rules Committee Democrats appointed since 1955 would have been close to the upper one-third mark in the seniority ladder by merely serving four years in their previous assignments.[58] In fact, three Democrats would have become chairman or ranking majority member of a standing committee by now, if they had remained in their previous assignments. All the Democrats except the four junior members who have come to Rules since 1973 would have had the option of becoming subcommittee chairmen or ranking minority members, if they had chosen to continue their previous committee assignments. The Democratic members have accepted the calculated risk of slower advancement in seniority and given up possible subcommittee chairmanships by accepting assignment to the Rules Committee.

Such is the recognition they have given to the importance of the Rules Committee.

On the Republican side of the aisle, however, the Rules Committee members have done better than they would have on their previous committees, perhaps because of the extremely small Republican membership on Rules which makes every step up the seniority ladder a significant one. In fact, since 1953 only Delbert Latta (R-Ohio) would have fared better on a previously assigned committee (by becoming second ranking Republican on Agriculture if he had remained on it instead of changing to Rules).

If this study is correct, the student of the committee should have little doubt that the Democratic recruitment process has long been an instrument employed by the majority leadership to satisfy its goal of gaining or keeping the loyalty of the Rules Committee. Neither of the other two exclusive committees has ever received such scrutiny from the Speaker with regard to its recruitment procedure. In fact, the Speaker's prerogative of choosing new Rules members always has been able to cancel out environmental constraints such as state, regional, and committee chairman expectations. The 1974 Democratic decision giving the Speaker the power to appoint the Democratic members has merely formalized his long-continued past practice.

NOTES

1. Interview, June 13, 1973.

2. Interview, November 30, 1971.

3. Telephone interview with D. B. Hardeman, former aide to Sam Rayburn, March 1, 1972.

4. Interview, July 30, 1973.

5. For a more detailed study on the Democratic leadership's role in recruitment for the Ways and Means and Appropriations committees see Richard Fenno, *The Power of the Purse: Appropriations Politics in Congress* (Boston: Little, Brown & Co., 1966); and John Manley, *The Politics of Finance: The House Committee on Ways and Means* (Boston: Little, Brown & Co., 1970).

6. Interview, November 1, 1971 (through his secretary, Edith B. Skinner).

7. Interview, August 3, 1971.

8. Fenno, *Power of the Purse*, pp. 68-70; and Manley, *Politics of Finance*, pp. 38-40.

9. Interview, August 3, 1971.

10. Interview, July 13, 1973.

11. Nicholas Masters, "Committee Assignments in the House of Representatives," *American Political Science Review*, June, 1961, pp. 345-57; Fenno, *Power of the Purse;* and Manley, *Politics of Finance.*

12. *Power of the Purse*, p. 58.

13. *Politics of Finance*, p. 51.

14. Interview, October 5, 1973.

15. Interview, March 11, 1971.

16. *Power of the Purse*, p. 58.

17. Interview, September 18, 1970.

18. Manley, *Politics of Finance*, p. 49. Freshman Democrat Harold Ford was elected after ten months in the House as a replacement for a fellow Tennessean, Richard Fulton, who resigned when elected mayor of Nashville.

19. Fenno, *Power of the Purse*, p. 58.

20. James A. Robinson, *The House Rules Committee* (Indianapolis: Bobbs-Merrill, 1963), p. 92.

21. Interview, July 30, 1973.

22. One factor which explains James Stanton's defeat in his contest with Morgan Murphy for a Rules Committee seat was his low party unity score of 59 and high disunity score of 25.

23. Four out of twenty-four Democratic appointees had below average scores from 1951 to 1966. Omar Burleson of Texas and James Corman of California were appointed in 1969 with low scores. See Manley, *Politics of Finance*, p. 51.

24. Democrats Thomas Cullen and Walter Lynch of New York served together on Ways and Means in the 78th Congress and Republicans Frank Crowther and Daniel Reed, also of New York, served in the 77th Congress.

25. Robinson, *House Rules Committee*, p. 101.

26. The geographic regions of Rules Committee members have been designated as follows: East — Massachusetts, New York; South — Florida, Georgia, Mississippi, Louisiana, Texas; Midwest — Illinois, Indiana, Nebraska, Ohio; Border — Missouri, Tennessee, Oklahoma; West — California, Hawaii.

27. Interview, June 19, 1973.

28. Interview, March 12, 1971.

29. Interview, November 1, 1971 (through his secretary, Edith B. Skinner).

30. Interview, March 12, 1971.

31. For more detailed study on geography and state delegation as variables for committee assignment, see George Goodwin, Jr., "The Seniority System in Congress," *American Political Science Review*, June, 1959, pp. 412-36; also see Charles Bullock, III, "The Influence of State Party Delegations on House Committee Assignments," *Midwest Journal of Political Science,* August, 1971, pp. 525-46.

32. Those seats mentioned are current state seats. The Democrats have held these seats, New York (1939-76) and Texas (1949-76); and the Republicans these, California (1961-76) and Illinois (1940-76), for many years.

33. Interview, December 30, 1970.

34. Interview, November 30, 1971.

35. Interview, July 30, 1973.

36. Interview, July 16, 1973.

37. *Politics of Finance,* p. 52.

38. *Power of the Purse,* p. 430.

39. Interview, August 3, 1971.

40. Interview, March 12, 1971.

41. Interview, July 13, 1973.

42. *Politics of Finance,* p. 52.

43. Interview, March 6, 1972.

44. Interview, July 12, 1973.

45. *Power of the Purse,* p.55.

46. Interview, March 6, 1972.

47. Interview, July 19, 1973.

48. Lester G. Seligman, "Recruitment in Politics," *Prod,* March, 1958, pp. 14-17.

49. David Rohde and Kenneth Shepsle, "Democratic Committee Assignments in the House of Representatives: Strategic Aspects of a Social Choice Process," *American Political Science Review,* September, 1973, p. 892.

50. Interview, October 5, 1973.

51. Interview, July 13, 1973.

52. Interview, March 6, 1972.

53. Interview, July 13, 1973.

54. Interview, December 1, 1970.

55. Interview, September 19, 1970.

56. Interview, July 12, 1973.

57. Robinson, *House Rules Committee,* p. 95.

58. The four-year time span was chosen for two reasons: 1) Two-thirds of the congressmen have completed their committee transferring process during the period of four years (see Charles Bullock, III, "Committee Transfers in the U.S. House of Representatives," paper prepared for the Midwest Political Science Association Annual Meeting, April 29–May 1, 1971, Chicago, p. 12); and 2) The average of Rules Committee members' congressional service prior to Rules appointment is 5 years (see Table 4.2, p. 154).

5

Committee Members' Goals

GOALS

Besides having their own goals as individual congressmen, members of the Rules Committee share the committee's goals and adapt themselves to meet the expectations of the House. They are also under the same House sanctions that constrain the committee.

The attractiveness or importance of a standing committee from the standpoint of an individual member can be measured in a number of ways. One way is the Eberhart Formula, which calls for the use of variables such as the length of the member's service when appointed, length of service on the committee, the holding power of the committee, the drawing power of the committee, and a combination of drawing and holding powers. The Eberhart Formula as a measure for ranking committees is well known to congressional scholars.[1] Another way is Charles Bullock's attempt to assess committee prestige on the basis of the number of transfers from a committee in relation to the number of transfers to it.[2]

INFLUENCE AND PRESTIGE

Fenno, on the other hand, spoke of members' goals in terms of influence within the House, good public policy, and reelection. He concluded that the members of the two money committees were influence- and prestige-oriented, stating: "To sum up, the vast majority of Appropriations and Ways and Means Committee members come to their committees seeking influence in the House.

Though dwarfed, in both cases, by the emphasis on House influence they display a secondary concern for furthering their policy preferences and their re-election."[3]

The Rules Committee members interviewed unanimously displayed a similar desire for influence and prestige. Tip O'Neill, even before he became majority whip and, subsequently, majority leader, suggested that "a member of the Rules Committee is almost as influential as a member of the leadership."[4] Richard Bolling, a senior Democrat on the committee, concurred by saying, "I think it would be easy to establish that the members of the Rules Committee have a little more power than some other members of the Congress."[5]

One can easily find the Republicans speaking in the same vein. For example, John Anderson joined the chorus by saying, "The Rules Committee is a powerful and prestigious committee, and I particularly think so since I have served on committees which are not regarded as major committees."[6]

CONSTITUENCY AND REELECTION BENEFITS

It would be grossly inaccurate to say that the desire for House influence would necessarily exclude or even reduce the desire for reelection. Fenno admitted the possibility of combining the goal of prestige in the House with that of constituency service by stating in his new book, "On Appropriations, the implication is, the Congressman can get funds for his constituency . . . while at the same time wielding a broader influence in the chamber."[7]

Certainly all the Rules Committee members entertained thoughts of reelection and constituency advantages when they joined the committee, as Richard Bolling has attested: "Members on the Rules Committee are generally considered people who can do relatively difficult work and are due some of the special treatment that a member of the leadership gets. I can see no harm in saying that we would use this special status to benefit our districts. If we didn't, I don't think we would be living up to our representative duties. I have always thought it was one of my jobs to get a little bit more for my people than anybody else could get for theirs."[8]

MEANS TO ATTAIN GOALS

An individual member of the Rules Committee shares its collective powers and environmental restraints (discussed in Chapters 2 and 3) with his fellow members. In addition, by virtue of his committee membership, he enjoys a substantial informal power of influence both within and without the committee.

INFLUENCE WITHIN THE RULES COMMITTEE

The comparatively small size of the Rules Committee (fifteen or sixteen members) and the realization by the members that they belong to "an exclusive club" generate some feeling of solidarity among the members. In fact, the members are generally responsive to each other's interests. These acts of mutual assistance usually manifest themselves in one of the following ways:

1. The granting of rules to bills in which members have a personal interest. In the light of what has already been learned about the prerogatives of the chairman in scheduling bills for committee consideration, one might expect the chairman to honor the reasonable requests of committee members for rules on their own bills. However, this was not always true before Colmer took the chair. Chairman Howard Smith, for example, was well known for the arbitrary manner in which he used this power of the chair to determine matters of scheduling. An experience related by Congressman Claude Pepper, a member of the committee, will illustrate this point: "I had a measure pending in the Rules Committee at one time which was endorsed by the administration and by the House leadership, and supported by the majority of the Rules Committee, but when I told the chairman, Judge Smith, that I wanted to call the matter up in the next committee meeting, he shocked me by saying, 'If that is the way you want to play the game, there won't be a meeting at all tomorrow.' "[9]

Chairman Smith's response constituted a real threat in view of his well-known proclivity to absent himself from the Hill to keep the committee from meeting. When queried about his policy of scheduling bills introduced by members of Rules, Smith said, "I would normally schedule bills for the Rules Committee members. However, if I were opposed to it I would not schedule it for anybody. On the other hand, I might schedule it, if I thought it would be turned down by the committee anyway."[10]

Chairman William Colmer was extremely cooperative in complying with the wishes of individual members of the committee. The members, on the other hand, while recognizing the prerogative of the chairman to set the agenda for committee meetings, have been quick to indicate their displeasure when individual members' wishes to schedule their bills were being ignored. For example, when Matsunaga was pushing his Egg Products Inspection Act amendment (H.R. 9020-92nd), which was urgently needed to aid the Hawaiian poultry farmers, Colmer refused to schedule it for committee action. He did so because of some staff misunderstanding. At this juncture, John Young (D-Tex.), a fellow member of the committee, without any solicitation on Matsunaga's part, openly expressed extreme displeasure at the chairman's treatment of Matsunaga's request. A week later the bill was scheduled. Colmer commented himself: "I would schedule hearings for all the bills sponsored by the Rules Committee members. But I would also make a distinction between members' bills and bills cosponsored by members just to show courtesy to noncommittee members. I would resist the scheduling of the latter should I be opposed to it."[11]

The authors checked all the bills (except bills originating in Rules) sponsored by Rules Committee members from the 88th Congress through the 92nd Congress against all the bills which failed to receive either hearings or rules during the same period (see Tables 5.1 and 5.2, p. 161). This check revealed that the members of Rules have succeeded in obtaining hearings for all bills sponsored by them in all five Congresses.

2. The postponement of committee action for a member's benefit. For official or personal reasons, a member might be unable to attend a business session of the Rules Committee on the day a bill of special importance to him had been scheduled for committee action. Since his failure to be recorded for or against such a measure might prove a source of embarrassment for him in his home district, he normally would request a postponement of final action

on the matter until he could attend. While there is no specific committee rule covering the situation, the request usually would be honored for the benefit and protection of the member. In this connection, Mary Spencer Forrest, assistant majority counsel of the committee from 1960 until 1972, observed, "I have never known the committee not to protect a member on a vote by request. However, this is done usually when a member has to be out of town for some good reason, in which case the vote will be delayed until his return."[12]

It should be noted, however, that emphasis here is to be placed on the term *request*. A member who absented himself without requesting a postponement of action would not reasonably expect to be protected. A classic example of the unprotected absentee can be found in the episode which found a committee member, Henry Latham (R-N.Y.), absent for a vote on a bill establishing rules of interpretation governing the limitation of federal court jurisdiction (H.R. 3-85th) in 1958. Latham's interest in the bill was generally known, but Latham's Republican colleague Clarence Brown (R-Ohio) opposed the postponement of action because of Latham's absence. He said in effect that though it should be the minority's duty to protect one of its own if he asked for it, in this instance it would not do so because it had not been so requested by Latham.

3. Floor managing the rule on popular and unpopular bills. Although handling an unpopular bill could hurt a member's reelection chances, floor managing a bill favored by his constituents could enhance the member's status by portraying him as its prime mover. With this in mind, the committee chairman makes his assignment of floor management to members on the majority side. Assignments to the minority members are made by its ranking member. Ordinarily, a request from a committee member to floor manage a specific rule is granted, unless a member with greater seniority has made a similar request. Matsunaga, for example, requested to be assigned to manage the rule for the Sugar Act extension bill (H.R. 8866-92nd), which was of significant interest to the people of Hawaii, but was preempted by a similar request from a senior member, Sisk of California. Matsunaga was, however, assigned to manage the rule on his own bill to repeal the Emergency Detention

Act (H.R. 234-92nd), which meant that he controlled the thirty minutes of debate time allotted to the majority side. The result was that he was able to present his case for the measure completely and successfully.

Conversely, a committee member may for his own safety at the polls or for any other reason refuse an assignment to manage a bill which is unpopular with his constituency. In discussing this issue, Robinson suggested that James Trimble's unfortunate acceptance of Chairman Smith's assignment to manage the debate on the rule to enlarge the committee was partially responsible for Trimble's defeat in 1966.[13] However, Smith himself stated, in an interview, "I usually gave a bill to someone who was for it. I couldn't give a bill to anyone who didn't want to handle it."[14] Chairman Colmer, too, respected the wishes of his committee members in this regard, and Chairman Madden has also. There appears to be an unwritten but strictly observed rule that a member may protect himself by refusing an assignment he really does not want.

4. The approval of resolutions introduced by committee members. Resolutions for which the Rules Committee has original jurisdiction appear to have a better chance of approval if introduced by committee members. Resolutions providing for the creation of House select committees, for example, must be approved by the Rules Committee in the first instance. Resolutions of this nature have generally been buried in the committee without ceremony.

As has been previously noted, members of the Rules Committee, especially Chairman Colmer, have taken a dim view of any proposal to establish or continue a select committee. Despite this prevailing attitude, in 1969 Congressman Pepper, a committee member, not only succeeded in obtaining approval of his resolution (H.Res. 7-91st) to create a select committee on crime (which he chaired), but also secured the committee's adoption of his resolution (H.Res. 155-92nd) to continue the crime-investigating committee for an additional term, even after it had spent one million dollars during its first short term. Under the circumstances, one can only surmise that Pepper's colleagues decided to make an exception in his case primarily because of his membership on the committee.[15] The decision to continue this select committee was not without criticism, however. In referring to this decision Chairman Colmer made this statement: "So far as I know, nothing new has been developed. We have a number of resolutions to set up other committees. We do not have room (office space) for them. I don't know how we can continue one committee and turn down new ones."[16] Membership on the committee makes the necessary difference in decisions of this kind.

5. The opportunity to cast a decisive vote. In view of the fact that Rules with its fifteen members is the smallest standing committee of the House, the vote of each member is crucial and frequently decisive. Every committee member, subject of course to his environmental restraints, is fairly often given the opportunity to cast a tie-breaking vote or a vote which decisively determines the outcome of a committee decision. Two examples of this kind of voting are as follows: Congressman James Delaney (D-N.Y.) has long been given credit for casting the decisive vote on July 18, 1961, to table the Kennedy public school aid bill (H.R. 7300-87th). He thus sided with the five committee Republicans and Smith and Colmer. The National Defense Education Act and a bill to aid colleges were also held up in the Rules Committee by the same vote.[17] Matsunaga had a chance to cast a decisive vote when, on May 14, 1974, he flew back to Washington from Honolulu especially to cast the tie-breaking vote to send the land use planning bill (H.R. 10294-93rd) to the floor.[18]

Table 5.3 (p. 162) shows that an individual Rules member was in a position to cast a decisive vote on from 10% (in the 89th Congress) to 44% (in the 86th Congress) of the roll-call votes. The titles listed in the table suggest that some of these bills contained important legislation.

STATUS OF RULES' MEMBERS OUTSIDE THE COMMITTEE

The very functions assigned to the Rules Committee in the legislative process make it necessary for those seeking a favorable rule for any legislation to appeal to the individual members of the sixteen-member committee. Because it takes only nine votes to win or lose the committee's approval, which necessarily must be had before a measure may be considered by the House, and because many controversial measures frequently win or lose approval by the margin of a single vote, individual members of the committee are regularly solicited for their assistance by interested members of the other committees of the House. Under the circumstances, an individual member is afforded many opportunities to elicit favors in return for a favorable vote. Since the chairmen, ranking minority members, and other senior members of the legislative committees are usually the prime movers of important bills and must appear before the Rules Committee to request favorable rules, it is clear that they are the ones with whom the Rules members have the greatest contact and the most influence. Frequently a member of the Rules Committee is requested by the chairman of a legislative committee to "carry the ball" for him in obtaining a favorable rule on a controversial measure. A Rules Committee member may agree to do this, as a personal favor to that chairman, even if he is not enthusiastically in support of the measure, in the hope that the legislative committee may expedite a bill in which he, the Rules member, has a personal interest. As a result, an individual member of the Rules Committee can be both more effective and more influential than other congressmen. For example, by helping obtain a rule for the controversial measure authorizing the foreign sale of U.S. passenger ships (H.R. 11589-92nd), a bill which had initially been tabled by the Rules Committee, Matsunaga won the gratitude of Edward Garmatz (D-Md.), former chairman of the Committee on Merchant Marine and Fisheries. Subsequently Garmatz agreed to become the principal sponsor of a Matsunaga proposal to develop the tuna fishing industry in the Pacific, thereby assuring favorable action by his own legislative committee.

GOAL SATISFACTIONS

INFLUENCE AND PRESTIGE

One could perhaps get a more accurate reading on the members' satisfactions by using objective criteria and extracommittee comments than by relying on interviews with the members themselves.

Congressional studies frequently contain appraisals of relative status by committee members. An example of this can be found in the following passage quoted by Fenno from an interview with a member of the Committee on Interior and Insular Affairs: "Some people say Appropriations is first, and I think I'd agree. Second, probably Ways and Means. I'd put Interior third. Yes, I think right behind Ways and Means — third."[19] If these remarks can be taken seriously, it would seem that this member, assigned to a committee which is classified as "minor" by the House rules, not as top-ranking by his own standards, must have been someone whose prestige goal could be easily satisfied. What about members of the Rules Committee, which the House has specifically classified as "exclusive"? Do they enjoy the prestige and influence that such classification would seem to indicate?

Both Fenno and Manley in their studies of the money committees leave their readers with the impression that the dual control of these committees over the "purse-string power" is primarily responsible for the prestige they enjoy in the House. On the other hand, the Rules Committee, serving in its capacity as an arm of the leadership, has gained its prestige and influence in the House through its pervasive knowledge of the business of the House and its sense of responsibility to the membership of the House as a whole. According to O'Neill, "The Rules Committee members are the most knowledgeable members of the House. Every important piece of legislation goes before them."[20] The ranking minority member, James Quillen, echoed O'Neill's statement, "I think it's good to be a member of the Rules Committee because you get a smattering of all legislative measures that go to the floor of the House."[21] While expertise alone is not synonymous with leadership, leadership cannot do without the expertise which is provided by Rules Committee members. In this role, in its role as a heat shield, and others, the Rules Committee assumes well-recognized leadership responsibilities. Congressman William Anderson, former member of the committee, acknowledged this leadership responsibility in this way: "In the Rules Committee especially, its members have a responsibility to their colleagues that is unique among the committees. And I think that each member has to keep that responsibility in mind."[22]

Have the Rules Committee members been in fact looked to as leaders of the House? The answer is yes. O'Neill, for one, observed that "the Rules Committee members sit in with the leadership longer and more frequently than others. And when you have a Democratic President, you are invited down to the White House more often than anybody else. You are like being part of the leadership."[23]

The Republicans recognized the leadership quality of their Rules Committee members by making every one a member of their Policy Committee, at least until 1963 when Gerald Ford assumed the minority leadership. As Republican Dave Martin related: "Every Republican Rules Committee member was on the Policy Committee before Ford. As Rules Committee members, actually they have more to say on the specific bills pending before the House than does the Policy Committee."[24] Ford's discontinuation of the practice of including all Republican Rules Committee members on his party's Policy Committee was not an indication of his loss of confidence in the leadership quality of these members. He explained that the reason for the change was to broaden the representation on the Policy Committee to include Republican members of other standing committees of the House.[25]

CONSTITUENCY AND REELECTION BENEFITS

Constituency

It has been hypothesized that the share of distribution of federal funds a congressman receives for his district may be a measure of the power and influence he wields in the Congress. If that hypothesis is valid, the members of the Rules Committee, the "Power Committee" of the House, should fare well in the federal outlays for their respective districts, even when compared with senior members of the legislative committees or leaders of the subcommittees of the Appropriations Committee. While much study of this hypothesis is needed, the authors have made an effort to put it to a test by calculating the Rules Committee members' district federal outlays to see if these outlays are a measure of the committee members' reputed power and influence. Two comparative schemes of study were devised, one based on members' shares of funds from various federal agencies, and the other based on the total allocation of federal funds to members' districts.

 1. Agency allocation scheme. For the purpose of this study, the authors selected seventeen federal agencies with a minimum average annual distribution of one billion dollars each. The figures used were taken from the Office of Economic Opportunity's publication *Federal Outlays*. Fiscal years 1968, 1969, and 1970 were used to strike an average.[26] The agencies which qualified were the Departments of Agriculture; Commerce; Defense; Health, Education and Welfare; Housing and Urban Development; Interior; Labor; Post Office; Transportation; and Treasury; and the Agency for International Development; Atomic Energy Commission; National Aeronautics and Space Administration; Office of Economic Opportunity; Railroad Retirement Board; and Veterans' Administration.

 One pair of leaders was chosen from each legislative committee with jurisdiction over the specific agency for comparison with the Rules Committee members. Whenever there was more than one committee with substantial legislative jurisdiction over an agency, all such committees were included in the study. Generally, the chairmen and ranking minority members of legislative committees in the 91st and 92nd Congresses were chosen. From the same Congresses, the authors also chose for comparison one pair of senior members from each Appropriations Committee subcommittee having jurisdiction over the agencies.

 In calculating the Rules Committee members' outlays, it was noted that six of the members had compact districts in which the counties were not shared with other congressmen, namely, Democrats Colmer, Young, and Anderson, and Republicans Anderson, Martin, and Quillen. Matsunaga's federal outlay averages were tabulated on the basis of 50% for each agency and year since he was one of two members elected at large to represent Hawaii during the three fiscal years studied.[27]

 The other eight members came from noncompact districts in which counties are split. This group was made up of Democrats Madden, Delaney, Bolling, O'Neill, Sisk, and Pepper, and Republicans Smith and Latta. The federal outlay for noncompact districts was calculated by determining what portion of each county a congressman represented according to the 1969 *Congressional Directory.* The 1970 census (Number of Inhabitants) was used to find the population of each county in a particular district; then, by dividing the population figure of that part of a county whose inhabitants fell in a congressman's district by the total population of that county, the percentage of that county's population in the congressman's district was obtained. By multiplying this percentage by the total federal outlay in the county, that portion of the total county outlay attributable to a congressman was determined. Where two or more counties were involved the figures were simply added together.

To illustrate the workings of the agency allocation scheme, let us look at the case of Rules Committee member Dave Martin. His Nebraska district received an average annual Agricultural Department outlay of $218,469,902, which was higher than that of any of the other fourteen Rules members' districts. This allocation from the Department of Agriculture was then compared with the highest outlays within the districts of the leaders of the House Agriculture Committee and the Subcommittee on Agriculture of the Appropriations Committee of both the 91st and 92nd Congresses. The results showed Martin's congressional district received more Agriculture Department funds than did the districts of the two leaders of the Agriculture Committee and the two senior members of the Appropriations subcommittee (see Table 5.4, p. 165).

The final results of this schematic comparison show that Rules Committee members' districts enjoyed the highest outlay figures for thirteen of the seventeen federal agencies. Highest district outlays from two of the agencies went to Appropriations subcommittee leaders, and from two of the agencies to the senior members of the legislative committees. This study, based on the allocation of funds by the seventeen federal agencies, appears to substantiate the hypothesis that a Rules Committee member wields substantial power and influence by virtue of his membership on the "Power Committee."

In an attempt to provide some control in this study, the authors ranked all fifty states on the basis of their per capita outlays by each of the seventeen agencies chosen. It was hypothesized that a state that ranked high on a particular agency's list should produce high-scoring congressmen. Comparing the state rank with the top scorer on each of the seventeen lists showed that ten high-scoring congressmen came from states among the top five in the per capita outlay rankings. Only Colmer (Defense) and Bolling (Veterans' Administration) came from low-ranking states (see Table 5.5, p. 166). These two members succeeded in obtaining large federal grants for their districts in a federal funding area in which their respective states had done very poorly.

As an additional control, the authors listed the average district outlay by a particular agency for each of the top scorer's states. The purpose of this control was to aid comparison of the top scorer's outlay with the district average of his own state (see Table 5.5). The result generally showed that the top scorer compared favorably with other members of his state delegation. Out of seventeen top scorers, only Delaney (Treasury) and Pepper (Civil Service) trailed (by less than half a million dollars each) when their district outlay was measured against the average district outlay of other congressmen in their states.

The authors also compiled the national average district outlay by every agency to contrast it with the top scorer's district outlay. The latter's top scores appear to be supported by the result that no single outlay in a top scorer's district is below the national district average.

Despite the controls, the authors were fully aware of the limitations and possible inaccuracies of their data. They were also cognizant of the following inadequacies:

a. The study was based on the hypothesis that a congressman should receive full credit for all federal distribution in his district. The work and contribution to his state of its U.S. Senators were completely disregarded.

b. The study failed to take into consideration the inherent economic factors of a district. In other words, controls for criteria that may affect the distribution of expenditures (e.g., need, capacity, etc.) are completely absent. Certain congressional districts, for example where large federal facilities are located, would continue to receive large sums of federal funds even though their congressmen might be junior in rank and noninfluential. In this regard Matsunaga would be the first to admit that Pearl Harbor has a direct relationship with the large defense outlay in his district. Moreover, the physical extent of a district may enter the picture: the fact that Dave Martin has sixty-one counties in his Nebraska district may partially account for his top score in Agriculture Department funding.

c. The study relied on *Federal Outlays* as its sole source of information, and the weaknesses of this publication should be noted. Its editors admit in the introduction of each volume that various discrepancies may be found in *Federal Outlays*. For example, for reasons of security, indiscriminate lumping together of trust funds and regular funds may occur.

d. The conclusions of this study are based on the assumption that chairmen or senior members of the legislative committees or the Appropriations subcommittees should receive more outlay dollars than junior members of those committees, an assumption which has not been tested. The authors took it for granted that a Rules Committee member was the top scorer if he compared favorably with the two senior members of the legislative committee and the Appropriations subcommittee with jurisdiction. Barry Rundquist has discovered in his study on military contracts, for instance, that junior Republican members of the House Armed Services Committee benefit more than the senior members of either party.[28]

Despite these shortcomings, the authors have presented these findings in the hope of encouraging more sophisticated studies of measuring congressional power and influence.

2. Total district outlay scheme. In this portion of the study, the authors used the fifteen Rules Committee members' districts. For comparative purposes, seventeen pairs of legislative committee leaders' districts were chosen, on the same basis as previously. Ten pairs of Appropriations subcommittee leaders were also chosen for the district federal outlay tabulation. In all cases, total district outlays were recorded. To facilitate the study, the authors computed a national mean for all congressional districts. For the three years studied the national average district outlay was $441,035,363 (see Table 5.6, 5.7, and 5.8, pp. 167, 168, 169).

The results of the study showed that a) six members of the Rules Committee (Colmer, Martin, O'Neill, Bolling, Smith, and Matsunaga) received more federal funds for their districts than the national average and that b) seniority in committee had no direct relationship to federal fund distribution. For example, Matsunaga (a junior member at the time) emerged as one of the top recipients with more federal outlays for his district than many of his senior colleagues on the committee.

As compared to the six of fifteen Rules Committee members (40%) who scored above the national average, only thirteen of the thirty-five legislative committee leaders (37.1%) did so. These thirteen senior members served on the following committees (listed in descending order of level of outlays): 1) Veterans' Affairs, 2) Science and Astronautics, 3) Merchant Marine and Fisheries, 4) Armed Services, 5) Agriculture, 6) Ways and Means, 7) Joint Committee on Atomic Energy, 8) Public Works, 9) Banking and Currency, and 10) Interstate and Foreign Commerce.

Using Richard Fenno's three-way classification of committees, one could conclude from these findings that a member of a public policy–oriented committee such as Judiciary, Foreign Affairs, or Education and Labor is not favored in obtaining large amounts of federal funds for his district.[29] Curiously, the senior members of the Veterans' Affairs and Merchant Marine committees (low-prestige committees according to Charles Bullock) are among the recipients of the highest federal outlays of all the legislative committee leaders studied.[30]

Seven of the twenty-one subcommittee leaders of the Appropriations Committee (33.3%) scored higher than the national average for federal district outlays. These seven served on the subcommittees for 1) State, Justice, Commerce, and Judiciary, 2) Public Works, 3) Defense, 4) Independent Offices and HUD, 5) Agriculture, and 6) Treasury, Post Office, and Executive Offices. Perhaps the most interesting and notable, if not astonishing, findings were that Chairman George Mahon of the prestigious and exclusive Appropriations Committee fell below the national average, and that Frank Bow, the late ranking minority member of that committee, scored the lowest in federal outlays among all Appropriations Committee leaders included in the study.

Reelection

Does membership on the Rules Committee mean reelection advantages? The answer to this question is apparently affirmative. The Rules Committee members' reelection records in the last twenty years compare favorably with those of members of the other two exclusive committees of the House — the Committee on Ways and Means and the Committee on Appropriations. Six (4.7%) of the Rules Committee members were defeated in the course of 128 contests from 1954 to 1974, and ten (also 4.7%) of the Ways and Means members were defeated in 213 contests in the same period. The Appropriations members fared worse, suffering twenty-nine defeats (6.4%) in 450 contests.[31]

The individual goals of attaining influence and prestige within the House and of acquiring constituency benefits can both be met providing independence of decision-making power is preserved. The evidence cited in this chapter seems to show that during the period studied the Democratic members have not lost their independent decision options, nor have they done poorly in satisfying their goals.

NOTES

1. Cited in George B. Galloway, *Congress at the Crossroads* (New York: Thomas Y. Crowell, 1946), p. 90.

2. Charles Bullock, III, "Committee Transfers in the U.S. House of Representatives" (Paper prepared for the Midwest Political Science Association Annual Meeting, April 29-May 1, 1971, Chicago), pp. 1-10.

3. Richard Fenno, "Congressional Committees: A Comparative View" (Paper presented at the American Political Science Association Annual Meeting, September 8-12, 1970, Los Angeles).

4. Interview, December 1, 1970.

5. Interview, August 13, 1970.

6. Interview, March 11, 1971.

7. Richard Fenno, *Congressmen in Committees* (Boston: Little, Brown & Co., 1973), p. 276.

8. Interview, August 13, 1970.

9. Interview, March 11, 1971.

10. Interview, July 18, 1973.

11. Interview, October 5, 1973.

12. Interview, October 10, 1971.

13. James A. Robinson, *The House Rules Committee* (Indianapolis: Bobbs-Merrill Co., 1963), p. 88.

14. Interview, July 18, 1973.

15. The resolution to continue Pepper's committee was carried by a 6–3 vote.

16. Minutes of the Executive Session of the Rules Committee, February 23, 1971.

17. For a more detailed study, see Richard Fenno, "The House of Representatives and Federal Aid to Education," in Robert Peabody and Nelson Polsby, eds., *New Perspectives of the House of Representatives* (Chicago: Rand McNally & Co., 1963), pp. 195-236.

18. Matsunaga left Washington for Honolulu for the state Democratic convention on May 13. In a long distance conversation with Speaker Albert that same evening Matsunaga learned that there would be a tie vote in the Rules Committee on the land use bill, which was scheduled for another vote the next day.

19. *Congressmen in Committees*, p. 274.

20. Interview, November 30, 1971.

21. Interview, November 25, 1970.

22. Interview, August 17, 1970.

23. Interview, December 1, 1974.

24. Interview, August 5, 1970.

25. Interview, September 18, 1970.

26. The OEO started to compile *Federal Outlays* in 1968. There was no change in the Rules Committee membership during the 90th, 91st, and 92nd Congresses, which made it convenient to use this time period.

27. In 1970 Hawaii was reapportioned into two congressional districts.

28. Barry Rundquist, "The House Seniority System and the Distribution of Prime Military Contracts" (Paper delivered at the American Political Science Association Annual Meeting, September 7-11, 1971, Chicago.).

29. Fenno, in his paper "Congressional Committees: A Comparative View" (p. 11) divided committees into House influence–, public policy–, and constituency benefit–oriented types.

30. Bullock, "Committee Transfers," Table 1.

31. The membership attrition record of the three committees is based on the ratio of the number of committee members who failed to return to Congress because of defeat at the polls to the total number of election contests, calculated from the total number of committee members minus the number of members retiring during each election year.

6

The Role of the Committee Chairman

THE CHAIRMAN'S POWERS

In the Rules Committee's efforts to serve the House leadership while preserving its own identity as the most powerful committee of the House, if not of the Congress, a major role is played by its chairman. Among the chairman's powers are those discussed in the following pages.

CALLING THE COMMITTEE INTO SESSION

Throughout the period when Howard Smith was its chairman, the Rules Committee never established a regular meeting day. This was, according to Robinson, "partly because its business depends on the unpredictable order in which legislative committees seek rules for their bills. In the absence of fixed times for meeting, it is within the Chairman's discretion to determine when to call the Committee together."[1] Chairman Smith used this discretion extensively and earned notoriety for refusing to call meetings of the committee by going on "fishing trips" and "barn fire missions" when measures he opposed were pending.

It was to avoid this type of arbitrary and capricious action by its chairman that the committee, taking advantage of Smith's defeat in the 1966 primary election, adopted rules establishing every Tuesday as the regular meeting day and providing that in the absence of the chairman the ranking majority member may call a meeting of the committee. The new rules further provided that by serving notice at one regular meeting any member could call up any measure pending before the committee for appropriate action at the next regular meeting.

SETTING THE AGENDA

Despite its membership enlargement and the adoption of its current restrictive rules under Chairman Colmer (see Appendix B), the Rules Committee still allows its chairman a considerable amount of latitude to facilitate, hamper, or prevent a bill's enactment through his agenda-setting power.

The chairman's prerogative of setting the committee agenda is almost unlimited. In practice he has even been permitted to kill a bill by refusing to schedule it for committee consideration (see Table 6.1, p. 171). Chairman Colmer, for example, exercised this prerogative of refusal to schedule hearings in order to kill the rural telephone bank bill (H.R. 7-91st) and the select committee on aging bill (H.Res. 850-91st). Again, in the case of the Equal Employment Opportunity Act (H.R. 17555-91st), the chairman expressed his strong personal objection to the measure in an executive session of the committee, and in effect obtained the committee's support of his refusal to schedule it for the committee's consideration. He did this in the closing days of the 91st Congress by gaining committee approval of his final agenda which omitted the civil rights bill. In his appeal to the committee members, Colmer spoke of his having been "very cooperative" with the leadership since he assumed the chairmanship, and then he suggested that he should be allowed to prevail against the leadership's wishes in this one instance. His wish prevailed.

In the last two years of Colmer's congressional career, he was resolutely opposed to the minimum wage bill (H.R. 7130-92nd), and he refused to schedule a hearing for it for nearly six months. Only after the Democratic leadership threatened him with a direct appeal to the Democratic members of his committee did Chairman Colmer hold hearings on the bill.

In contrast, the new chairman, Ray Madden, has scheduled nearly all bills since the beginning of the 93rd Congress. He explains his policy in this way: "I have not refused to schedule any bill because I think the House should be allowed to exercise its will on all measures. However, I've postponed and delayed the scheduling of a few bills until more information on them became available."[2]

Even after the decision has been reached to schedule a bill for a hearing, the chairman may still exercise a large degree of control of the legislative process through the device of timing. Depending on his position on a bill, he can schedule it early in the session when support for or opposition to the bill has not yet built up; or he can wait until late in the session to bring the pressure of adjournment to bear on the committee members. One chairman scheduled hearings on a bill at a time so inconvenient for its proponents that they failed to appear before the committee to present their case. This was conveniently interpreted as lack of support for the measure.

In the 90th Congress, Chairman Colmer established a precedent by setting a deadline by which all legislative committees had to submit a request for a rule on any bill they had reported out if they wanted to receive Rules Committee action. The deadline was set at July 9 in 1968 and at October 1 in 1971. This meant that Chairman Colmer, with the consent of the majority of the Rules Committee members, and the tacit agreement of the House leadership, was now virtually empowered to determine the date of adjournment of Congress by closing its agenda.[3] "Emergency measures," as determined by the leadership and agreed to by the committee, were exempted from the deadline. However, the chairman has been very reluctant to place any bills in this emergency category because "to open it up for one would mean we would have to open it up for others." The committee has supported his reluctance in this matter.

It should be noted that the chairman's agenda-setting power is not absolute because it can be overridden by a majority vote of the committee. However, the traditional respect for the norm of the House would discourage any dissenting committee majority from taking action to overrule its chairman.

PARLIAMENTARY PREROGATIVES

In presiding over committee meetings, the chairman has powers which may appear to be minor on the surface, but which are, in fact, important in determining the fate of a bill. Until January,

1975, the committee rules provided, *inter alia,* that a majority of the committee membership constituted a quorum at any meeting of the committee. The rules now provide that while a majority of the members still constitutes a quorum at any business meeting of the committee, seven members make up a quorum at any committee hearing. The chairman observes this requirement meticulously or selectively, depending upon his wish to continue or to adjourn a meeting. He can expedite action on any measure by disregarding the lack of a quorum, or he can delay proceedings on any bill to which he is opposed by declaring the lack of a quorum and adjourning the meeting even though the absence of a quorum may be merely momentary.

The strength of this parliamentary prerogative is exemplified by an incident which occurred in the closing days of the 91st Congress. A hearing was in progress on the prevailing rate pay system for government employees (H.R. 17809-91st), a bill which Chairman Colmer and the Republicans opposed. Madden, one of the committee members who favored the bill, left the committee room just for a moment to confer with a visiting constituent. Dave Martin, who was opposed to the bill, seized the opportunity to raise a point of order that a quorum was not present. Chairman Colmer, instead of sending for Madden, who was within voice range in the adjoining hallway, promptly adjourned the meeting for lack of a quorum.

Another interesting incident involving the lack of a quorum occurred on September 14, 1959. At one point during that day's discussion of the Mutual Security Appropriations Act of 1960 (H.R. 8385-86th), William Colmer left the committee room and went into the chairman's office. A while later, Hamer Budge (R-Idaho) left the committee room and joined Colmer. With Colmer and Budge absent from the room, there were only six members present out of a total of twelve, which did not constitute a quorum. After waiting for a considerable time, Chairman Smith led the remaining five members into his office to reestablish a quorum and act on the bill there. It was reported that Colmer was so displeased with Smith's action that he was not on speaking terms with him for over six months.

The chairman may also exercise his prerogative to entertain or not to entertain a motion to grant a rule to any bill pending before the committee at any given time. Although this prerogative is not of material significance under the normal routine, it can be used to hinder or help a bill's chances when special circumstances warrant (see Table 6.2, p. 175). The chairman can, for example, deliberately delay the vote on any motion for the purported benefit of an interested member who is not able to attend the scheduled meeting. By entertaining a motion and putting it to a vote during the absence of the necessary number of supporters of a bill pending before the committee, the chairman can also maneuver unfavorable action on a bill he opposes. The Consumer Protection Act of 1970 (H.R. 18214-91st) appears to have suffered this treatment. A motion to grant it a rule died on a 7-7 tie vote taken in the absence of Richard Bolling, a supporter of the measure.

HOUSEKEEPING POWER

Rule 4 of the committee rules provides that "The professional and clerical staffs of the Committee shall serve under the general supervision and direction of the Chairman, who shall establish and assign the duties and responsibilities of the members of the staffs and delegate such authority as the Chairman deems appropriate, with the exception of the Minority Staff, who shall serve under the general supervision and direction of the Ranking Minority Member of the Committee."[4] Pursuant to this rule, the chairman alone hires and fires, assigns, and commands the employees on the majority professional and clerical staffs. While the members of the staff serve the committee members, individually and collectively, in the area of routine business, their primary loyalty is to the person of the chairman who alone holds the power of hiring and firing them. This control over the working staff is jealously guarded by the chairman, for it is through his staff that he maintains control over the committee's files, records, and written communications, which are so necessary to his exercise of leadership. For example, early in the 92nd Congress former Chairman Colmer demonstrated his extreme sensitivity to any infringement of this prerogative of the chairman when, during an executive session of the committee, he accused committee member Matsunaga of "ordering the staff" to put his (Matsunaga's) bill on the committee agenda. This alleged action of Matsunaga, Colmer explained, was the reason for his refusal to schedule Matsunaga's bill for a hearing, a refusal which in effect amounted to a penalty for infringement upon the chairman's prerogative. It should be noted that the committee, in June, 1975, voted to permit each member to hire a personal assistant.

Post–Committee Action Power

Until 1923, the chairman could refuse to file a resolution with the House even after the committee had adopted a resolution to grant a rule to a bill. Since then House rules have made it mandatory for the chairman to report such a resolution, and accordingly the chairman's post–committee action power has been substantially curtailed.

However, through his prerogative to assign himself or any other majority member to present the resolution providing for a rule, the chairman may exert considerable influence to defeat a rule to which he is opposed. He may present the resolution himself and speak against it while doing so, or assign the presentation to a member who is opposed to the measure. Unfair as such maneuvering may seem, it is permitted under present committee and House rules. This power to assign the floor management of a resolution also provides the chairman with opportunities to reward or penalize a member of the committee. The unpleasant task of managing a resolution providing for the consideration of an unpopular bill on the floor can be assigned to a recalcitrant member, who may, as a consequence of the assignment, suffer at the polls in his bid for reelection. Congressman James Trimble (D-Ark.) may have been an unwitting victim of Chairman Smith's exercise of this power in the 87th Congress. Trimble was given the assignment (which he did not refuse) of managing the Rules Committee enlargement resolution (H.Res. 127-87th), a bill which was extremely unpopular in the South. Perhaps Chairman Smith's action contributed to Trimble's defeat in 1966. A cooperative member, on the other hand, is assigned the management of popular measures only, to the enhancement of his own popularity.

It was precisely this power of assigning rule management that prompted liberal members of the committee to extract a promise from Chairman Smith that he would assign the second ranking majority member, Ray Madden (D-Ind.), a liberal, to manage the rule for the twentieth century's first meaningful civil rights act, H.R. 6127-85th, on August 26, 1957. Having learned that the chairman might stop at nothing to kill the bill and even floor manage the rule himself, Congressman Richard Bolling, with the support of all the non-Southerners on the committee, threatened to move to restrict Smith's exercise of this prerogative by specifying that Madden manage the rule. Chairman Smith averted such a formal decision on the part of the committee by stating that it would be best if it were "understood" by the committee that he would make the necessary designation and that he would be inclined in doing so to designate Madden. A formal resolution to restrict the chairman's power to assign a rule manager would have been extraordinary. As has been noted, if it will accomplish the same purpose the normal procedure of the House or the committee is always preferred to the extraordinary.

CENTER OF COMMUNICATION

As the person in charge of the committee, the chairman is the best-informed member on matters pertaining strictly to it. In the name of the committee and with the assistance of his staff, he receives and dispatches all committee communications. Even if the leadership has a "personal representative" on the committee (e.g., Richard Bolling and Homer Thornberry for Speaker Sam Rayburn and Thomas P. O'Neill for Speaker John McCormack) who serves as the leadership's eyes and ears on the committee, the chairman still has the prerogative of communicating directly with the majority membership, the legislative committee chairmen, and even the minority leaders and members. As chairman of this powerful committee, he commands greater attention than any of the other committee members or practically any other House member.

Legislative Initiative

As previously noted, the Rules Committee can seize and has on occasion seized the legislative initiative from legislative committees by introducing a bill of its own. Along the same line, the chairman, by the mere threat of holding hearings on a bill, can force a legislative committee to act. In this connection the most talked about incident in recent times concerned the anti-riot bill which was being held up in the Judiciary Committee in the 90th Congress. Chairman Colmer, with the support of former Ranking Minority Member Allen Smith (R-Calif.) announced that he would hold hearings on the issue anyway, and this action prompted Chairman Celler of the Judiciary Committee to report out his own bill. This type of initiative probably would not be tolerated by the House if it were being abused; nevertheless, the power is there for the Rules Committee chairman to exercise when necessary.

The Rules Committee chairman's considerable prerogatives remain in spite of new committee rules. True, he can no longer arbitrarily absent himself to "go fishing," as Chairman Smith used to do, for in his absence the ranking majority member may now assume the chair and conduct any regularly scheduled meeting. Nevertheless, the chairman has certain residual powers. He may call special meetings to expedite the consideration of bills he favors, or refuse to call such meetings in order to delay action on measures he opposes. By exercising his prerogative to schedule witnesses he may reduce their numbers to expedite the consideration of measures he favors, or lengthen the list of witnesses, summoning them by personal invitation, to delay final action on measures he opposes. Because of the long-standing policy of the committee of allowing every member of the House the privilege of being heard, objections are hardly ever raised to the chairman's decision to continue any hearing, however lengthy. He may even go to the extent of inviting non-House witnesses, such as senators, Cabinet members, and officials of the executive branch, to lengthen and delay the proceedings.

In the final analysis, the chairman, of course, can only be as powerful as his colleagues on the committee, the House leadership, the majority caucus, and the House membership will allow. In conformity with the principle that no power status is permanent, fixed, and unchangeable, the power of the chairman and his influence on the overall legislative process has varied from time to time, and from chairman to chairman.

POWER AND INFLUENCE OF RULES COMMITTEE CHAIRMEN, 1955-74

The Rules Committee has long been known by its chairman's reputation, especially since Howard Smith assumed the chairmanship in 1955. In conformity with this well-known image, the authors divided the tenures of the three chairmen during the twenty years studied, 1955-74, into five periods entitled independence, semi-independence, courtesy, subordination, and restoration of prestige.

INDEPENDENT PERIOD — HOWARD SMITH, 1955-60

Because Chairman Adolph Sabath (D-Ill.) had had the reputation of being subservient to the House leadership and even more so to President Roosevelt, Howard Smith assumed the chairmanship in 1955 with the goal of attaining an independent course of action. He justified the greater prestige and power which this independence brought himself and the committee by saying: "I will not pledge my support blindfolded to any unknown measures, to any person, or any subject, but will use my best judgement and discretion after careful study and concentration, and vote for such measures as I believe to be in the interest of the welfare of our country and in conformity with the wishes of my constituents."[5]

Smith set out to achieve his goal of independence by using several tactics, among them the following:

1. Refusal to call meetings of the committee. Despite the great amount of notice Smith received during his chairmanship for his failure to call meetings when crucial bills were pending, the instances in which he forestalled meetings through his own disappearance, although widely publicized, were comparatively few. The authors have gone through the committee minutes laboriously and discovered that Chairman Smith, surprisingly enough, held

more meetings than had any of his predecessors. His meetings were shorter but more frequent. Refusal to hold meetings, it appears, was not really an important tactic of Smith's.

2. Failure to schedule bills to which he was opposed. This omission was probably the most important single device in Smith's design to gain independence. The fact that frequent committee meetings were held did not mean that measures desired by the leadership or the House majority were being scheduled by Smith. Confident in the belief that the committee would not take the extraordinary step of overruling him, out of respect for committee tradition and the lack of sufficient opposing votes (Smith, Colmer, and four Republicans assured him a 6-6 tie vote), Smith refused to schedule an average of thirty bills per Congress from 1955-60, as compared to Chairman Leo Allen's twenty measures (83rd Congress) and Chairman Sabath's eleven measures (82nd Congress) (see Table 6.1, p. 171).

3. Legislative bargaining. Realizing that he, as chairman of the Rules Committee, could not continuously frustrate the expectations of the leaders without their seeking House sanctions against him, Smith resorted to bargaining with Speaker Rayburn on a give-and-take basis. Maneuvered into an impossible situation, Rayburn took the initiative of bargaining with Smith. As Smith recalled: "I went to Texas to see my family and purposely did not tell anyone where I was. When I returned after a week, my staff told me that everyone was looking for me. The Speaker left a message saying that he wanted to do some 'trading and trafficking' with me. I called him and Sam asked me to meet with him in the Capitol."[6]

A former Rules staff member remembers that "the Judge was always very serious in his bargaining sessions with the Speaker. One day he came back to the office smiling and saying, 'he wanted to have five bills to start with and we settled on only three.'" The Speaker was not the only one with whom Smith bargained. From time to time he would strike a deal with a legislative committee chairman for the latter's support of a Smith-sponsored bill. In exchange he would support a measure which was under the legislative chairman's sponsorship and which was pending before the Rules Committee.

One celebrated example of this kind of bargaining occurred when Chairman Smith traded support with former Chairman Emanuel Celler of the Judiciary Committee. Celler agreed to expedite action on the federal court jurisdiction limitation bill (H.R. 3-85th), which Smith was seeking to get out of the Judiciary Committee, when Smith promised to support a rule for the pre-merger notification bill (H.R. 7698-85th), pending in the Rules Committee. Robinson related the story as follows: Ranking Minority Member Clarence Brown of Ohio "spoke again to say he did not believe in 'horse-trading,' but wondered what could be done to expedite H.R. 3. Celler admitted to a liking for 'horse-trading' and implied he might hasten action on Smith's bill if the Chairman of the Rules Committee could see his way clear to assist in granting a rule on the so-called pre-merger notification bill. Smith allowed that 'I am a horse-trader and the son of a horse-trader.' "[7]

By any yardstick, Chairman Howard Smith must be credited with the successful achievement of his goal of committee independence. Much has been written about the great power he exercised as the chairman of the Rules Committee during the period 1955-60. Raymond Moley made the following observation about Smith in 1958: "Even beyond the potent Speaker, he is the man to be reckoned with by any member or interest with an axe to grind. Officially, his present power is as chairman of that exalted court of first instance, the Committee on Rules. Bills do not reach the floor without a 'rule' from that body unless the House, on a rare occasion, votes otherwise."[8]

As was clearly stated in the chapter on House sanctions, the House system would never permit the Rules Committee to frustrate its (the House's) expectations for too long a period. It happened that John F. Kennedy's nomination and election in 1960 provided the occasion for the large Democratic majority in the House to impose an extraordinary sanction on Chairman Smith and his coalition on the committee. Sanction was imposed by enlarging the committee. Its membership was increased from twelve to fifteen by adding two leadership-oriented Democrats (B. F. Sisk of California and Carl Elliot of Alabama) and one Republican.

SEMI-INDEPENDENT PERIOD — HOWARD SMITH, 1961-66

After the enlargement of the Committee on Rules, Smith had to operate under a new threat of restraint, i.e., a committee which could overrule its chairman at will. Consequently, he was forced to reduce his expectations by accepting a goal of semi-independence. This meant that, on the one hand, he would not submit to the leadership's wishes at all times while, on the other, he would not continually frustrate the expectations of the House majority, the leadership, or the committee majority to the extent that new extraordinary sanctions would be imposed on him.

While the chairman's power to call meetings, set agendas, etc., was not formally curtailed by the committee following the enlargement, Smith was quite aware of his new limitations. This awareness was reflected in a drastic reduction in the number of bills which he declined to schedule for committee action. The average number of such bills dropped to nineteen per Congress after enlargement from thirty per Congress before enlargement. As noted in the chapter on decisions (Chap. 7, p. 122), Smith also greatly improved his agreement score after the enlargement. To attain some tangible degree of independence, Smith now relied on parliamentary strategies. As Robert Peabody observed, "Howard W. Smith was able to utilize his still very sizeable discretion as chairman and his almost universally admired skills as a parliamentary strategist to protect and further many of the interests held by himself and a substantial bloc of southern conservatives."[9] To Peabody's observation may be added Robinson's: "Judge Smith is universally acknowledged as an able parliamentarian, one of two or three of the keenest in modern times. His knowledge of the *Rules* probably nearly matches that of Clarence Cannon (D-Mo.), who codified them, and his experience with the Rules has likely been engulfed only by the late Sam Rayburn."[10]

Bolling cites one example of Smith's parliamentary finesse in a maneuver to shield House Republicans from almost unavoidable embarrassment on the floor:

> During the Eisenhower Administration the Democratic-controlled Education and Labor Committee brought out a bill that did not conform to the recommendations of the President. The

Republicans in floor debate supported their President's viewpoint. Therefore they said they could not even consider the committee's version of the bill. Once the Republicans had taken this position, Democrats managing the bill staged a prearranged retreat. They announced they would accept the President's version down to the last semicolon. This embarrassed Republicans who, privately opposed to any such education bill, hitherto had felt safe in giving it verbal support.

Smith and Halleck got the point of this Democratic maneuver. They hastily conferred on the floor — in the open. Moments later, Smith offered a privileged motion that stopped debate. The motion, if adopted, would have struck out all the provisions after the opening enacting clause. The motion carried by five votes, thereby killing the bill before the Republicans' embarrassment could be recorded in the form of a roll call on the ungutted bill.[11]

A Democratic member of Congress is quoted as saying, "Howard Smith was a terribly powerful chairman right up until the 89th Congress. At times he was even more powerful than the Speaker himself."[12] To this assessment a White House aide added, "Make no mistake, the judge is [still] a force to be reckoned with."[13] Don Oberdorfer, a journalist and long-time Smith observer made the following observations about Smith after the committee's enlargement:

> The hypothetical one-vote margin reckons without illnesses, absenteeism, log-rolling, occasional displays of political independence and sincere dissent. Nor does it compensate for the enormous discretion which Smith has exercised as chairman. The committee majority has not seen fit to mount the battle it would take to strip him of his position. The result is that Smith is dethroned but not deposed. He has had to give up his former monarchy for something resembling the French Parliament in its complexity, but he continues to take a toll of liberal measures by a combination of shrewd coalition-building, the inertial force of leadership and sheer brass.[14]

The conclusion is clear that Chairman Smith attained his goal of semi-independence for the Rules Committee, but only by establishing himself as a skillful, effective chairman. As a Democrat, however, he failed to meet the expectations of the House majority and its leadership. Consequently, the Democrats imposed an extraordinary sanction on the committee in 1965 when they won the largest majority in twenty years. The political climate in the 89th Congress was too liberal to approve the Smith-engineered, semi-independent status of the committee, so the House, not surprisingly, adopted the 21-day rule to serve notice on the committee that it could be by-passed. The committee's wings of independence were formally clipped to the satisfaction of the House majority and its leadership.

Period of Courtesy — William Colmer, 1967-72

Congressman William Colmer (D-Miss.) was never viewed as a cooperative member of the Rules Committee by the House Democratic leadership. Perhaps because of his still-unpleasant memory (he had been considered by the leadership for purge from the committee in 1961), Colmer registered his worst agreement scores (see p. 122) during the Smith semi-independent period. Congressman Trent Lott, former administrative assistant to Colmer and now a member of the Rules Committee, explained: "As chairman after enlargement, Smith still had to deal with the leadership and be somewhat cooperative. On the other hand, Colmer could vote the way Smith would have voted. That's why Colmer had more deviations."[15] From the moment he was seated as chairman, Colmer changed his noncooperative aim into a cooperative one, as dictated by his desire to survive as chairman. His decision was further prompted by two environmental factors:

1. Colmer was the lone confirmed conservative of the ten Democrats serving on the committee. He related what he told Howard Smith at one of their reunions after he assumed the chairmanship: "I told Howard that he had it made when he was chairman. He could always look to me for support and assistance on the Democratic side. I now have no one. And the leadership will always have the votes to override me."[16] Bearing out this pessimism of Colmer's, one experienced newspaperman said: "The fact is the Chairman doesn't have a hell of a lot of power today except when a majority of the members go along with him. Once he doesn't have the votes, it's all over. The days of the powerful Rules Committee Chairman are gone."[17]

2. The Rules Committee, for the first time, adopted rule operation at the beginning of the 90th Congress (see Appendix Although the committee's action was not opposed by Chairma Colmer, and was in fact supported by him, the adoption of such rules served to restrain the powers of the chairman in such areas as calling meetings, ascertaining quorums, etc.

Under this new set of environmental restraints, there was only one way for Colmer to survive: get along with the leadership and with the committee members. His goal was survival through co-operation, but he was confronted with the bitter truth that no respectable committee chairman could live on the meager political bread and water of complete subordination to the House leadership. Colmer, seeking *some* degree of independence as a reasonable goal, found himself working for a balance between his own expectations and those of the leadership and the committee Democrats. He was not geared to accept complete subordination, not even to preserve his long-cherished and coveted chairmanship.

Colmer planned to accomplish his objective by using the following tactics:

1. Courtesy. Courtesy to his colleagues and tolerance of the bills he abhorred was one of the strategies Colmer adopted. In describing Chairman Colmer's willingness to accommodate himself to the new situation a committee staff member observed: "The Chairman goes out of his way to be fair and likes to do things by unanimous consent. He usually lets the Committee make up its own mind on when to hear a bill or what to do with it. His favorite phrase is, 'What's the Committee's pleasure?' "[18]

Colmer did not often use his prerogative as chairman to block measures to which he was opposed, even though he would have fought them if he had been but a member of the committee. One member commented on Colmer's spirit of tolerance as follows: "He [Colmer] has fought hard against the bills which he personally believes are wrong and has taken strong stands, but on the other hand he doesn't block them by not scheduling hearings."[19] Under the heading of courtesy, Colmer included and emphasized the "heat-shield" function of the committee, that is to say its function of protecting the leadership and the members of the House (see p. 29).

~n through his scheduling power to any
.e was happy to serve as a buffer for his
extra-House elements. From his point of
.ng noncooperative when refusing to schedule
.i were supported by Democrats but which the
.eadership really opposed.

.er studiously employed courtesy to gain support from his
and thus stability for his position as chairman, what method
.i he use to maintain some degree of independence for himself?
Let him speak for himself: "I would stall and delay the scheduling
of a piece of legislation to which I objected strongly just to the
limit beyond which I would be overruled. The theory is that we
need a cooling-off period for the sponsors to think it over. They
may change their minds and would want to at least modify the measure. Among others, I am opposed to bills which would cause infla-
tion. It has been my pet peeve."[20] As the former chairman spoke
those words at his Mississippi beach home ten months after his
retirement, he spoke as a man who knew with great precision how
far he could go in the game of delaying measures which he opposed.

The degree of satisfaction of Chairman Colmer's goal of survival
can best be measured in the context of committee, leadership, and
House expectations. In view of the philosophical differences between
Colmer and his fellow Democrats on the committee, he was not
expected to vote in frequent conformity with the party line as a
Democratic member of the committee. Nonetheless, he was expected
to be fair, cooperative, and nonobstructionist with the committee
members and the leadership.

All members of the Colmer Rules Committee interviewed (except
H. Allen Smith and Delbert Latta) described their chairman as
being fair to them. Even the well-established Democratic liberals on
the committee, Madden, Bolling, O'Neill, Pepper, and Matsunaga,
all of whom at the time obviously held a political philosophy different from that of Colmer, agreed in this regard. Perhaps John
Anderson, a moderate liberal Republican member of the committee,
summed it up best in this observation: "Take Richard Bolling for
example; he [Colmer] and Dick get along well. Yet you could not
find two people with more dissimilar views."[21] Bolling observed that
"Chairman Colmer is cooperative with the leadership and party

members on the committee."[22] O'Neill expressed his views as follows: "I have found that Chairman Colmer, while not in agreement with much of the philosophy of the party, understands and appreciates his relationship with the responsibility to the leadership and his fellow Democrats. Consequently, he has never been an obstructionist. He has been fair and effective."[23]

Pepper said, "Chairman Colmer is held in high esteem by the individual members of his committee, even when they disagree with his vote or his position on a measure. He has, I know, brought up for consideration many measures that he personally does not approve."[24] In the eyes of these liberal Democrats, Colmer's high score on cooperativeness was apparently based on his willingness to schedule bills to which he was personally opposed.

For the same reason, Colmer received excellent marks from his own Democratic leaders on the question of whether or not he was cooperative as the chairman of the Rules Committee. Speaker McCormack referred to Colmer as "a good and very cooperative chairman."[25] Despite his unsuccessful efforts to restore the 21-day rule in the 92nd Congress, Speaker Albert indicated that he had received "very good," and even "excellent" cooperation from Colmer in the latter's role as Rules Committee chairman.[26] The late Majority Leader Hale Boggs echoed a similar sentiment: "Chairman Colmer has excellent rapport with the House leadership and committee members. He has strong feelings on some subjects but he is realistic and cooperative."[27]

On the question of fairness, there was nothing but praise for Colmer from the Republican members of the committee as well. Anderson observed: "His relationship with the other members of the Rules Committee is very congenial. He is a courtly Southern gentleman by disposition and nature. Much of his success is due to his ability to cultivate very warm relationships with the members of the committee."[28] Dave Martin added, "He is effective and fair. He operates differently from Judge Smith. He deals with all the members rather than just some."[29] The Republican leaders of the House were also satisfied with Colmer's performance, as evidenced by the remarks of Gerald Ford, when he was minority leader: "I think that Mr. Colmer is a responsible chairman. I have no objection to the current performance of the Rules Committee under his leadership."[30] Colmer evidently established a reputation for fair dealing among those who appeared most often as witnesses before his committee. All nine committee chairmen and nine ranking minority members interviewed by the authors in 1971-72 unanimously agreed that Colmer had been fair in his dealings with them. The comment of "very fair with me" by Chairman Harley Staggers (D-W.Va.) of the Commerce Committee was typical.[31] Former Ranking Minority Member William Springer (R-Ill.) of the Commerce Committee echoed a familiar view about Colmer's having lived up to the expectations of the House committee leaders: "I know that in many instances he did not agree with much of the legislation that had come from our committee. However, there are no instances that I know of in which the chairman attempted to hold up any bills from our committee."[32]

Sample interviews with congressmen identified with both philosophical extremes of the political spectrum in the House failed to reveal any serious criticism of Colmer as chairman. However, contrasting impressions of Colmer's performance as chairman of the committee were noted. For example, ultraliberal Shirley Chisholm (D-N.Y.) expressed the view that "Mr. Colmer tends to impede controversial bills from reaching the floor,"[33] while ultraconservative former Representative Durwood Hall (R-Mo.) judged Chairman Colmer as being "not as effective as former Chairman Howard Smith in keeping undesirable controversial bills from reaching the floor."[34]

If any conclusion is to be drawn, it is that Chairman Colmer, despite his difference in political philosophy with the Democratic leadership, made a real effort to be chairman of the Rules Committee in the manner that would be expected of a member of the majority party. Colmer has been given "fair," "good," or even "excellent" ratings, depending mainly on how well he served the leadership and the committee as a chairman. Unlike Howard Smith, Colmer harbored a sense of responsibility to the House leadership as chairman of the "Power Committee." In assuming this responsibility, he sublimated his concern for his own prestige, power, and political philosophy. In other words, he convincingly demonstrated that he was fundamentally the leadership's chairman first and Colmer's chairman second.

Was Colmer's goal of achieving partial independence also met successfully? In answering this question it cannot be overlooked that Colmer, through his control of the committee's weekly agenda, did manage to frustrate the leadership's wishes on a few major pieces of legislation. In the 91st Congress, for example, despite repeated appeals from the Speaker and the majority leader for a rule on the Equal Employment Opportunity Act (H.R. 17555-91st) Colmer demonstrated his adamant opposition by refusing to schedule it for committee consideration. His delay in scheduling the minimum wage bill (H.R. 7130-92nd) and his efforts in prolonging the gun control bill (H.R. 17735-90th) hearings were also well-known instances in which he manifested his independent spirit.

By showing courtesy to his committee peers, Colmer earned their respect, which in turn entitled him to a certain amount of deference from his colleagues. Their attitude then helped the chairman to attain partial independence. There was in fact, a mutual exchange of courtesies. The following remarks of a staff member illustrate this point: "When you're respected as a man as well as a legislator you're given a lot of deference, and this represents a significant power. The members will stand behind their Chairman — even the administration supporters would go along with the Chairman if they thought the leadership was trying to embarrass him. Even when the members were drafting rules at the beginning of the Congress they were careful not to embarrass him."[35]

A favorite exercise of students of the Rules Committee in recent years has been to compare Chairman Smith and Chairman Colmer with respect to their fairness to their colleagues on the committee, their cooperativeness with the leadership, and their general effectiveness as chairman. By and large these studies conclude that while Colmer emerges as the fairer and more cooperative of the two, he is rated less effective in wielding the power vested in the committee chairmanship. In fairness to Colmer, it should be noted that he became chairman with a set of more restrictive rules and a membership altered by the replacement of two conservatives with two liberals. It should also be noted that effectiveness in the chair does not necessarily correlate with independence and noncooperativeness, as most studies of the committee seem to indicate.

PERIOD OF SUBORDINATION — RAY MADDEN,
JANUARY, 1973–SEPTEMBER, 1973

Ray Madden assumed the chair after Colmer's voluntary retirement at the beginning of the 93rd Congress. As a regular and liberal Democrat of long standing, and a labor union advocate, Madden has always held the view that the Rules Committee is an arm of the leadership and the majority party. With the exit of Colmer, Tip O'Neill, and William Anderson from the committee, Speaker Albert found himself able at one stroke to appoint three new, presumably loyal, members (see p. 53). These appointments insured a cooperative chairman and a Democratic membership free of conservatives for the first time in recent years. Chairman Madden's goal is simple and easy to comprehend: subordination to the Democratic Party and its leadership. He stated his own concept of this goal by saying:

> If the Speaker thinks that there is a bill pending before the Rules Committee that the party is for and he wants to get it up, all he has to do is get on the telephone and call me up and say, "There is a bill we would like to have heard by the Rules Committee because the Democratic members want to have it brought on the floor of the House." After all, the Democratic Party is a political party with national goals. If we have a chairman of the Rules Committee who tries to stifle legislation that the party supports, it would create dissension and not help us or the Democratic Party in the general election.[36]

A chairman does not need much strategy of his own if he chooses to be subordinate to the leadership. This is especially so if the majority of the committee members are in the same frame of mind. The extent to which Madden was willing to go in order to be loyal to the leadership is best illustrated by the following incident: On April 11, 1973, Congressman B. F. Sisk was assured that there would be no committee meeting on the next day to take up the economic stabilization bill (H.R. 6168-93rd), one in which he had a serious interest. With this understanding, Sisk was on his way to California on the morning of Friday, April 12, unaware that upon the request of the leadership Madden had scheduled a meeting anyway. Learning upon his arrival in Los Angeles about this hastily called session, Sisk telephoned the committee in an attempt to speak to the chairman about the possibility of a postponement. Madden refused to take the call. He convincingly demonstrated his preference for loyalty to the leadership over accommodating committee members, despite the long-standing tradition of protecting absent committee members. Sisk commented on this episode as follows: "I thought we had a thorough understanding one day, this was in connection with the economic stabilization bill. The next morning he completely reversed direction. He was going 180° in the opposite direction. As a result, we took action which I felt was very embarrassing to the leadership and the Democrats."[37]

As will be discussed in Chapter 7, during the first nine months of the 93rd Congress the Democrats on the Rules Committee compiled a Rice Index of Cohesion score of 82, twenty-five points higher than that of any of the previous nine Congresses (see Table 7.1, p. 177). (The 87th Congress had showed the previous high score of 57.) Their agreement score of 91% for the same period is also the highest of those nine Congresses and twelve points higher than the previous high, which was 79% for both the 88th and 89th Congresses. Chairman Madden, along with Sisk, Pepper, and Matsunaga, recorded a 100% agreement score for this period. This meant that on the basis of all the committee roll-call votes studied, whenever a comparison could be made, Madden invariably voted in conformity with the leadership's position as expressed on the House floor. Available statistics clearly show that during his first nine months as chairman of the Rules Committee, Ray Madden was completely successful in satisfying his goal of being loyal to the leadership and to the Democratic Party.

RESTORATION OF PRESTIGE — RAY MADDEN, OCTOBER, 1973–DECEMBER, 1974

As previously noted, the total convergence of the leadership's and the committee's expectations would essentially mean the loss of the committee's separate identity. Furthermore, the complete convergence of the leadership's and Rules Committee chairman's expectations would relegate the chairman to impotency. The fact that

Madden failed to gain the prestige or notoriety of his immediate predecessors as chairman during the "subordination period" could have prompted him to change his initial goals. However, the following environmental factors were probably more responsible for his change of attitude in the fall of 1973:

1. By the end of September, 1973, resolutions reported out of the Rules Committee had suffered ten defeats and one near-defeat (H.Res. 256, 197-196). The majority of the House had rejected the decisions of the Rules Committee more times within that nine-month period than it had in all the sessions of the previous four Congresses (see Table 3.4, p. 151). Since there was complete convergence of leadership and committee expectations, one could only conclude that either the leadership had not assessed the mood of the House accurately or the leadership purposefully wished to test its strength on the floor, regardless of success. In any event, the defeats did not reflect well on Chairman Madden. Both he and his committee had become the subject of ridicule. Republican Congressman Elford Cederberg, ranking minority member of the Appropriations Committee, remarked: "Whenever the Rules Committee brings out rules almost in violation of the basic norms and traditions of the House, as they have been doing recently, they should be made to look ridiculous, and that they have been."[38] Committee member Sisk lamented: "There is just no question that the Rules Committee has been rolled over by being voted down on the previous question more times in the last six months than it has been in the last nineteen years I've been in Congress. I think it is a sad situation."[39]

2. The development of the energy crisis in late 1973 made it difficult for the three Democrats of the committee from the oil-producing states, Young, Long, and McSpadden, to be in continuous agreement with the leadership on various crisis-initiated bills. They naturally preferred to attend to constituency interests before those of the party and of the leadership. Consequently, Madden was beginning to have problems in obtaining a committee majority to support the leadership.[40]

To meet these new situations, Chairman Madden set up a new goal for himself and his committee, to restore the lost prestige of the chairman and the committee by establishing a semi-independent posture. Having given his total loyalty to the leadership for roughly nine months, the chairman now attempted to attain a delicate balance between committee expectations, leadership expectations, and those of the House majority.

How can a loyal Democratic chairman who is a liberal go about acquiring some degree of independence vis-à-vis his leadership? To attain this goal the chairman must first become aware of the following environmental conditions: 1) There are no real philosophical and ideological differences between the goals of the leadership and those of the chairman. At most, there could be mere tactical discrepancies between the two sets of goals. 2) It is obvious that the expectations of the Democratic leadership are not always the same as those of the House majority, as evidenced by the defeat in the House of a number of leadership-sponsored rules.

Postponement of favorable action on controversial measures until such time as the House majority favored it appears to have been the strategy adopted by Madden. He used the age-old argument of constituency interest (see p. 79) to justify such actions by his committee and to dissipate possible doubt of his loyalty to the leadership. Madden described his own new strategy as follows: "We are going along like the Rules Committee should go along. We go along with the leadership, but when bills come along that look like they are going to be upset on the floor, we hold them up until some more work can be done on them."[41]

Asked whether his goal was still loyalty to the leadership and his party, Madden replied: "Yes, but there is a difference in degree of loyalty. I've always aimed to go along more or less as a chairman with what the leadership sponsors. Of course, the Rules Committee is not bound by any rule or law and any member of the Rules Committee is not bound by any rule of the House to go along with the leadership. In fact, we are elected to come down here and represent our district and our nation."[42]

In its editorial of March 9, 1974, the *Washington Post* wrote, "Once again the House Rules Committee has acted arbitrarily and denied the full House a chance to work its will on an important piece of domestic legislation. Last week the victim was the land use bill. This week the Rules panel, egged on by the Nixon administration, refused to approve a rule to facilitate debate on the conference report on emergency urban mass transit aid."[43] This bore a remarkable resemblance to many *Post* editorials during the Howard Smith period of the sixties, but the quoted editorial was written in 1974 and the chairman of the committee was Madden. By holding up rules on the land use bill (H.R. 10294-93rd) and the mass transit conference report (S. 386-93rd), two bills supported by the leadership, the Rules Committee and Madden certainly "regained the image of independence."[44] Despite this postponement, Madden retained his loyalty image by eventually reporting the held-up bills. H.R. 10294 was given a rule on May 14 with Matsunaga casting the tie-breaking vote and the S. 386 conference report was cleared for floor action on July 24.

Madden did not go back on his word which he gave to the leadership when he informed it that he was only trying to postpone action on the aforementioned bills. With the change in Madden's strategy the House majority evidently became more inclined to approve Rules Committee decisions, for it defeated only five rules in the period of fifteen months (October, 1973–December, 1974), as compared to ten in the first nine-month period (January–September, 1973).

NOTES

1. James A. Robinson, *The House Rules Committee* (Indianapolis: Bobbs-Merrill Co., 1963) p. 84.

2. Interview, March 14, 1974.

3. For example, the Speaker asked the committee to consider four emergency measures (H.R. 7248, higher education; H.R. 8628, political broadcasting; H.R. 11060, campaign expenditures limitations; H.R. 2266, school desegregation assistance) after the October deadline in 1971. The Rules Committee refused to consider H.R. 11060.

4. U.S. Congress, House, *Rules*, 92nd Cong., annotation to Rule XI, 27(d) (1).

5. Quoted in Robinson, *House Rules Committee*, p. 83.

6. Interview, July 18, 1973.

7. *House Rules Committee*, p. 14.

8. Raymond Moley, "Smith of Virginia," *Newsweek*, August 25, 1958, p. 80.

9. Robert Peabody, "The Enlarged Rules Committee," in Robert Peabody and Nelson Polsby, eds., *New Perspectives on the House of Representatives* (Chicago: Rand McNally & Co., 1963), p. 157.

10. *House Rules Committee,* p. 84.

11. Richard Bolling, *House Out of Order* (New York: E. P. Dutton & Co., 1965), pp. 86-87.

12. Quoted in R. L. Pratt, "The Taming of the Shrew: Myth and Politics in the House Committee on Rules" (B.A. thesis, Wesleyan University, 1969), p. 140.

13. Quoted in Don Oberdorfer, "Judge Smith Moves with Deliberate Drag," *New York Times Magazine,* January 12, 1964, p. 13.

14. *Ibid.,* p. 85.

15. Interview, July 17, 1973.

16. Interview, October 5, 1973.

17. Quoted in Pratt, "Taming of the Shrew," p. 139.

18. Quoted in *ibid.,* p. 138.

19. Quoted in *ibid.,* p. 118.

20. Interview, October 5, 1973.

21. Interview, March 12, 1971.

22. Interview, August 13, 1970.

23. Interview, December 10, 1970.

24. Interview, March 11, 1971.

25. Interview, December 22, 1970.

26. Interview, August 10, 1975.

27. Interview, December 1, 1970.

28. Interview, March 12, 1971.

29. Interview, August 1, 1970.

30. Interview, September 18, 1970.

31. Interview, March 10, 1971.

32. Interview, June 26, 1971.

33. Interview, April 16, 1971.

34. Interview, March 11, 1971.

35. Quoted in Pratt, "Taming of the Shrew," p. 138.

36. Interview, July 16, 1973.

37. Interview, July 17, 1973.

38. Interview, June 19, 1973.

39. Interview, July 17, 1973.

40. This was the situation during consideration of the Emergency Petroleum Allocation Act (H.R. 9861-93rd), the Daylight Saving Act (H.R. 11324-93rd), and the National Energy Emergency Act (H.R. 11450-93rd).

41. Quoted in *Congressional Quarterly Weekly Report,* March 30, 1974, p. 804.

42. Interview, March 14, 1974.

43. *Washington Post,* March 9, 1974.

44. For an excellent account of the committee's activities in the 93rd Congress, see Alan Ehrenhalt, "House Rules Committee Regains Image of Independence," *Congressional Quarterly Weekly Report,* March 30, 1974, pp. 804-10.

7

Committee Decisions

LEADERSHIP-COMMITTEE AGREEMENT STUDIES

To measure the Rules Committee's performance in service to the two parties' leaderships, the authors compared the members' committee roll-call votes with those of the leaders on the floor on a "help or hinder" basis. Several hypotheses about Rules Committee behavior, based largely on the analysis of this book, were examined in light of the results of the vote comparison. Although the votes of the members in committee and the votes of the leaders on the floor do not tell the whole story, the comparative study revealed some interesting as well as unexpected facts about the Rules Committee during the chairmanships of the three men covered by this study (see Table 7.1, p. 177).

INDEPENDENT PERIOD — HOWARD SMITH, 1955-60

Hypothesis I: The Democratic majority of a reputedly independent Rules Committee would show a high degree of disagreement with the Democratic leadership of the House.

The results of the study repudiate this hypothesis almost completely. In fact, the committee Democrats voted in agreement with the leadership's position an average of 78.1% of the time in the 85th Congress and 73.1% of the time in the 86th. These averages compare favorably with the Democratic Rules membership's record in subsequent Congresses. In fact, if the consistently negative votes of Chairman Smith and Congressman Colmer were disregarded, the other six committee Democrats, with almost perfect scores, would have given the Rules Committee of this period (1955-60) the best performance as the true arm of the leadership. The only major deviations found among the six loyal Democrats were the votes of James Trimble (D-Ark.) and Homer Thornberry (D-Tex.) against the 1957 Civil Rights Act (H.R. 6127-85th) and the 1960 Civil Rights Act (H.R. 8601-86th). As representatives of border and southern states in 1957 and 1960, Trimble and Thornberry could not have voted differently and survived.

From this study of leadership agreement, it seems that a chairman with an independent mind does not, even in his prime, have the power or influence to transform his committee into an independent organ, one opposed to, or free from, control of the House leadership. Theoretically at least, the committee remains an effective arm of the leadership so long as the leaders enjoy the support of the committee majority, regardless of the chairman's predisposition.

Hypothesis II: An independent Democratic chairman who supports the House Republican leadership and the Republican Rules Committee membership from time to time helps to promote a high degree of agreement between the Republican committee members and the House Republican leadership.

According to the study, the Republican Rules Committee members scored a high percentage of agreement with the Republican leadership — 78.7% in the 85th Congress and 85.8% in the 86th. The 85.8% record was the highest of all the scores in the nine Congresses studied. This may have been due not only to the Republican leaders having found an ally in the person of the Democratic chairman, but also to having a Republican President and a comparatively homogenous Republican membership on the committee.

Semi-Independent Period — Howard Smith, 1961-66

Hypothesis III: The enlargement of the committee and the addition of two pro-leadership Democrats to the Rules Committee would increase the agreement scores of the Democratic committee members.

Enlargement of the committee did in fact improve the Democratic members' agreement scores. The scores of this post-enlargement period were 78%, 79%, and 79.3% respectively. The improvement over the independent period (78.1% and 73.1%) was, however, considerably less than expected. The reason for this unimpressive showing was that William Colmer, then ranking Democrat on the committee, persisted in his extreme reluctance to cooperate with the leadership. In the 87th Congress, he disagreed with the Democratic leadership on every roll-call vote. Colmer's individual agreement score for that Congress stood at zero (0%), the only such score for any member during the entire twenty-year period studied. His scores for the 88th and 89th Congresses were 25% and 11% respectively, which were lower than his own scores for the previous Congresses (34% in the 85th and 14% in the 86th) and lower than those of Howard Smith (20%, 25%, and 27% for the 87th-89th Congresses). Colmer was apparently acting as the representative of conservatism on the committee and in this respect outperforming Chairman Smith, who had resigned himself to a role of semi-independence after losing the coalition majority.

Hypothesis IV: The impact of enlargement and "packing" of the committee would force the Republicans into a higher level of agreement to offset the strengthening of the Democratic leadership's influence.

Contrary to expectations and the hypothesis, the Republicans reduced their agreement scores, with 60.2%, 77.6%, and 78.8% respectively for the 87th, 88th, and 89th Congresses. The findings for the 87th Congress may be misleading because they are based on a very limited sampling. Only three out of a total of sixteen committee roll-call votes (18.7%) were used for this agreement study. The rest of the roll-call votes were omitted because either they lacked corresponding floor votes or the floor votes of the Republican leadership were split. In spite of this inadequacy, it may safely be concluded that there was a lack of improvement in agreement on the part of the Republicans. The fact that a Democrat replaced a Republican in the White House during the period of the 87th, 88th, and 89th Congresses may have contributed to increased Republican disagreement. The Democratic President's appeal for bipartisan support of his programs was heeded by the Republican leadership in some instances. The Peace Corps Act of 1961 (H.R. 7500-87th) serves as a good illustration. President Kennedy wanted to establish the Peace Corps both to improve the U.S. image abroad and to provide opportunities for service to those citizens dedicated to international mutual aid. The proposal proved attractive and acceptable to the Republican leaders, Ford and Arends, but not to the more conservative Rules membership. In fact, all five Republicans on the Rules Committee voted against the measure both in the committee and on the floor, in flat opposition to their leadership's announced support of it.

PERIOD OF COURTESY — WILLIAM COLMER, 1967-72

Hypothesis V: The departure of Howard Smith, an ultraconservative, and his replacement by Spark Matsunaga, a liberal Democrat, would no doubt help improve the Democrats' agreement scores.

The study showed that Democrats did not fare as well in their agreement score as had been expected. They scored only 73.9% in the last two years of the Johnson administration, despite Colmer's high score of 63%. Their scores dropped to 65.2% and 65.8% for the 91st and 92nd Congresses respectively (during the first Nixon term), the lowest in the entire nine-Congress period studied. Apparently, the failure of Messrs. Madden, Delaney, and Sisk to agree with the Democratic leadership more frequently contributed to the poor showing in the 90th Congress. In fact, all three had a lower agreement score than Colmer. Then, when the Nixon administration was installed in the 91st Congress and the Democratic leadership lost some of its legislative initiative, every single Democrat lowered his agreement score except Sisk and Young, who increased theirs. The impact of general national discontent may be another reason the Democratic agreement score remained so low in the 92nd Congress.

Hypothesis VI: With a Republican President, Richard Nixon, in office at the beginning of the 91st Congress, the Republicans on the Rules Committee would rally behind their leaders to support administration policy and legislation.

The study showed that the inauguration of President Nixon indeed helped the Republican members of the Rules Committee to raise their agreement scores from 57% in the 90th Congress to 84% in the 91st Congress. Three of the five members scored 90%, having voted in agreement with the Republican leadership nine out of ten times. Nevertheless, the score of the Republicans fell to a low of 65% in the 92nd Congress, despite the fact that a Republican President was still in office. As will be discussed later, there was widespread disenchantment on a national scale which moved both Democrats and Republicans to ignore their respective party leaders (see p. 134).

PERIOD OF SUBORDINATION — RAY MADDEN, JANUARY, 1973–SEPTEMBER, 1973

Hypothesis VII: With a loyal Democrat in the chair for the first time since 1955, with the departure of a Southern conservative, and with three new members handpicked by the Speaker, the Democrats on the Rules Committee would certainly register a very high leadership agreement score.

The study showed that Democratic members of the Rules Committee most assuredly were on a honeymoon with the leadership during the first nine months of the 93rd Congress. Four out of ten members had a perfect score of 100%, and five had a minimum of 85%. These scores were amazingly high because the highest average agreement score for the other eight Congresses studied was only 79%. The committee's new practice of holding open business sessions, begun in the 93rd Congress, may also have encouraged the Democrats to maintain a united front in the public eye.

Hypothesis VIII: With President Nixon having overwhelmingly won a second term in office, the Republicans on the Rules Committee would strive for a higher degree of agreement with the Republican leadership to implement administration policies and to offset the rejuvenated strength of the Democrats.

The study revealed that Republicans of the 93rd Congress did in fact maintain a high agreement score of 81%, an improvement of sixteen points over their low of 65% in the previous Congress. Even the liberal Anderson garnered a score of 79% and almost consistently voted in agreement with the other four Republicans on the committee. The newcomer Del Clawson, having been assigned to the committee on the recommendation of H. Allen Smith (R-Calif., recently retired), fitted almost perfectly into the Republican ranks.

RESTORATION OF PRESTIGE — RAY MADDEN,
OCTOBER, 1973–DECEMBER, 1974

Hypothesis IX: The Rules Committee Democrats, along with Chairman Madden, having been rebuffed and ridiculed for their blind loyalty to the leadership during the opening session of the 93rd Congress, would now seek independence from the leadership.

Led by McSpadden, who was running for governor of Oklahoma in 1974, Long, Matsunaga, Pepper, Young, and even Chairman Madden fell in their agreement scores. The Democrats in the second period of the 93rd Congress registered an average agreement score of 80.6%, roughly ten points less than that of the first period of the 93rd Congress. Madden's decision to be more independent, the energy crisis, and the fact that McSpadden and Long, both Albert's personal choices, were stepping out of ranks and disagreeing with the leadership all contributed to the lower scores. In the exercise of their new-found independence, the Democrats in the 93rd Congress did not go as far as Howard Smith and William Colmer, who opposed the leadership on practically all issues.[1]

Hypothesis X: Although the Watergate scandal began to develop to its climax in the spring of 1974, and Gerald Ford had been replaced by John Rhodes as the minority leader in late 1973, the Republican lineup on the Rules Committee remained the same, with none of them from an oil-producing state. Their agreement scores should, therefore, have been similar to those of the Madden subordination period.

One of the biggest surprises of the Republican membership turned out to be that its agreement score (59%) was one of the lowest in eighteen years. This phenomenon can be attributed to individual constituency and philosophical considerations. An instance of the former was Ranking Minority Member Dave Martin's disagreement with his own leadership on the all-year Daylight Savings Time bill

(H.R. 11324-93rd) because Nebraska is in two time zones. This bill's adoption would have inconvenienced a group of his constituents because they would not, under its provisions, have had sunrise until after 9:00 A.M. A case of the latter involved the waiving of points of order for any and all amendments to the conference report on the military procurement authorization bill (H.R. 9286-93rd), namely, amendments proposed by the conferees in excess of their authority. The entire Republican membership went against its leadership in this case. While the Republican leadership was trying to save the bill by supporting the waiver, the Rules Committee Republicans voted unanimously and repeatedly, both in the committee and on the floor, against the general waiver which would have permitted floor amendments on public health and hospitals and other provisions supported by political liberals.

CONSISTENCY STUDIES

Robinson observed in his study of 1963 that: "Roll-call votes on the House floor may be different from votes in the Rules Committee. Some members occasionally vote to report a bill but reserve the right to vote against it on the floor. The frequency of this 'divided vote' is not known, but its existence is well known."[2] In the hope of arriving at some meaningful analysis of the "divided vote," the authors compared all the roll-call votes in the Rules Committee of the 85th through 93rd Congresses with the roll-call votes cast by the Rules Committee members on the House floor. To compare these, of course, it was necessary to select only those bills on which roll-call votes were taken both in the committee and on the floor. It was also necessary to determine the most important vote in the committee, the one which either hindered or helped the eventual passage of the bill (not necessarily the final vote), as well as the final roll-call vote on the floor for the same bill. By this process of elimination, the authors ended up with nine groups of votes, ranging from a set of five for the 87th to a set of twenty-five for the 93rd Congress, to be used to study the Rules Committee members' voting consistency in the committee and on the floor.

In making this consistency study, the authors were made aware of the following limitations: a) Crucial votes in the committee are not necessarily by roll call. As David Truman suggested:

> Not all votes are taken by roll call, of course, but it is rarely the case that a matter of real controversy, or one of importance in other respects, is disposed of in either chamber without at least one vote recording the preferences of the individual senators and representatives. . . . Reservations properly can and should be registered, however, against an uncritical reliance upon roll calls as indicators of the full range of legislative behavior. They are unmistakably a record of decisions taken, of choices made, but they are evidence of only the most public choices.[3]

Thus, there is always the probability of missing an important unrecorded vote. b) At times more than one critical roll-call vote determines the fate of a bill in committee, as when an amendment in the nature of a substitute bill is offered, and a decision has to be made by the student of the committee as to which is the most important vote. This subjective decision is open to possible challenge by other students of Congress provided with the same data, and, by the same token, the choice of the final floor vote to be considered is subject to the same type of criticism. c) Bills approved in committee by seemingly critical roll-call votes are at times passed on the floor of the House without a roll-call vote. d) The current study, being limited to only nine Congresses, may not be comprehensive enough to enable the authors to draw valid conclusions.

Contrary to the general impression conveyed by Robinson and others, the conclusion drawn from the consistency study is that committee members very seldom vote to grant a rule to a bill in the committee and then proceed to the floor to vote against its passage. Democratic members had the highest divided-vote score, 12%, in the 86th Congress, and the Republicans had their highest, 11.8%, in the 91st Congress. The Democrats voted to support measures in the committee and then opposed them on the floor only six out of forty-nine possible times. The Republicans did so only six times out of fifty-one. The Rules Committee members' frequency of casting divided votes is not too much more than 10% of their opportunities for doing so per Congress (see Table 7.1, p. 177). Among the common reasons for casting these divided votes were the following:

1. Discrepancies in committee and floor versions. More often than not the substance of a bill reported out by the Rules Committee was altered on the floor, sometimes beyond recognition. Thus, a member who supported the original version and voted for its clearance in committee might find himself unable to approve the House-passed version. The Republican Rules Committee members, for example, unanimously voted to give an open rule to the public debt ceiling increase bill (H.R. 11104-93rd). When the final figures were set by the Democratic majority, the ceiling was not as high as President Nixon desired. Consequently, three of the four Republicans switched their votes from Yea to Nay.

2. Decision to permit the House to work its will. Depending on the circumstances and the individual, a member sometimes voted to send a bill to the floor to let the House work its will, despite the fact that he was opposed to the bill. The theory of letting the House work its will was explained by Chairman Madden as follows: "When a bill is reported out of a committee, the majority of that committee must think well of that bill. There are 435 members of Congress. Why should eight members of the Rules Committee deprive all the members of Congress of the right to vote on that bill? We are just observing a democratic principle. If the original committee that held hearings thought enough of it to report it out, why should eight members of our committee have the power to keep 435 members from legislating on it?"[4]

As has been observed, Madden remained true to these words in the first nine months of the 93rd Congress when he voted to clear every single bill pending before Rules, regardless of whether it had the support of the House majority or not. Nonetheless, on at least three occasions he changed his committee vote of "help" to a floor vote of "hinder."[5]

3. Submission to a legislative committee's demand for a particular type of rule. Here there was no question of support for a bill. Presumably a member was in general support of the substance of the bill. At this point a legislative committee chairman demanded

a specific rule which would permit only the original committee to take the bill to the floor. The Rules member, confronted with the option of either supporting the specific rule requested or not having a bill at all, voted for the rule in the committee but went against it on the floor.

The classical example of this was the Trade Act of 1970 (H.R. 18970-91st). Tip O'Neill, then a member of Rules, was supporting the bill and an open rule. Chairman Mills of the Ways and Means Committee then served notice on the leadership and the Rules Committee that he would withdraw the bill rather than accept an open rule. An open rule would indeed have been adopted on an 8-7 vote if it hadn't been for the fact that O'Neill changed his vote from support for the open rule to opposition to it. Although O'Neill supported the closed rule in the committee to please Mills and to save the bill, he had no reason to vote for such a rule on the floor and so did not.

4. Serving as an arm of the leadership by casting the divided vote. The major reason for this phenomenon was that the members voted in conformity with the leadership's wishes in committee to fulfill their obligation to the leaders, but voted independently on the floor to signal their constituent sentiments or political convictions, or both. Leadership on either side of the aisle rarely had any need to expect its Rules membership to "toe the line" on the floor, since each member's vote there was, naturally, only one out of 435 in contrast with one out of fifteen in the committee.

McSpadden, who most often deviated from the Democratic majority in the 93rd Congress stated, in this connection: "As a member of the Committee on Rules, I may be opposed to some bills on the floor, but I would vote for them in the committee in accordance with the Speaker's wishes. I don't think this will be betraying a trust. Carl Albert said to me at the time of my appointment, 'There may be times when I would like to ask your cooperation as a member of the committee but you could always vote with your district on the floor.' "[6] Anderson of Illinois, the liberal Republican on the committee, confirmed this possibility of vote choices from his vantage point: "On some bills I would go along with members of my party in the Rules Committee just to demonstrate a united front, even though I may have reservations about the particular pieces of legislation. But the committee is not the final arbiter, and I would then be opposed to the bills on the floor.[7]

The record shows that members of both parties have cast divided votes. When Matsunaga, an ardent opponent of the draft law (H.R. 6531-92nd), made it known that he would oppose the requested rule in committee, Speaker Albert beckoned him to the Speaker's desk during debate on another matter on the House floor. Albert began by asking Matsunaga, "Sparky, you're OK on the rule for the draft conference report, aren't you?" When Matsunaga responded that he was intent on opposing the rule in committee because of his basic opposition to the draft, Albert pleaded with him on the basis of the seriousness of the situation. It was a case, he said, of either having the general waiver or not having a conference report at all, and he inquired whether or not Matsunaga could see his way clear to reporting the rule out of committee and then opposing it on the floor. Realizing that the House leadership would find itself in an embarrassing position if unable to move a nationally important and highly publicized issue to the floor, Matsunaga agreed to the Speaker's suggestion.

The School Construction Assistance Act (H.R. 10128-86th) and the Urban Renewal Improvement Act amendments (S. 57-86th) were not very popular in the southern and border states in 1959-60. Consequently, former Congressman James Trimble (D-Ark.) and Homer Thornberry (D-Tex.) voted to support the rules for these bills in the committee yet voted against the bills on the floor. Two Republicans did the same thing with the Family Assistance Act (H.R. 16311-91st). Ranking Minority Member H. Allen Smith and James Quillen supported a closed rule for the bill at the request of the Republican leadership in the committee, but voted against the measure on the floor.

By using the divided vote, a Rules Committee member can serve the House leadership in a most tangible manner. However, the use of this device has been very limited. The authors will attempt to explain why the divided vote was not used more often for this purpose:

1. The lack of secrecy of the committee voting record. Even when executive (closed) sessions were the usual order of the day for Rules Committee meetings, a member who wished to comply with the request of the leadership and thus vote against his constituents' interests found no refuge behind the supposed secrecy of the executive session. There was no real secrecy about the committee roll-call vote, for despite the committee's denial of public access to committee minutes, the news media were always able to poll the members individually to learn the lineup of the votes. (The committee's own rules in the 91st Congress specifically provided that minutes, including roll-call votes, could be released to committee members only. The rules in the 92nd Congress, however, made the roll-call votes public information.) In the 93rd Congress, the committee made a practice of holding open business meetings. With this turn of events, a member who was concerned with constituency repercussions obviously was not in a position to remain loyal to the leadership. Bereft of that veil of secrecy which formerly shielded Rules Committee members, he was forced to vote in support of constituent interests. As former Congressman William Anderson (D-Tenn.) put it: "You know how much we Tennesseans are opposed to any form of gun control. When we worked on the Gun Control Act (H.R. 17735-90th) for Speaker McCormack, I remember that was about the only time that the leadership contacted me; and yet it was one of the few times when I just couldn't go along, because my district was so strongly against it. The reporters would find out how I voted in the committee anyway, and I'd be in deep water."[8]

Use of the divided vote by Democrats dropped suddenly in the 92nd Congress (1.4%) when the committee roll-call votes were made open to the public. The lifting of secrecy on committee voting records has just about eliminated the divided vote as a method of showing loyalty to the leadership. There were 140 opportunities for committee Democrats to cast divided votes, but only in the case of the bill to authorize foreign sale of passenger vessels (H.R. 11589-92nd) did two Democrats (Madden and Pepper) cast divided votes.

2. The reluctance on the part of the leadership to impose its will on the Rules membership. The divided vote only served a purpose when there was a need for such a vote. The need was apparent only

when two conditions prevailed: either there was a close vote expected in the committee, or there was an important issue on which the leadership had taken a strong position.

If need is a criterion for the divided vote, then the Republicans on the committee, being in the minority party since the 84th Congress, have not been required to cast the divided vote as often as the Democrats. As John Anderson explained, "In view of the fact that the minority leadership does not have the function of programming legislation, I don't think that the minority Rules members are bound by the same degree of responsibility to it as the majority members are to the majority leadership."[9] The record shows, in fact, that while the Republicans' high divided-vote score of 11.8% in the 91st Congress closely paralleled that of the Democrats' 12% in the 90th Congress, the Republicans scored zero in three out of the nine Congresses studied. On the average, therefore, the Republican members, finding no real need for divided votes, voted more consistently than their Democratic counterparts.

RICE INDEX OF COHESION STUDIES

The well-known Rice index of cohesion is designed to indicate whether members of the same party have been voting in unison (partisan) or in opposition to each other (nonpartisan).[10] Because the House and the party leaders expect the Rules Committee members to be loyal to their respective parties, the application of the Rice index to the Rules Committee members would seem especially meaningful. This was done by the authors, using all the roll-call votes taken during the period of the nine Congresses, from 1957 to 1974.

INDEPENDENT PERIOD — HOWARD SMITH, 1955-60

In the 85th and 86th Congresses, with a Democratic membership of eight in the Rules Committee, it would have taken the persistent disagreement of only two of its members with the majority to drop its cohesion index down to 50. Howard Smith and William Colmer supplied this dissension. Three members voting consistently against the other five would have further reduced the cohesion index of the Democrats to 25. This decline in the score was accentuated by the Civil Rights Act of 1957 (H.R. 6127-85th) and the constituency-oriented Natural Gas Act (H.R. 8525-85th), which created enough of a division within the Democratic ranks to produce one of the lowest cohesion indexes in the eighteen-year period — 34.7 for the 85th Congress. However, the Democrats raised their average to 45.6 in the 86th Congress. (The Democrats' cohesion index fell between 43.5 and 48.7 in five of the nine Congresses studied.)

With only four Republicans on the Rules Committee during the corresponding period, the consistent deviation of one Republican from the minority ranks would have reduced their Rice cohesion index to 50, yet the Republicans showed enough solidarity within the committee to produce the comparatively high indexes of 57.8 and 66.7 for the 85th and 86th Congresses respectively. The Republicans enjoyed the advantage of not having any member who was consistently "out-of-line" among their ranks.

SEMI-INDEPENDENT PERIOD — HOWARD SMITH, 1961-66

The enlargement of the Rules Committee in the 87th Congress had a strong impact on its Democratic majority and its Rice index rose to 57.1, its highest during the period studied, except for that reached in the 93rd Congress. Although both Smith and Colmer remained on the committee during this period, it would have taken the persistent deviation of three of its members to drop the index of the Democrats to below 50, since there were ten of them. The fact that Chairman Smith sided with the majority in five out of a total of sixteen roll-call votes to show his "good faith" to his party leadership also contributed to the higher cohesion index.

When four new Republican members were appointed to the Rules Committee in the 87th Congress, Republican party solidarity reached unprecedented heights and produced the highest cohesion index ever attained by the Republicans — an incredible 94. There were only two dissenting votes (one each by two members) cast in a total of fifteen roll-call votes in the committee. However, the Republican index did drop to 76.6 and 80 in the subsequent Congresses studied.

PERIOD OF COURTESY — WILLIAM COLMER, 1967-72

The Democratic leadership, having appointed Matsunaga of Hawaii and William Anderson of Tennessee as new members to fill the two vacancies left by the defeats of Smith and Trimble, hoped to experience a greater cohesion in the Rules Committee of the 90th Congress. However, constituency interests prevailed over party loyalty whenever the two came into conflict. During consideration of the Gun Control Act (H.R. 17735-90th) and the Interstate Commerce Taxation Act (H.R. 2158-90th), for example, partisan loyalty fell victim to district pressures, and the Democrats split their votes 5-4 on H.R. 2158 and 5-5 on the crucial Casey amendment to H.R. 17735.

The Democratic cohesion index of 33 in the 92nd Congress should be of special interest to students of the Rules Committee because it was the lowest Democratic score in all Congresses studied. The Democratic members joined only once in a 10-0 partisan vote (H.R. 16810-92nd) and twice in a 9-1 vote out of a total of twenty-two roll-call votes. Seven times they split their votes 5-5 or 5-4. Perhaps the best explanation of these splits is the one given by William Anderson, who retired at the end of the 92nd Congress: "The 92nd Congress was marked by the lingering war in Vietnam, the Watergate discovery, and, all in all, the wide spread of public discontent. The members felt that they were never under so much pressure from a diversity of constituents. Consequently they tended to let their own assessments, convictions, and philosophies on the various problems supersede those of the leadership and their colleagues."[11]

The Republicans on the Rules Committee of the 90th Congress also experienced difficulty in attaining high cohesion and ended up with one of the lowest scores — 62.4 on the Rice index. As in the case of the Democrats, partisan loyalty yielded to constituency considerations. For example, in voting on the previously mentioned constituency-oriented gun control bill and the Interstate Commerce Taxation Act the Republicans split 3-2. It is plain that regardless of party affiliation or who occupies the committee chairmanship, when there is a conflict between constituency interests and party loyalty the former is likely to prevail.

PERIOD OF SUBORDINATION — RAY MADDEN,
JANUARY, 1973–SEPTEMBER, 1973

As has been previously noted, the first time that the Democratic membership on the Rules Committee was freed of philosophical conservatives was in the 93rd Congress. The Democratic committee's solidarity during this period, evidenced by a cohesion index of 82.1, heartened every party loyalist. On the average only one Democrat out of ten deviated from the majority throughout a total of thirty-four roll-call votes in committee. More surprising was the fact that in twenty-one instances, nearly two-thirds of all roll-call votes, the ten Democrats cast votes in unanimity. That the committee had a liberal chairman, that it was given three Speaker-recommended new members, and that it was free of die-hard conservatives are three reasons why the very high cohesion index was attained.

The high level Democratic cohesion would seem to suggest that the issues faced by the committee during this nine-month period were noncontroversial. The truth of the matter is that controversial issues *were* considered. The Republicans' solid vote against the Democratic majority was one evidence of this. The Republicans registered a high cohesion index of 86 by casting twenty-one unanimous votes. In only two instances did the Republican members all agree with the Democrats: 1) in providing a rule for the Little Cigar Act (H.R. 7482-93rd) and 2) on an insignificant deadline question for the Joint Budget Committee (H.R. 7130-93rd). Aside from these two bipartisan votes, the Republicans voted against the Democratic majority on each and every one of the thirty-four questions put to a record vote. Democratic unity under Madden's chairmanship seemed to cause increased Republican solidarity.

RESTORATION OF PRESTIGE — RAY MADDEN,
OCTOBER, 1973–DECEMBER, 1974

Constituent interests seemed to prevail over party loyalty during the latter part of the 93rd Congress. As a consequence, the Democrats recorded a much lower cohesion index, 54. The Republicans, too, were affected by various constituency considerations during this period, but they managed to maintain their solidarity and registered a lower but still high cohesion index of 71.

The study clearly showed that throughout all these periods the chairman, regardless of his personality and mode of operation, could at best be only one of the many factors contributing to committee members' voting behavior. He could neither dictate to, nor greatly influence, the members in their voting on crucial issues. There were just too many other constraints on the members for the chairman to exert any effective influence or control. While there was nothing to prevent a member from conforming as a result of coincidence, occasional courtesy, or philosophical rapport, the member of the majority party was not under any obligation to his chairman to conform to the latter's image. The Democratic members (except Colmer) voted almost in unison in support of the House leadership in the 85th and 86th Congresses, in spite of the independent image of the committee chaired by Howard Smith (see p. 120), and the Democrats had the lowest agreement score in the 92nd Congress, despite the fact that Chairman Colmer successfully projected his own and the committee's image of cordial cooperation with the leadership (see p. 123). The authors suggest that while the chairman often determined the committee image, it was not necessarily through the collaboration of his own party members on the committee. Instead, he formed the committee image primarily on the model of his own attitudes and actions.

This analysis of the roll-call votes also confirmed the impression that even a loyal member of the Rules Committee frequently deserted his leadership in favor of his constituency when forced to make a choice. The rationale was that a member could hardly be accused of being disloyal to his party if his failure to heed the call of his respective leaders was based on genuine grounds of constituency pressures. The minimal presence of the divided vote shown by the consistency studies, the extremely low Republican leadership agreement score in the Madden "restoration of prestige period," and the low Democratic Party cohesion index all presented striking evidence of the importance of the members' constituency with respect to their votes in committee and on the House floor.

FEDERAL DISTRICT OUTLAY STUDIES

In the hope of gaining a better understanding of the relation between constituency interests and the decision behavior of Rules Committee members, the authors used the federal district outlay studies (see Tables 5.4-5.8, pp. 165-69) to identify those members who received more than the national average of outlay from any particular agency. The authors' analysis (see Table 7.2, p. 178) also ascertained that a higher than "ideal" number of high-involvement states were represented on the Rules Committee. This can perhaps be accounted for by the fact that eight of the thirteen states represented on Rules are big states with high-involvement status in at least half of the agency areas. The number of high-involvement member districts was also "overrepresented" for ten of the seventeen agencies studied.

Theoretically, if the committee had had more high-involvement members than the ideal number for any agency, it should have had a decision bias favoring legislation beneficial to that agency. While the results were conclusive when the authors used the *Federal Outlay* figures to show that the Rules members had fared well in getting federal funds for their respective districts (see Chapter 5), the authors were not able to discern a definite relationship between the committee's high involvement with agencies and its behavior in the 90th through 92nd Congresses. For example, the committee should have had an urban bias since it had a very high HUD involvement status, but the housing and urban development bill (H.R. 16704-92nd), a distributive bill, was in fact deferred indefinitely by the Rules Committee.[12]

The committee should also have had an agricultural bias, since there were at least two members more than the number expected who were highly involved with the Agriculture Department. However, the rural telephone bank bill (H.R. 12066-90th), the supplemental rural electrification bill (H.R. 10190-90th), and the potato bill (H.R. 15030-90th), all Agriculture Committee bills, were denied rules by the Rules Committee.[13]

In spite of the inconclusiveness of this study, the student can still legitimately draw the inference that a member's high involvement in federal outlays does not necessarily affect his voting decision.

NOTES

1. A possible exception may be found in the action of the oil-state Democrats in joining Republicans to oppose the Democratic majority. See the conference report vote on the Emergency Energy Act's (S. 2589-93rd) price roll-back provisions, February 20, 1974.

2. James A. Robinson, *House Rules Committee* (Indianapolis: Bobbs-Merrill Co., 1963), p. 108.

3. David Truman, *The Congressional Party* (New York: John Wiley & Sons, 1959), p. 12.

4. Interview, July 16, 1973.

5. In the cases of H.R. 6168-93rd (Economic Stabilization Act), H.Res. 205-93rd (Atlantic Union delegation), and S. 1989-93rd (Federal Salary Act amendments).

6. Interview, June 12, 1973.

7. Interview, July 23, 1973.

8. Interview, June 12, 1973.

9. Interview, March 13, 1971.

10. "The Rice index of cohesion has been widely used, partly because it is quite simple to compute and understand. When the party or subgroup is split 50-50, the index is at 0. As the group becomes more and more united, the index rises to 100. To derive the index of cohesion, simply convert the "yeas" and "nays" into percentages of the total number of group members voting. The index of cohesion is the absolute difference between the two percentage figures. Thus, if 60 Democratic Senators split 45 for (75%) and 15 against (25%), the index of cohesion is 75 − 25, or 50. If 40 Republican Senators split 12 for (30%) and 28 against (70%), the index of cohesion is 70 − 30, or 40." Ralph K. Huitt and Robert L. Peabody, *Congress: Two Decades of Analysis* (New York: Harper and Row, 1969), p. 47n.

11. Interview, June 12, 1973.

12. The four high-involvement members who voted against a rule for the bill were Madden, with grants totaling $21,559,178; Bolling, with $19,100,601; Anderson of Illinois, with $25,379,453; and Colmer with $22,218,271. The national district average for grants from HUD was $17,226,447.

13. The high-involvement members who voted against the rural telephone bank bill were Colmer with grants of $36,649,870, Latta with $34,219,019, and Martin with $218,469,902. Martin was the top scorer in agricultural outlays for all committee leaders. The national average was only $29,444,818.

During the three Congresses studied (90th-92nd, during which there was no change in Rules Committee membership), of the twenty-six bills denied rules by the Rules Committee the only distributive bills for agencies overrepresented on the committee were the HUD bill mentioned (H.R. 16704-92nd) and the three Agriculture bills cited.

8

Conclusion

As the House leadership's expectations clash, reconcile, and converge with those of the majority members of the Rules Committee in the congressional environment, the Rules Committee chronicles its own development through the various phases of independence, semi-independence, cooperation, and subordination.

Chairman Howard Smith's effective use of his prerogative of setting the agenda, coupled with the 6-6 conservative-liberal makeup of the committee over which he presided, made the Rules Committee basically independent of the Democratic leadership from 1955 to 1960 (84th-86th Congresses) (see Table 8.1, p. 179). Smith succeeded in withholding action on an average of thirty bills per Congress, and 31% of the committee Democrats voted consistently to disagree with the leadership, that is to say, 2½ out of the 8 Democrats were invariably in disagreement with the leadership. The cohesion indexes of 35 and 46 in the 85th and 86th Congresses, respectively, also mean that two or three Democrats consistently dissented from the majority. These Democrats, voting in concert with the four Republicans, were able to block, in the Rules Committee, most of the legislation desired by the Democratic leadership.

In recognizing the Rules Committee's independent image, one should not overlook the fact that an independent chairman may not necessarily be able to influence his colleagues to support him. In fact, except for Smith and the conservative William Colmer, all Democrats were extremely loyal to the leadership, showing agreement scores of almost 100%.

The election of President Kennedy and a Democratic majority in 1960 provided the leadership with an environment in which to enlarge the Rules Committee. After the addition of two loyal Democrats to the committee in 1961, on the average only 20% of the Democrats voted against the leadership. The two aforementioned Democratic dissenters thus did not have enough leverage to oppose the leadership successfully, even with the aid of the five-member Republican minority. Nevertheless, Chairman Smith continually used his scheduling power and cleverly employed parliamentary maneuvers to frustrate the leadership's legislative program. In 1961-62, Smith managed to kill nineteen bills by not holding hearings on them, and in 1963-64, eighteen bills suffered similar treatment. This blatant display of semi-independence by the Rules Committee prompted the unusually large House Democratic majority of the 89th Congress to adopt the 21-day rule to bypass the committee. The maneuver was effective to the extent that eight bills that otherwise could have been blocked in the committee were taken by the leadership directly to the House floor by use of the 21-day rule.

The enlargement of the Rules Committee in the Kennedy Congress of 1961-62 resulted in an improvement of eleven points in the Democratic cohesion index (from the 86th Congress's 46 to the 87th's 57) as a greater percentage of Democrats voted together.

The failure of Smith to win reelection to the 90th Congress meant that a new and untried chairman would be presiding over the semi-independent Rules Committee. This fact, coupled with the widespread feeling among the Democrats that the 21-day rule was abused by legislative committee chairmen in the 89th Congress, prompted the House to repeal the 21-day rule.

The new Rules Committee chairman, Colmer, showed extreme courtesy to the leadership and to his more liberal colleagues on the committee and withheld action on a minimum of legislative measures. The enlarged and heavily Democratic Rules Committee, even with two liberal additions in the 90th Congress failed, however, to improve its agreement score (73%) and suffered an all-time low agreement score of 65% during the first term of the Nixon administration. This meant that 35% of the Democrats (3½ out of 10) consistently voted against the leadership in the 91st and 92nd

Congresses. Furthermore, in the 92nd Congress, the Democratic cohesion index dropped to 33, a low for the nine Congresses studied, which indicates that the Democrats had never before been so disunited.

National discontent, as expressed by constituents, may have contributed to this disunity, but concluding that the committee will exert its independence regardless of the leadership, if circumstances warrant it, is unavoidable. It was with full knowledge of this characteristic of the Rules Committee that Carl Albert, after becoming Speaker of the House, promptly proposed the reinstatement of the 21-day rule, modified with a 10-day additional grace period to enhance its acceptability. His proposal failed for reasons discussed earlier.

By 1973, a loyal Democrat, Madden, had replaced Colmer as chairman of the Rules Committee, and Speaker Albert had at one stroke appointed three additional loyalists to it. Not surprisingly, then, the first nine months of the 93rd Congress produced that high agreement score of 91%, which signified that only one of ten Democrats disagreed with the leadership on all the recorded votes. The cohesion index for the 93rd Congress (82), the computation of which is less subjective, also supports this conclusion, showing that only one out of ten Democrats deviated from the majority.

This level of agreement represents an almost total convergence of the leadership's expectations and those of the committee. The committee's new composition and its members' willingness to cooperate more closely with the leaders have probably contributed to this convergence more than has any pressure from the House. In fact, the majority of House members, unlike the majority of House Democrats (which supported eight of the ten), disapproved of ten decisions of the committee in a period of nine months, a disapproval rate greater than for all four previous Congresses put together. (On six occasions a conservative coalition was victorious.)

The Rules Committee's prestige suffered as a result of these floor defeats. In addition, there was a very real danger that total convergence would reduce the activity of the committee to rubber-stamping the leadership proposals. Even if the House overwhelmingly sanctioned a Speaker-dominated committee, if the independence expectations of the committee were completely suppressed the committee might be eliminated altogether because it would no longer have a function.

It was time for the Rules Committee to give up its subordinate role, and the energy crisis and McSpadden's gubernatorial campaign in Oklahoma provided the impetus. The committee began to display greater independence in the second portion of the 93rd Congress (October, 1973–December, 1974). The constituent interest factor was used by Chairman Madden and other Democrats to justify the more independent posture of the committee and its decisions, which were becoming more acceptable to the House majority. The change in committee posture was reflected in the drop in the Democratic agreement score in this fifteen-month period to 81% and in the decline of the cohesion index to 54. Thus the committee once again regained its semi-independence, and with such vigor that when the Democratic Caucus made an attempt to circumvent it by giving the Speaker the power to call any bill reported out of a legislative committee, the House majority, joined by the Speaker himself, voted to frustrate this effort.

The election of seventy-five new Democrats to the House and the revival of a powerful operational Democratic Caucus in the 94th Congress provided fresh incentives to push the committee into subordination. The committee's Democratic membership had expanded to eleven in direct proportion to the increased number of Democrats in the House, giving the incumbent Speaker an additional appointee. Then came the caucus's decision to give the Speaker the power to reappoint all the Democratic Rules members at the beginning of each Congress. While the Speaker has always had the prerogative of filling the Democratic Rules Committee vacancies, he was now vested with the power to remove a renegade incumbent member of his own party at the end of each Congress. Consequently, although the complete record of Democratic agreement and cohesion for the 94th Congress is not yet available, one can reasonably assume that the Rules Committee will undergo another period of subordination in the 94th Congress.

These recent changes, however, should be viewed within the light of these two qualifications: 1) The Democrats on the committee will still have a certain degree of independence on most of the issues coming before it, since the Speaker is not expected to make his influence felt on each and every issue (the adoption of the Hansen proposal would have been a worse constraint on the committee); and 2) The caucus's decision was made without the benefit of a House vote. One may always assume that the House majority may not be in agreement with the Democratic Caucus.

The authors conclude that this study supports the position that the history of the Rules Committee is one of the committee's accommodating the leadership on the one hand and seeking independent status on the other. The majority leadership, the chairman of Rules, and the Rules majority, of course, are all important protagonists in this historical play. If complete committee independence can be defined as that situation in which the leadership lacks the basic majority (of the committee itself) to control the committee, and if total committee subordination can be interpreted as the complete convergence of the two sets of expectations, that is to say, the Speaker's and those of the committee, then it would seem that the life of the Rules Committee is most secure when it is assuming a semi-independent posture. This study (of the past twenty years of the Rules Committee's history) showed that the Rules Committee's independence lasted for only three Congresses (84th–86th) before the committee was enlarged and became semi-independent. The study further revealed that the subordinate status of the committee ended in 1973 after only nine months. The study also showed that the committee in six and a half out of nine Congresses could very well be designated as semi-independent in its relationship with the leadership (87th–92nd and 2nd session, 93rd).

The fact that the House environment is decisive in shaping the leadership-committee relationship is the basis for another dimension of this analysis. The authors conclude that the committee's survival clearly depends on the House majority's approval of its decisions; there is no doubt that drastic sanctions would be imposed on the committee by the House if the House majority failed to agree with the committee's decisions, regardless of its relationship with the leadership. For example, the independent Rules Committee of the 86th Congress found it difficult to accommodate itself to the change in its environment caused by a substantial increase in Democratic membership; as a result, early in the 87th (in 1961), the Rules Committee was enlarged, which was an extraordinary sanction by the House. In 1973, on the other hand, a subordinated Rules Committee, after sitting nine months, became painfully aware of the fact that the House majority had deflated a significant number of its decisions. It is, of course, true to say that even a semi-independent committee, the most stable form of all, cannot survive free from major House sanctions, if, for example, the House acquires a larger Democratic contingent and becomes too liberal to tolerate the committee's existing ways, as it did in 1965. At that time the 21-day rule was the sanction adopted to bypass the committee at the beginning of the 89th Congress.

The authors further submit that the Rules Committee achieves stability when it is semi-independent and at the same time enjoys the approval of the House majority. The Smith period after the committee's enlargement (87th and 88th Congresses) and the Colmer period in its entirety (90th–92nd Congresses) are classical examples of this stability.

Despite the fact that the Rules majority was constantly in disagreement with the leadership as a result of the national discontent in the 91st Congress, and the beginning of the 92nd Congress, the leadership failed to obtain the adoption of a 31-day rule proposal. Here again the House majority showed its approval of the Rules Committee's semi-independent performance by its decisive rejection of the Hansen proposal in October, 1974.

Generally, the committee's stature definitely suffers when it assumes either a subordinate or an independent role in relation to the leadership. The record discloses that although the committee's decisions met with the House's approval in the 84th and 85th Congresses, the committee had been frustrating the expectations of the leadership during this period. The leadership, therefore, had no alternative but to strive for a more cooperative Rules Committee. It did this until it succeeded in subordinating the committee through a change of the House environment in 1961. The theoretically subordinate status of the committee of the 94th Congress is to be found in the power the Speaker has over it. However, the Speaker has not, up to the present time, exercised this power to any marked extent. It would be fair to say, therefore, that there is, at present, a subordination of the Rules Committee merely in theory, not in practice.

To survive, the Rules Committee must maintain a semi-independent posture which will satisfy both its expectations and those of the leadership. Above all, it must ultimately have the general approval of the House majority. As long as the membership of the House remains as large as it now is and the legislative issues before the House remain as complicated as they now are, the leadership will probably need a Rules Committee to share its burden of planning legislative programs. Speaker Albert stated precisely this position in one of his very rare floor speeches on October 3, 1974:

> Of equal importance, it seems to me, is that if the Rules Committee does not have this authority, it is reduced almost to a nonentity in the House, and it would throw burdens upon the leadership of the House which would require an unconscionable amount of time in deciding which bills shall be brought up and in what order, or it would require the leadership, the Speaker, to have a staff to do it, and we would have the programming of legislation, as I see it, that would perhaps be done by an appointed bureaucracy rather than by Members of the House on an important committee.[1]

NOTE

1. *Congressional Record,* Daily Edition, October 3, 1974, p. H9891.

Tables

Table 2.1 *Regulations on Legislative Committees' Travel Established by Rules Committee (93rd Congress)*

Committees with Authority to Travel Only in the U.S.	Committees with Limited Authority to Travel without the U.S.		Committees with Blank Authority to Travel without the U.S.
		Justification for Travel without U.S.	
District of Columbia	Agriculture	Public Law 480	Armed Services
Interior & Insular Affairs	Veterans' Affairs	Investigations of medical facilities, hospitals, counseling programs, and veterans' benefits for American veterans and servicemen in the Philippines, Japan, South Korea, Cambodia, Laos, and South Vietnam.	Banking & Currency
			Education & Labor
			Foreign Affairs
			Government Operations
		Investigations of present counseling programs, the quality of medical care, and the operation of educational, pension, and other programs for American veterans and servicemen in Canada, Mexico, the United Kingdom, West Germany, the Netherlands, Luxembourg, France, Spain, Italy, and Greece.	Interstate & Foreign Commerce
			Judiciary
			Merchant Marine & Fisheries
			Post Office & Civil Service
			Public Works
		Investigations of cemeteries of the U.S. in which veterans of any war or conflict may be buried, whether in the U.S. or abroad, except those cemeteries administered by the Secretary of the Interior.	Science & Astronautics

Table 3.1   *Rules Committee Roll-Call Votes on Previous Question Motions on Adoption of 21-Day Rule, 31-Day Rule, and Hansen Proposal*

Pro-posed Rule	Con-gress	Yeas		Nays	
		Democrats	*Repub-licans*	*Democrats*	*Republicans*
21-day rule	81st (1949)	Sabath, A. (Ill.) Madden, R. (Ind.) Lyle, J. (Tex.) McSweeney, J. (Ohio) Delaney, J. (N.Y.) 41.7%	none	Cox, E. (Ga.) Smith, H. (Va.) Colmer, W. (Miss.)	Allen, L. (Ill.) Brown, C. (Ohio) Wadsworth, I. (Ill.) Herter, C. (Mass.)
21-day rule	89th (1965)	Madden, R. (Ind.) Delaney, J. (N.Y.) Trimble, J. (Ark.) Bolling, R. (Mo.) O'Neill, T. (Mass.) Sisk, B. (Calif.) Pepper, C. (Fla.) 46.7%	none	Smith, H. (Va.) Colmer, W. (Miss.) Young, J. (Tex.)	Brown, C. (Ohio) Smith, H.A. (Calif.) Anderson, J. (Ill.) Martin, D. (Nebr.) Quillen, J. (Tenn.)
31-day rule	92nd (1971)	Madden, R. (Ind.) Bolling, R. (Mo.) O'Neill, T. (Mass.) 20%	none	Colmer, W. (Miss.) Delaney, J. (N.Y.) Sisk, B. (Calif.) Young, J. (Tex.) Pepper, C. (Fla.) Matsunaga, S. (Hawaii) Anderson, J. (Tenn.)	Smith, H.A. (Calif.) Anderson, J. (Ill.) Martin, D. (Nebr.)[a] Quillen, J. (Tenn.) Latta, D. (Ohio)
Hansen proposal	93rd (1974)	Bolling, R. (Mo.) 7.1%	none	Madden, R. (Ind.) Delaney, J. (N.Y.) Sisk, B. (Calif.) Young, J. (Tex.) Pepper, C. (Fla.) Matsunaga, S. (Hawaii) Murphy, M. (Ill.) Long, G. (La.) (McSpadden, C. (Okla.) — not voting)	Martin, D. (Nebr.) Anderson, J. (Ill.) Quillen, J. (Tenn.) Latta, D. (Ohio) Clawson, D. (Calif.)

[a] Martin paired against.

Table 3.2   *Privileged Reports of Committees*

Appropriations Committee
1. General appropriation bills

House Administration Committee
1. Right of a member to his seat
2. All matters referred to it on printing for the use of the House or the two Houses
3. All matters of expenditure of the contingent fund of the House
4. Enrolled bills

Interior and Insular Affairs Committee
1. Bills for the forfeiture of land grants to railroad and other corporations
2. Bills preventing speculation in the public lands
3. Bills for the reservation of the public lands for the benefit of actual and bona fide settlers
4. Bills for the admission of new states

Public Works Committee
1. Bills authorizing the improvement of rivers and harbors

Standards of Official Conduct Committee
1. Resolutions recommending action by the House of Representatives with respect to an individual member, officer, or employee of the House of Representatives as a result of any investigation by the committee relating to the official conduct of such member, officer, or employee of the House of Representatives

Veterans' Affairs Committee
1. General pension bills

Ways and Means Committee
1. Bills raising revenue

SOURCE: U.S. Congress, House, *Rules,* 92nd Cong., XI, 22, § 726.

Table 3.3 *Discharge Petitions Filed against the Rules Committee*

Congress	Date	Bill No. (Res. No.)	Title of Bill	Dis-charged
85th	4/29/57	H.R. 6127 (H.Res. 221)	Civil Rights Act of 1957	no
	5/15/57	H.R. 2474 (H.Res. 249)	Postal Service salary increase	yes
	8/7/57	H.R. 2462 (H.Res. 373)	Federal employees' salary increase	no
	8/7/57	H.R. 5836 (H.Res. 380)	Postal rate readjustment policy	no
	8/23/57	H.R. 6127 (conf) (H.Res. 398)	Civil Rights Act of 1957	no
86th	7/30/59	H.R. 4630 (H.Res. 320)	District of Columbia home rule	no
	8/20/59	H.R. 4633 (H.Res. 339)	District of Columbia home rule	no
	9/7/59	H.R. 8601 (H.Res. 359)	Civil Rights Act of 1959	no
	4/6/60	H.R. 4700 (H.Res. 483)	Social Security amendments of 1959	no
	5/17/60	H.R. 1253 (H.Res. 521)	Federal Trade Commission Act amendment	no
	6/2/60	H.R. 9883 (H.Res. 537)	Federal employees' pay increase	yes
87th	8/30/61	H.R. 4658 (H.Res. 419)	Aid to schools in areas affected by federal activities	no
	4/16/62	H.R. 3745 (H.Res. 585)	Pensions of World War I veterans	no
	6/28/62	H.R. 11327 (H.Res. 693)	To provide an appointed governor and secretary for the District of Columbia	no
88th	7/9/63	H.J.Res. 9 (H.Res. 407)	Constitutional amendment to permit prayer in public schools	no
	9/10/63	H.R. 2332 (H.Res. 496)	Pensions for World War I veterans	no
	12/9/63	H.R. 7152 (H.Res. 574)	Civil Rights Act of 1963	no

(Continued on next page)

Table 3.3 (cont.)

Congress	Date	Bill No. (Res. No.)	Title of Bill	Dis- charged
89th	3/9/65	H.R. 7 (H.Res. 243)	Repeal of the retailer's excise taxes on toilet preparations	no
	8/24/65	H.R. 4644 (H.Res. 515)	Elected mayor, city council, and nonvoting delegate to House of Representatives for District of Columbia	yes
90th	8/2/67	H.R. 7 (H.Res. 752)	Classification in the postal field service	no
	10/26/67	H.R. 655 (H.Res. 94)	Reduction of depletion allowance for oil and gas	no
91st	9/14/70	H.R. 18279 (H.Res. 1169)	Organized Crime Control Act of 1970	no
	12/9/70	H.R. 17555 (H.Res. 1273)	Equal employment opportunities for American workers	no
	12/18/70	H.R. 18214 (H.Res. 1294)	Consumer Protection Act	no
92nd	10/4/71	H.J.Res. 620 (H.Res. 610)	Proposed amendment to Constitution	no
	5/11/72	H.J.Res. 253 (H.Res. 950)	Amend the Constitution to allow for representation of the District of Columbia in Congress	no
93rd	7/16/74	H.R. 14782 (H.Res. 1217)	World War I veterans' pension	no
94th	10/7/75	H.R. 7590 (H.Res. 746)	Authorize the General Accounting Office to audit the Federal Reserve Board and others	no

Table 3.4   *Rules Committee Resolutions Defeated on the Floor*

Congress	Date	Bill No. (Res. No.)	Title
85th	3/27/57	H.Res. 85	Banking & currency investigations
	8/7/57	H.R. 7244 (H.Res. 362)	Agriculture, meat promotion
	6/26/58	H.R. 12954 (H.Res. 609)	Agriculture Act of 1958
	7/24/58	H.R. 4504 (H.Res. 485)	Agriculture, wholesale terminal market
	8/1/58	S. 3497 (H.Res. 650)	Extend housing loan program
86th	5/15/60	H.R. 2331 (H.Res. 488)	National parks, Chesapeake & Ohio Canal
87th	None		
88th	5/14/63	H.Res. 340	Travel authority for Committee on Labor and Education
	10/28/63	H.Res. 314	Travel authority for Committee on Labor and Education
	10/1/64	H.R. 1183 (H.Res. 892)	Continuing appropriation 1965
89th	4/20/66	H.Res. 756	Expresses disapproval of House for Reorganization Plan #1
90th	7/20/67	H.R. 11000 (H.Res. 749)	Rat Extermination Act of 1967
	6/20/68	H.Res. 1222	Rejects Senate amendments to H.R. 15414
	9/18/68	H.R. 15890 (H.Res. 1253)	Providing for GS 16, 17, 18 positions for federal employees
91st	2/26/70	H.R. 12025 (H.Res. 799)	National Forest Timber Conservation and Management Act, 1969
92nd	5/25/71	S.Res. 108 (H.Res. 411)	Reorganization Plan #1
	5/26/71	H.Res. 155	Creates a select committee on energy resources
	2/8/72	H.Res. 164	Creates select committee on privacy, human values and democratic institutions
	6/22/72	H.R. 14163 (H.Res. 1019)	Predator indemnities
	8/16/72	H.Res. 1094	Provides for consideration of conference reports the same day as reported

(Continued on next page)

Table 3.4 (cont.)

Congress	Date	Bill No. (Res. No.)	Title
93rd	2/28/73	H.Res. 257	District of Columbia Committee travel
	4/10/73	H.J.Res. 205 (H.Res. 348)	Atlantic Union delegation
	4/16/73	H.R. 6168 (H.Res. 357)	Economic Stabilization Act
	4/18/73	H.R. 4204 (H.Res. 360)	Emergency Employment Act
	5/10/73	H.R. 7447 (H.Res. 389)	Second supplemental appropriations
	6/13/73	H.R. 8410 (H.Res. 437)	Public debt limit
	7/3/73	S. 1989 (H.Res. 512)	Federal Salary Act amendments
	7/24/73	H.R. 8929 (H.Res. 495)	Educational & cultural postal amendments
	8/3/73	S. 1264 (H.Res. 518)	Eisenhower College proceeds
	9/11/73	S. 1697 (H.Res. 511)	Emergency eucalyptus assistance
	10/17/73	H.R. 9286 (H.Res. 601)	Military procurement
	2/22/74	S. 2589	Emergency Energy Act — conference report
	4/4/74	H.R. 12565 (H.Res. 1026)	Department of Defense supplemental authorization
	5/8/74	H.R. 8053 (H.Res. 929)	Post card registration
	6/11/74	H.R. 10294 (H.Res. 1110)	Land use planning
	12/9/74	H.R. 5385 (H.Res. 1485)	Surface transportation
94th	4/1/76	H.J.Res. 606	Atlantic convention
	5/17/76	H.R. 10210	Unemployment compensation amendments

Table 4.1 *Tangible Qualifications of Rules Committee Appointees*[a]

Members	Year Appointed	Average of Popular Vote Percentage for Two Elections Preceding Appointment	Average of Party Unity Scores for Two Congresses Preceding Appointment	Average of Party Dis-unity Scores for Two Congresses Preceding Appointment
Democrats				
Colmer, W. (Miss.)	1940	100	not available	
Madden, R. (Ind.)	1949	56.7	88	6.5
Delaney, J. (N.Y.)	1949	58.1	91	9
Trimble, J. (Ark.)	1955	100	86	6
Thornberry, H. (Tex.)	1955	78	84	12.5
Bolling, R. (Mo.)	1955	57.5	93	3.5
O'Neill, T. (Mass.)	1955	73.8	85	5
Elliot, C. (Ala.)	1961	100	80.5	10.5
Sisk, B. (Calif.)	1961	90.5	92	6.5
Young, J. (Tex.)	1964	85.2	78.7	10.7
Pepper, C. (Fla.)	1965	61.7	70	2
Matsunaga, S. (Hawaii)	1967	80.5	81	1.5
Anderson, W. (Tenn.)	1967	78.9	84	5
Murphy, M. (Ill.)[b]	1973	72	74	11
Long, G. (La.)[c]	1973	66.2	71	12
McSpadden, C. (Okla.)[d]	1973	71.1	..	..
Moakley, J. (Mass.)	1975	67	88	9
Young, A. (Ga.)	1975	63	85	6
Republicans				
Scott, H. (Pa.)	1953	53.5	60	18
Nicholson, D. (Mass.)	1953	59.1	96	3
Chenoweth, J. (Colo.)	1953	57.7	91	6
Reece, B. (Tenn.)	1953	65.9	96	3
Budge, H. (Idaho)	1959	57.5	83.5	9.5
St. George, K. (N.Y.)	1961	58.5	78.5	5
Smith, H. (Calif.)	1961	78	88	8
Hoffman, E. (Ill.)	1961	64	79	8
Avery, W. (Kan.)	1961	57.2	63	27.5
Anderson, J. (Ill.)	1964	64.6	82.5	9.5
Martin, D. (Nebr.)	1964	58.4	81	6.5
Quillen, J. (Tenn.)	1965	62.8	83	7
Latta, D. (Ohio)	1965	70.6	83.5	12.5
Clawson, D. (Calif.)	1973	62.4	71	8
Lott, T. (Miss.)	1975	69.1	80	14

[a] Including all incumbent members and former members appointed to the committee after 1953.

[b] Murphy's unity and disunity scores are based on one Congress only. He was first elected to Congress in 1970.

[c] Long served in the 88th Congress (1963-64). He was not elected again until 1972. His popular vote percentage is the average of the 1962 and 1972 elections. Long's unity and disunity scores are based on the 88th Congress only.

[d] McSpadden was elected to Congress in 1972. His popular vote percentage is based on the 1972 election.

NOTES: The minimum average popular vote percentage is 56.7% for the Democrats and 53.5% for the Republicans.

The minimum average party unity score is 70 for the Democrats and 60 for the Republicans.

The maximum average party disunity score is 12.5 for the Democrats and 27.5 for the Republicans.

Party unity and disunity scores are based on *Congressional Quarterly* sources.

Table 4.2 *Years Rules Committee Members Served*
in Congress before Appointment[a]

Member	Year of Appointment	Years Served
Democrats		
Colmer, W. (Miss.)	1940	7
Madden, R. (Ind.)	1949	6
Delaney, J. (N.Y.)[b]	1949	2
Trimble, J. (Ark.)	1955	10
Thornberry, H. (Tex.)	1955	6
Bolling, R. (Mo.)	1955	6
O'Neill, T. (Mass.)	1955	2
Elliot, C. (Ala.)	1961	12
Sisk, B. (Calif.)	1961	6
Young, J. (Tex.)	1964	7
Pepper, C. (Fla.)	1965	2
Matsunaga, S. (Hawaii)	1967	4
Anderson, W. (Tenn.)	1967	2
Murphy, M. (Ill.)	1973	2
Long, G. (La.)[c]	1973	2
McSpadden, C. (Okla.)[d]	1973	0
Moakley, J. (Mass.)	1975	2
Young, A. (Ga.)	1975	2

Average number of years for Democrats = 4.44

Member	Year of Appointment	Years Served
Republicans		
Scott, H. (Pa.)	1953	12
Nicholson, D. (Mass.)	1953	6
Chenoweth, J. (Colo.)[e]	1953	2
Reece, B. (Tenn.)[f]	1953	2
Budge, H. (Idaho)	1959	8
St. George, K. (N.Y.)	1961	14
Smith, H. (Calif.)	1961	4
Hoffman, E. (Ill.)	1961	2
Avery, W. (Kan.)	1961	6
Anderson, J. (Ill.)	1964	3
Martin, D. (Nebr.)	1964	3
Quillen, J. (Tenn.)	1965	2
Latta, D. (Ohio)	1965	6
Clawson, D. (Calif.)	1973	10
Lott, T. (Miss.)	1975	2

Average number of years for Republicans = 5.4

Average number of years for all Rules Committee members = 5.2

[a] Including all incumbent members and former members appointed to the committee after 1953.
[b] Delaney was elected first to the 79th Congress in 1944. However, he was defeated for a seat in the 80th Congress. Upon election to the 81st Congress, he was given a seat on Rules.
[c] Long was elected first to the 88th Congress in 1962. He was defeated in 1964. After his election to the 93rd Congress he was appointed to the Rules Committee.
[d] McSpadden was elected to the 93rd Congress in 1972.
[e] Chenoweth was elected first to the 77th Congress in 1940. He continued to serve until the 81st Congress in which he was defeated in his reelection bid. Chenoweth returned to the House for the 82nd Congress. After his election to the 83rd Congress he was appointed to the Rules Committee.
[f] Reece was elected first to the 67th Congress in 1920. He continued to serve until his defeat in 1930. In 1932 he was elected to the 73rd Congress where he remained until the 80th Congress in which he was not a candidate. From 1946 to 1948, Reece was chairman of the National Republican Committee. In 1948 he was defeated in his senatorial campaign. However, Reece was successful as a congressional candidate in 1950. He was reelected to the 83rd Congress and was given a seat on Rules in 1953.

Table 4.3 *Members of 93rd Congress "Qualified"
to Serve on Rules Committee*[a]

DEMOCRATS

Eliminated for Geographic Reasons (18)[b]

Burton, P. (Calif.)	Symington, J. (Mo.)
Corman, J. (Calif.)	Badillo, H. (N.Y.)
Danielson, G. (Calif.)	Bingham, J. (N.Y.)
Edwards, D. (Calif.)	Brasco, F. (N.Y.)
Rees, T. (Calif.)	Koch, E. (N.Y.)
Roybal, E. (Calif.)	Podell, B. (N.Y.)
Waldie, J. (Calif.)	Rangel, C. (N.Y.)
Mink, P. (Hawaii)	Rosenthal, B. (N.Y.)
Sullivan, L. (Mo.)	Eckhardt, B. (Tex.)

*Eliminated Because of Seniority or
Exclusive Committee Assignment (16)*[c]

Udall, M. (Ariz.)	Rodino, P. (N.J.)
Yates, S. (Ill.)	Thompson, F. (N.J.)
Burke, J. (Mass.)	Stokes, L. (Ohio)
Donohue, H. (Mass.)	Green, W. (Pa.)
Dingell, J. (Mich.)	Moorhead, W. (Pa.)
Fraser, D. (Minn.)	Tiernan, R. (R.I.)
Karth, J. (Minn.)	Kastenmeier, R. (Wis.)
Daniels, D. (N.J.)	Reuss, H. (Wis.)

Selected for Possible Rules Committee Assignment (22)

Matsunaga, S. (Hawaii)[d]	O'Hara, J. (Mich.)
Culver, J. (Iowa)	Melcher, J. (Mont.)
Annunzio, F. (Ill.)	Minish, J. (N.J.)
Murphy, M. (Ill.)[e]	Carney, C. (Ohio)
Madden, R. (Ind.)[d]	Seiberling, J. (Ohio)
Long, G. (La.)[e]	Eilberg, J. (Pa.)
Harrington, M. (Mass.)	Nix, R. (Pa.)
Mitchell, P. (Md.)	Rooney, F. (Pa.)
Sarbanes, P. (Md.)	St. Germain, F. (R.I.)
Kyros, P. (Maine)	Meeds, L. (Wash.)
Ford, W. (Mich.)	Aspin, L. (Wis.)

REPUBLICANS

Eliminated for Geographic Reasons (19)[b]

Arends, L. (Ill.)	Clancy, D. (Ohio)
Collier, H. (Ill.)	Devine, S. (Ohio)
Crane, P. (Ill.)	Keating, W. (Ohio)
Derwinski, E. (Ill.)	Harsha, W. (Ohio)
Erlenborn, J. (Ill.)	Miller, C. (Ohio)
Michel, R. (Ill.)	Minshall, W. (Ohio)
McCollister, J. (Nebr.)	Wylie, C. (Ohio)
Thone, C. (Nebr.)	Duncan, J. (Tenn.)
Ashbrook, J. (Ohio)	Kuykendall, D. (Tenn.)
Brown, C. (Ohio)	

(Continued on next page)

Table 4.3 (cont.)

Eliminated Because of Seniority or
Exclusive Committee Assignment (35)[c]

Dickinson, W. (Ala.)	Hutchinson, E. (Mich.)
Edwards, J. (Ala.)	Nelsen, A. (Minn.)
Rhodes, J. (Ariz.)	Sandman, C. (N.J.)
Steiger, S. (Ariz.)	Conable, B. (N.Y.)
Hosmer, C. (Calif.)	McEwen, R. (N.Y.)
Pettis, J. (Calif.)	Grover, J. (N.Y.)
Talcott, B. (Calif.)	Broyhill, J. (N.C.)
Teague, C. (Calif.)	Ruth, E. (N.C.)
Veysey, V. (Calif.)	Goodling, G. (Pa.)
Brotzman, D. (Colo.)	Johnson, A. (Pa.)
Blackburn, B. (Ga.)	Schneebeli, H. (Pa.)
Bray, W. (Ind.)	Scherle, W. (Iowa)
Myers, J. (Ind.)	Archer, B. (Tex.)
Gross, H. (Iowa)	Broyhill, J. (Va.)
Skubitz, J. (Kans.)	Robinson, J. (Va.)
Shriver, G. (Kans.)	Wampler, W. (Va.)
Cederberg, E. (Mich.)	Davis, G. (Wis.)
Chamberlain, C. (Mich.)	

Selected for Possible Rules Assignment (40)

Buchanan, J. (Ala.)	Vander Jagt, G. (Mich.)
Hammerschmidt, J. (Ark.)	Martin, D. (Nebr.)[d]
Clawson, D. (Calif.)[e]	Mizell, W. (N.C.)
Goldwater, B. (Calif.)	Hunt, J. (N.J.)
Rousselot, J. (Calif.)	Hastings, J. (N.Y.)
Wiggins, C. (Calif.)	Kemp, J. (N.Y.)
Wilson, C. (Calif.)	King, C. (N.Y.)
Burke, J. (Fla.)	Lent, N. (N.Y.)
Frey, L. (Fla.)	Camp, J. (Okla.)
Young, C. W. (Fla.)	Latta, D. (Ohio)[d]
Mayne, W. (Iowa)	Eshleman, E. (Pa.)
Dennis, D. (Ind.)	Ware, J. (Pa.)
Hillis, E. (Ind.)	Williams, L. (Pa.)
Zion, R. (Ind.)	Spence, F. (S.C.)
Sebelius, K. (Kans.)	Quillen, J. (Tenn.)[d]
Winn, L. (Kans.)	Collins, J. (Tex.)
Carter, T. (Ky.)	Price, R. (Tex.)
Snyder, M. (Ky.)	Whitehurst, G. (Va.)
Hogan, L. (Md.)	Mallary, R. (Vt.)
Brown, G. (Mich.)	Thomson, V. (Wis.)

[a] The following criteria were used to screen all 435 members of the House:
1) The member must not be a freshman.
2) A Democrat must have had a minimum average popular vote percentage of 56.7% in the 1968 and 1970 elections and a Republican must have had 53.5% in those elections.
3) A Democrat must have had a minimum party unity score of 70 for the 90th and 91st Congresses and a Republican must have had 60 (data based on *Congressional Quarterly* sources).
4) A Democrat must have had a maximum average party disunity score of 12.5 for the 90th and 91st Congresses and a Republican must have had 27.5.

[b] Geographic variable: No state is entitled to more than one Rules member from the same party.

[c] Seniority and exclusive committee variable: Members who enjoy seniority ranking over the top one-fourth of the members of the same party on any standing committee or who are members of one of the other exclusive committees are presumably not interested in service on the Rules Committee.

[d] Incumbent members of the Rules Committee, start of 93rd Congress.

[e] Appointed to Rules Committee in 93rd Congress.

Table 4.4 *Comparison of Rules Committee Members' Probable and Actual Advancement*

Members and Previous Assignments	Date of Rules Appointment	Ranking at Rules Appointment		Ranking 4 Years Later		Ranking 8 Years Later		Ranking in 1975		Probable Responsibility, Previous Comm. 1975
		Previous Comm.	Rules	Probable Previous Comm.	Rules	Probable Previous Comm.	Rules	Probable Previous Comm.	Rules	
Democrats										
COLMER	1940									
Census		5 of 11	8 of 10	3 of 11	7 of 9		off	(off Rules 1973)		
Immigration & Naturalization		3 of 12		2 of 11						
Rivers & Harbors (Public Works)		6 of 14		3 of 15						
MADDEN	1949									
Education & Labor		7 of 10	5 of 8	4 of 12	3 of 4	4 of 17	3 of 8	1	1	chairman
DELANEY	1949									
Census		8 of 10	8 of 8		off		4 of 8		2 of 11	chairman
Territories		7 of 11								
Elections No. 1		5 of 5								
Rivers & Harbors (Public Works)		9 of 16		6 of 13		5 of 19		1		
TRIMBLE	1955									
House Administration		5 of 10	5 of 8	2 of 16	5 of 8	2 of 15	5 of 10	(off Rules 1967)		
Public Works		4 of 13		4 of 22		4 of 20				
THORNBERRY	1955									
Interstate & Foreign Commerce		10 of 14	6 of 8	4 of 21	6 of 8	4 of 20	6 of 10	(off Rules 1963)		
BOLLING	1955									
Banking & Currency		10 of 14	7 of 8	7 of 19	7 of 8	6 of 17	7 of 10	2 of 24	3 of 11	ranking majority

(Continued on next page)

Table 4.4 (cont.)

Members and Previous Assignments	Date of Rules Appoint-ment	Ranking at Rules Appointment Previous Comm.	Rules	Ranking 4 Years Later Probable Previous Comm.	Rules	Ranking 8 Years Later Probable Previous Comm.	Rules	Ranking in 1975 Probable Previous Comm.	Rules	Probable Responsibility, Previous Comm. 1975
O'NEILL Merchant Marine & Fisheries	1955	12 of 13	8 of 8	6 of 20	8 of 8	6 of 19	8 of 10	(off Rules 1973)		
ELLIOT Education & Labor House Administration	1961	6 of 20 11 of 15	9 of 10	3 of 19 9 of 14	8 of 10	(off Rules 1965)				
SISK Interior & Insular Affairs Science & Astronautics	1961	8 of 20 6 of 16	10 of 10	6 of 23 3 of 21	8 of 10	4 of 20 3 of 18	6 of 10	2 of 29 2 of 25	4 of 11	ranking majority ranking majority
YOUNG (Tex.) Public Works	1964	13 of 20	10 of 10	8 of 18	7 of 10	8 of 23	7 of 10	3 of 27	5 of 11	subcommittee chairman
PEPPER Banking & Currency	1965	13 of 19	10 of 10	10 of 20	8 of 10	10 of 22	6 of 10	10 of 29	6 of 11	subcommittee chairman
MATSUNAGA Agriculture Post Office & Civil Service	1967	13 of 24 12 of 17	9 of 10	7 of 22 6 of 15	9 of 10	15 of 20 6 of 15	7 of 11	3 of 29 6 of 20	7 of 11	subcommittee chairman subcommittee chairman
ANDERSON (Tenn.) Science & Astronautics Interstate & Foreign Commerce	1967	16 of 21 16 of 19	10 of 10	8 of 18 13 of 25	10 of 10	(off Rules 1973)				

	Year								
MURPHY									
Foreign Affairs	1973	20 of 21	8 of 10			..	..	15 of 25	8 of 11
Science & Astronautics		16 of 18				..	..	8 of 25	
LONG									
Interstate & Foreign Commerce	1973	24 of 24	9 of 10			..	..	18 of 29	9 of 11
MOAKLEY									
Banking & Currency	1975	16 of 29	10 of 11			..	..	16 of 29	10 of 11
Post Office & Civil Service		11 of 19				..	..	11 of 19	
YOUNG (Ga.)									
Banking & Currency	1975	15 of 29	11 of 11			..		15 of 29	11 of 11
Republicans									
SCOTT									
Interstate & Foreign Commerce	1953	9 of 13	5 of 8	5 of 15	4 of 4	(off Rules 1959)			
NICHOLSON									
Banking & Currency	1953	8 of 12	6 of 8	(off Rules 1955)					
CHENOWETH									
Interstate & Foreign Commerce	1953	11 of 13	7 of 8	(off Rules 1955)					
REECE									
Foreign Affairs	1953	12 of 12	8 of 8	9 of 15	off	5 of 13	2 of 2	(off Rules 1961)	
BUDGE									
Appropriations	1959	18 of 20	4 of 4	(off Rules 1961)					
ST. GEORGE									
Armed Services	1961	11 of 14	3 of 5	(off Rules 1965)					
Post Office & Civil Service		9 of 9							
SMITH									
Judiciary	1961	6 of 11	3 of 5	6 of 14	1	4 of 15		(off Rules 1973)	
Veterans' Affairs		6 of 8		5 of 9		5 of 11			

(Continued on next page)

Table 4.4 (cont.)

Members and Previous Assignments	Date of Rules Appointment	Ranking at Rules Appointment		Ranking 4 Years Later		Ranking 8 Years Later		Ranking in 1975		Probable Responsibility, Previous Comm. 1975
		Previous Comm.	Rules	Probable Previous Comm.	Rules	Probable Previous Comm.	Rules	Probable Previous Comm.	Rules	
HOFFMAN Merchant Marine & Fisheries	1961	11 of 11	5 of 5	(off Rules 1964)						
AVERY Interstate & Foreign Commerce	1961	6 of 11	5 of 5	(off Rules 1964)						
ANDERSON (Ill.) Government Operations	1964	7 of 12	5 of 5	2 of 15	2 of 5	2 of 16	2 of 5	1	1[a]	ranking minority
MARTIN Education & Labor	1964	6 of 10	5 of 5	5 of 14	3 of 5	3 of 16	3 of 5	(off Rules 1975)		
QUILLEN Public Works	1965	11 of 14	4 of 5	4 of 15	4 of 5	3 of 14	3 of 5	2 of 13	1[a]	subcommittee ranking minority
LATTA Agriculture Government Operations	1965	6 of 11 6 of 11	5 of 5	4 of 15 4 of 15	5 of 5	3 of 13 2 of 18	4 of 5	3 of 14 4 of 16	3 of 5	subcommittee ranking minority
CLAWSON Appropriations	1973	18 of 22	5 of 5	..	..	..	..	9 of 18	4 of 5	
LOTT Judiciary Merchant Marine & Fisheries	1975	8 of 11 7 of 13	5 of 5	.. ..	..	.. ..	..	8 of 11 7 of 13	5 of 5	

[a] Although Anderson is actually the senior Republican on the Rules Committee, he has stepped aside to allow Quillen to act as the ranking minority leader. Anderson has done this so he can remain on the committee and act as chairman of the Republican Conference.

Table 5.1 *Number of Bills Sponsored by Rules Committee Members*
Denied a Hearing (1963-72)

Congress	Number of Bills Denied a Hearing[a]	Number of Bills Sponsored by Rules Members Denied a Hearing	Percent-age of Total
88th	25 (7 suspensions, 0 consent)	0	0
89th	52 (5 suspensions, 3 consent)	0	0
90th	42 (15 suspensions, 3 consent)	0	0
91st	32 (20 suspensions, 8 consent)	0	0
92nd	30 (14 suspensions, 1 consent)	0	0
	181	0	0

[a] Including bills which reached the floor by suspension or consent.

Table 5.2 *Number of Bills Sponsored by Rules Committee Members*
Denied a Rule (1963-72)

Congress	Total Number of Bills Denied a Rule	Number of Bills Sponsored by Rules Members Denied a Rule	Percent-age of Total
88th	7	0	0
89th	5	0	0
90th	6	3	50
91st	6	1	16.7
92nd	2	0	0
	26	4	15.4

Table 5.3   *Rules Committee Roll-Call Votes Tied or Decided by One Vote*

Congress	Percent of Total Committee Roll-Call Votes	Bill Number	Title	Vote
85th	27.3	H.R. 3	Federal court jurisdiction limitation	6–5
		H.R. 6127	Civil Rights Act	6–6
				5–6
86th	44.4	H.R. 2575	Appropriations for 3rd Pan American Games	4–3
		S. 57	Housing and urban renewal amendments	6–6
		H.R. 5752	Legal holidays for government employees	5–6
		H.R. 12341	Extension of marketing standards	6–6
87th	16.7	H.Res. 233	Fiscal policies of the U.S.	7–8
		H.R. 5741	Mine safety bill	7–6
		H.R. 7927	To adjust postal rates	7–7
88th	37.0	H.R. 4996	Area Redevelopment Act amendments	7–6
		H.R. 8720	Manpower development training	7–7
		H.R. 7152	Civil rights bill	8–7
				8–7
				7–8
		H.Res. 789	Agree to Senate amendments to H.R. 7152 (civil rights)	6–7
		H.R. 11377	Poverty bill	7–8
		H.R. 904	Potato bill	8–7
		H.Res. 814	To send H.R. 8139 to conference	8–7
		S. 1164	Area Redevelopment Act amendments	7–8
				8–7
		H.R. 1096	Ice Age national scientific reserve	8–7
		H.R. 12318	Classification of House employees	6–5
89th	10.0	H.R. 2362	Education bill	8–7
		H.R. 14544	Sale of participations in government agency loan pools	7–7
		S. 2934	Rural Community Development Act	7–6

Congress	Percent of Total Committee Roll-Call Votes	Bill Number	Title	Vote
90th	27.3	H.R. 2158	Taxation of interstate commerce	7–7
		H.R. 6649	Export-Import Bank	7–7
				7–7
		H.Res. 1100	Civil Rights Act	8–7
		H.R. 17735	Gun control	8–7
91st	29.8	H.R. 8298	Water carrier mixing	6–7
		H.Res. 840	Educational quality	8–7
		H.R. 17867	Foreign aid appropriations	7–7
		H.Res. 914	Senate amendments on voting rights	8–7
		H.R. 18970	Trade Act	8–7
				8–7
		H.R. 18214	Consumer protection	7–7
				7–7
92nd	20.0	H.R. 1163	Grain storage	8–7
				8–7
		H.Res. 796	Dock strike settlement	8–7
		H.R. 14370	Revenue sharing	8–7
		H.R. 16656	Highway bill	8–7
93rd	20.7	H.R. 9682	District of Columbia self-government	7–7
		H.Res. 582	Deploring the outbreak of hostilities in the Middle East	8–7
		H.R. 9681	Emergency Petroleum Allocation Act	7–6
				7–8
		H.R. 7130	Budget control legislation	6–7
				6–6
		H.R. 11104	Public debt ceiling increase	7–7
		H.R. 11450	National Energy Emergency Act	7–6
				6–7
		H.R. 15263	Rice Act of 1974	6–6
		S. 2589	Conference report on Emergency Energy Act	7–7
				7–7
		H.R. 10294	Land use planning	7–8

(Continued on next page)

Table 5.3 (cont.)

Congress	Percent of Total Committee Roll-Call Votes	Bill Number	Title	Vote
		H.R. 16090	Federal Election Campaign Act amended	7–6
		S. 1868	Import of Rhodesian chrome	8–7
		H.Res. 988	Committee reform	5–6
		S. 386	Urban mass transit	6–6
		H.R. 13320	Civil defense emergency authority	7–7
		S.J.Res. 247	Suspend certain laws with regard to resolution of Cyprus conflict	6–7
		H.R. 5050	Securities Act amendments of 1974	6–6
				7–6
		H.R. 77	Jointly administered trust funds for legal services plans	6–7
		H.R. 2990	Annual authorization of appropriations for U.S. Postal Service	6–5
		H.R. 8410	Public debt limit	6–7

Table 5.4 Rules Committee Members and Legislative Committee Leaders Receiving Highest Federal District Outlays, by Agency[a]

Department or Agency	Rules Committee Member	Committee Leader	Appropriations Subcommittee Leader
Agriculture	*Martin, D. (Nebr.)* $218,469,902	Poage, W. (Tex.) $129,785,556	Andrews, M. (N.D.) $185,823,223
Commerce	*Colmer, W. (Miss.)* 35,941,099	Staggers, W. (W.Va.) 4,623,017	Sikes, R. (Fla.) 1,014,045
Defense	*Colmer, W. (Miss.)* 473,217,910	Rivers, M. (S.C.) 354,589,000	Lipscomb, G. (Calif.) 235,745,720
Health, Education & Welfare	*O'Neill, T. (Mass.)* 139,476,948	Perkins, C. (Ky.) 104,880,737	Flood, D. (Pa.) 111,989,309
Housing & Urban Development	*Pepper, C. (Fla.)* 35,727,184	Patman, W. (Tex.) 18,810,786	Jonas, C. (N.C.) 20,393,499
Interior	Sisk, B. (Calif.) 26,267,970	Aspinall, W. (Colo.) 48,444,079	*Hansen, J. (Wash.)* 52,523,047
Labor	*Martin, D. (Nebr.)* 34,593,232	Perkins, C. (Ky.) 13,721,588	Flood, D. (Pa.) 2,882,922
Post Office	*O'Neill, T. (Mass.)* 30,997,294	Corbett, R. (Pa.) 22,193,113	Robison, H. (N.Y.) 12,445,389
Transportation	*Matsunaga, S. (Hawaii)* 40,718,916	Springer, W. (Ill.) 31,385,771	McFall, J. (Calif.) 28,762,866
Treasury	*Delaney, J. (N.Y.)* 141,980,332	Mills, W. (Ark.) 40,537,518	Robison, H. (N.Y.) 89,361,153
Agency for International Development	*Young, J. (Tex.)* 13,309,970	Mailliard, W. (Calif.) 5,522,559	Rooney, J. (N.Y.) 489,057
Atomic Energy Commission	Bolling, R. (Mo.) 60,866,369	Holifield, C. (Calif.) 2,459,112	*Evins, J. (Tenn.)* 241,725,733
Civil Service Commission	*Pepper, C. (Fla.)* 12,102,527	Henderson, D. (N.C.) 7,972,968	Steed, T. (Okla.) 5,880,188
National Aeronautics & Space Administration	*Smith, H. (Calif.)* 64,477,415	Miller, G. (Calif.) 3,525,560	Rhodes, J. (Ariz.) 929,762
Office of Economic Opportunity	O'Neill, T. (Mass.) 3,884,017	*Perkins, C. (Ky.)* 4,395,293	Flood, D. (Pa.) 2,969,723
Railroad Retirement Board	Martin, D. (Nebr.) 6,775,698	*Springer, W. (Ill.)* 9,001,110	Flood, D. (Pa.) 6,513,909
Veterans' Administration	*Bolling, R. (Mo.)* 51,090,879	Dorn, W. (S.C.) 17,036,714	Boland, E. (Mass.) 50,679,789

[a] Based on 1968, 1969, and 1970 figures from *Federal Outlays*, published by the Office of Economic Opportunity. The name of the congressman receiving the highest outlay from each agency is italicized.

Table 5.5   *Analysis of Leading Federal District Outlays, by Agency*[a]

Agency	Representative with Highest Federal District Outlay	State	State Rank[b]	District Average within Top Scorer's State	Top Scorer's District	National District Average
Agriculture	Martin, D.[c]	Nebr.	2	$145,584,431	$218,469,902	$29,444,818
Commerce	Colmer, W.[c]	Miss.	4	8,785,512	35,941,099	2,760,648
Defense	Colmer, W.[c]	Miss.	20	126,974,467	473,217,910	140,890,918
Health, Education & Welfare	O'Neill, T.[c]	Mass.	6	121,107,699	139,476,948	107,827,001
Housing & Urban Development	Pepper, C.[c]	Fla.	4	27,839,772	35,727,184	17,226,447
Interior	Hansen, J.	Wash.	11	16,219,196	52,523,047	4,722,231
Labor	Martin, D.[c]	Nebr.	2	15,504,314	34,593,232	4,614,042
Post Office	O'Neill, T.[c]	Mass.	2	20,020,260	30,997,294	15,399,197
Transportation	Matsunaga, S.[c]	Hawaii	2	40,718,916	40,718,916	15,118,834
Treasury	Delaney, J.[c]	N.Y.	1	142,391,817	141,980,332	32,983,026
Agency for International Development	Young, J.[c]	Tex.	6	3,866,283	13,309,970	2,950,374
Atomic Energy Commission	Evins, J.	Tenn.	5	32,053,291	241,725,733	6,052,969
Civil Service Commission	Pepper, C.[c]	Fla.	4	12,540,740	12,102,527	8,170,256
National Aeronautics & Space Administration	Smith, H.[c]	Calif.	1	34,530,248	64,477,415	38,167,196
Office of Economic Opportunity	Perkins, C.	Ky.	7	3,802,964	4,395,293	2,372,671
Railroad Retirement Board	Springer, W.	Ill.	12	5,449,709	9,001,110	3,727,173
Veterans' Administration	Bolling, R.[c]	Mo.	24	24,717,220	51,090,879	26,080,162

[a] Only Rules Committee members, legislative committee leaders, and appropriations subcommittee leaders were studied. Based on 1968, 1969, and 1970 figures from *Federal Outlays*, published by the Office of Economic Opportunity.
[b] State rank based on per capita outlay for each of the fifty states.
[c] Rules Committee member. Thirteen of seventeen top scorers (76.5%) were Rules Committee members.

Table 5.6   *Ranked Total Federal District Outlays, by Position*[a]

Rules Committee Members		*Committee Leaders (continued)*	
Colmer, W. (Miss.)	$762,265,569	Gross, H. (Iowa)	$341,796,949
O'Neill, T. (Mass.)	554,786,849	Saylor, J. (Pa.)	305,005,896
Martin, D. (Nebr.)	511,351,048	Belcher, P. (Okla.)	302,844,096
Bolling, R. (Mo.)	488,230,091	Dorn, W. (S.C.)	284,070,641
Smith, H. (Calif.)	478,417,160	Price, M. (Ill.)[c]	277,199,412
Matsunaga, S. (Hawaii)	465,742,840	Quie, A. (Minn.)	275,689,962
———[b]		Perkins, C. (Ky.)	272,190,751
Young, J. (Tex.)	380,056,449	Blatnik, J. (Minn.)	254,414,823
Sisk, B. (Calif.)	378,173,467	Staggers, W. (W.Va.)	243,666,285
Delaney, J. (N.Y.)	356,183,320	Harsha, W. (Ohio)[c]	234,725,324
Pepper, C. (Fla.)	348,890,093	Byrnes, J. (Wis.)	205,054,719
Quillen, J. (Tenn.)	312,174,433	Morgan, T. (Pa.)	179,888,154
Anderson, J. (Ill.)	247,415,526	Dulski, T. (N.Y.)	169,446,867
Anderson, W. (Tenn.)	227,884,757		
Latta, D. (Ohio)	203,894,672	13 of 35 (37.1%) above mean	
Madden, R. (Ind.)	180,474,954		

6 of 15 (40%) above mean

Appropriations Subcommittee Leaders

Committee Leaders			
Teague, C. (Calif.)	$807,498,452	Sikes, R. (Fla.)	$652,494,637
Miller, C. (Calif.)	648,966,313	Rhodes, J. (Ariz.)	607,302,843
Mailliard, W. (Calif.)	642,956,004	Lipscomb, G. (Calif.)	606,957,859
Hébert, F. (La.)[c]	636,441,631	Evins, J. (Tenn.)	512,074,064
Teague, O. (Tex.)	592,254,186	Andrews, M. (N.D.)[c]	504,244,662
Poage, W. (Tex.)	586,739,329	Steed, T. (Okla.)	492,691,305
Mills, W. (Ark.)	586,333,361	Robinson, H. (Kan.)	485,017,309
Holifield, C. (Calif.)	558,149,465	———[b]	
Rivers, M. (S.C.)	543,719,835	Mahon, G. (Tex.)	372,715,615
Garmatz, E. (Md.)	525,958,807	McFall, J. (Calif.)[c]	361,489,420
Cramer, W. (Fla.)	512,365,936	Winshall, W. (Ohio)	338,450,619
Patman, W. (Tex.)	482,685,292	Hansen, J. (Wash.)	313,823,064
Springer, W. (Ill.)	459,066,626	Michel, R. (Ill.)	300,711,509
———[b]		Reifel, B. (S.D.)	300,613,414
Windnall, W. (N.J.)	396,817,421	Langen, O. (Minn.)	298,729,865
Arends, L. (Ill.)	395,108,138	Whitten, J. (Miss.)	287,094,474
Henderson, D. (N.C.)	379,079,500	Rooney, J. (N.Y.)	283,458,239
Aspinall, W. (Colo.)	377,859,883	Jonas, C. (N.C.)	260,888,009
Mahon, G. (Tex.)	372,715,615	Flood, D. (Pa.)	254,673,847
Corbett, R. (Pa.)	346,371,116	Passman, O. (La.)	238,857,724
Fulton, J. (Pa.)	346,371,116	McDade, J. (Pa.)[c]	236,181,162
Adair, E. (Ind.)	344,496,586	Bow, F. (Ohio)	223,828,138

7 of 21 (33.3%) above mean

[a] Based on 1968, 1969, and 1970 figures from *Federal Outlays,* published by the Office of Economic Opportunity.
[b] ——— = national mean ($441,035,361).
[c] Held position in 92nd Congress. Others held position in 91st Congress.

Table 5.7   *Total Federal District Outlays above National Mean*[a]

Congressman	District Outlay	Committee and Position
Teague, C. (Calif.)	$807,498,452	Veterans' Affairs–Ranking Minority (91st)
Colmer, W. (Miss.)[b]	762,265,569	Rules–Chairman (91st)
Sikes, R. (Fla.)	652,494,637	Appropriations–Ranking Minority, State, Justice, and Commerce Subcommittee (91st)
Miller, G. (Calif.)	648,966,313	Science and Astronautics–Chairman(92nd)
Mailliard, W. (Calif.)	642,956,004	Merchant Marine–Ranking Minority (91st)
Hébert, F. (La.)	636,411,631	Armed Services–Chairman (92nd)
Rhodes, J. (Ariz.)	607,362,843	Appropriations–Ranking Minority, Public Works Subcommittee (91st)
Lipscomb, G. (Calif.)	606,957,859	Appropriations–Ranking Minority, Defense Subcommittee (91st)
Teague, O. (Tex.)	592,254,186	Veterans' Affairs–Chairman (92nd)
Poage, W. (Tex.)	586,739,329	Agriculture–Chairman (91st)
Mills, W. (Ark.)	586,333,361	Ways and Means–Chairman (91st)
Holifield, C. (Calif.)	558,149,465	Joint Committee on Atomic Energy–Chairman (91st)
O'Neill, T. (Mass.)[b]	554,786,849	Rules (91st)
Rivers, M. (S.C.)	542,719,835	Armed Services–Chairman (91st)
Garmatz, E. (Md.)	525,958,807	Merchant Marine–Chairman (91st)
Cramer, W. (Fla.)	512,365,936	Public Works–Ranking Minority (91st)
Evins, J. (Tenn.)	512,074,064	Appropriations–Chairman, Independent Offices and Department of Housing and Urban Development Subcommittee; Ranking Majority, Public Works Subcommittee (91st)
Martin, D. (Nebr.)[b]	511,351,048	Rules (91st)
Andrews, M. (N.D.)	504,244,662	Appropriations–Ranking Minority, Agriculture Subcommittee (92nd)
Steed, T. (Okla.)	492,691,305	Appropriations—Chairman, Treasury, Post Office Subcommittee (91st)
Bolling, R. (Mo.)[b]	488,230,091	Rules (91st)
Robison, H. (N.Y.)	485,017,309	Appropriations–Second Ranking Minority, Treasury, Post Office Subcommittee (91st)
Patman, W. (Tex.)	482,685,292	Banking and Currency–Chairman (91st)
Smith, H. (Calif.)[b]	478,417,160	Rules–Ranking Minority (91st)
Matsunaga, S. (Ha.)[b]	465,742,840	Rules (91st)
Springer, W. (Ill.)	459,066,626	Interstate and Foreign Commerce–Ranking Minority (91st)

[a] Only Rules Committee members, legislative committee leaders, and appropriations subcommittee leaders were studied. Based on 1968, 1969, and 1970 figures from *Federal Outlays,* published by the Office of Economic Opportunity. The national mean for this period was $441,035,361.

[b] Rules Committee member.

Table 5.8 *Total Federal District Outlays below National Mean*[a]

Congressman	District Outlay	Committee and Position
Windnall, W. (N.J.)	$396,817,421	Banking & Currency–Ranking Minority (91st)
Arends, L. (Ill.)	395,108,138	Armed Services–Ranking Minority (91st)
Young, J. (Tex.)[b]	380,056,449	Rules (91st)
Henderson, D. (N.C.)	379,079,550	Post Office & Civil Service–Ranking Majority (91st)
Sisk, B. (Calif.)[b]	378,173,467	Rules (91st)
Aspinall, W. (Colo.)	377,859,883	Interior & Insular Affairs–Chairman (91st)
Mahon, G. (Tex.)	372,715,615	Appropriations–Chairman; Chairman, Department of Defense Subcommittee (91st)
McFall, J. (Calif.)	361,489,420	Appropriations–Chairman, Transportation Subcommittee (92nd)
Delaney, J. (N.Y.)[b]	356,183,320	Rules (91st)
Pepper, C. (Fla.)[b]	348,890,093	Rules (91st)
Corbett, R. (Pa.)	346,371,116	Post Office & Civil Service–Ranking Minority (91st)
Fulton, J. (Pa.)	346,371,116	Science & Astronautics–Ranking Minority (91st)
Adair, E. (Ind.)	344,496,586	Foreign Affairs–Ranking Minority (91st)
Gross, H. (Iowa)	341,796,949	Post Office & Civil Service–2nd Ranking Minority (91st)
Minshall, W. (Ohio)	338,450,619	Appropriations–Ranking Minority, Transportation Subcommittee (91st)
Hansen, J. (Wash.)	313,823,064	Appropriations–Chairman, Interior Subcommittee (91st)
Quillen, J. (Tenn.)[b]	312,174,433	Rules (91st)
Boland, E. (Mass.)	309,625,177	Appropriations–Chairman, HUD Subcommittee (92nd)
Saylor, J. (Pa.)	305,005,896	Interior & Insular Affairs–Ranking Minority (91st)
Belcher, P. (Okla.)	302,844,096	Agriculture–Ranking Minority (91st)
Michel, R. (Ill.)	300,711,509	Appropriations–Ranking Minority, Labor, HEW Subcommittee (91st)
Reifel, B. (S.D.)	300,613,414	Appropriations–Ranking Minority, Interior Subcommittee (91st)
Langen, O. (Minn.)	298,729,865	Appropriations–Ranking Minority, Agriculture Subcommittee (91st)
Whitten, J. (Miss.)	287,094,474	Appropriations–Chairman, Agriculture Subcommittee (91st)
Dorn, W. (S.C.)	284,070,641	Veterans' Affairs–Ranking Majority (91st)
Rooney, J. (N.Y.)	283,458,239	Appropriations–Chairman, State, Justice, Commerce & Judiciary Subcommittee (91st)
Albert, C. (Okla.)	281,743,753	House Speaker (92nd); Majority Leader (91st)
Price, M. (Ill.)	277,199,412	Joint Committee on Atomic Energy– House Vice Chairman (92nd)
Quie, A. (Minn.)	275,689,962	Education and Labor–2nd Ranking Minority (91st)

(Continued on next page)

Table 5.8 (cont.)

Congressman	District Outlay	Committee and Position
Perkins, C. (Ky.)	$272,190,751	Education and Labor–Chairman (91st)
Jonas, C. (N.C.)	260,888,009	Appropriations–2nd Ranking Minority; Ranking Minority, Independent Offices & Housing & Urban Development Subcommittee (91st)
Flood, D. (Pa.)	254,673,847	Appropriations–Chairman, Labor, HEW Subcommittee (91st)
Blatnik, J. (Minn.)	254,414,823	Public Works–Ranking Majority (91st)
Anderson, J. (Ill.)[b]	247,415,526	Rules (91st)
Staggers, W. (W.Va.)	243,666,285	Interstate & Foreign Commerce– Chairman (91st)
Passman, O. (La.)	238,857,724	Appropriations–Ranking Majority, Treasury, Post Office Subcommittee (91st)
McDade, J. (Pa.)	236,181,162	Appropriations–Ranking Minority, Interior Subcommittee (92nd)
Harsha, W. (Ohio)	234,725,324	Public Works–Ranking Minority (92nd)
Anderson, W. (Tenn.)[b]	227,884,757	Rules (91st)
Bow, F. (Ohio)	223,828,138	Appropriations–Ranking Minority; Ranking Minority, State, Justice, Commerce & Judiciary Subcommittee (91st)
Ford, G. (Mich.)	221,523,386	Minority Leader (91st)
Byrnes, J. (Wis.)	205,054,719	Ways & Means–Ranking Minority (91st)
Latta, D. (Ohio)[b]	203,894,627	Rules (91st)
Madden, R. (Ind.)[b]	180,474,954	Rules (91st)
Morgan, T. (Pa.)	179,888,154	Foreign Affairs–Chairman (91st)
Dulski, T. (N.Y.)	169,446,867	Post Office & Civil Service –Chairman (91st)

[a] Only Rules Committee members, legislative committee leaders, and appropriations subcommittee leaders were studied. Based on 1968, 1969, and 1970 figures from *Federal Outlays,* published by the Office of Economic Opportunity. The national mean for this period was $441,035,361.

[b] Rules Committee member.

Table 6.1   *Bills Denied Rules Committee Hearings Which Did Not
Reach Floor by Other Means*

Congress	Bill Number	Title	Committee
82nd	11 bills	(A detailed listing of bills from the 82nd Congress through the 86th Congress is not available.)	
83rd	20 bills		
84th	4 bills		
85th	28 bills		
86th	31 bills		
87th	H.R. 2017	Relating to withholding taxes imposed by certain cities on compensation of federal employees	Ways & Means
	H.R. 207	Limitation of liability for vessel owners	Merchant Marine & Fisheries
	H.R. 6759	Relief of Prince Georges County School Board, Md.	Judiciary
	H.R. 10946	Davis-Bacon Act amendments	Education & Labor
	S. 1124	Educational opportunities for migrant workers	Education & Labor
	H.R. 12070	Assistance in the field of special education to institutions of higher learning	Education & Labor
	H.R. 11158	Urban Mass Transportation Act	Banking & Currency
	H.R. 3	Pre-emption of state laws	
	H.R. 11537	Amend the Labor-Management Relations Act	Education & Labor
	H.R. 11707	Racial discrimination in land grant colleges	Education & Labor
	H.R. 11888	Improvement of Educational Quality Act	Education & Labor
	H.R. 10056	Racial discrimination in schools receiving federal assistance	Education & Labor
	H.R. 11340	University extension bill	Education & Labor
	H.R. 12306	Occupational safety programs	Education & Labor
	S. 1132	National Citizens Council on Migratory Labor	Education & Labor
	H.R. 13204	National Defense Education Act	Education & Labor
	H.R. 8354	Youth Conservation Corps	Education & Labor
	H.R. 10144	Federal Equal Employment Opportunities Commission	Education & Labor
	H.J.Res. 538	To reimburse House members and staff for travel expenses	House Administration
88th	H.R. 405	FEPC bill	Education & Labor
	H.R. 7771	Racial discrimination in schools receiving federal assistance	Education & Labor
	H.R. 6289	Chicago Skyway	Public Works
	H.R. 3850	Additional Secretary of Agriculture	Agriculture

(Continued on next page)

Table 6.1 (cont.)

Congress	Bill Number	Title	Committee
88th (cont.)	H.R. 6600	Re appointments of members to joint chiefs of staff	Armed Services
	H.R. 7351	Public Works Acceleration Act	Public Works
	H.R. 11522	Labor standards for employees of federal contractors	Education & Labor
	H.R. 10088	Older Americans Act	Education & Labor
	H.R. 5690	Re collective bargaining agreements	Education & Labor
	H.R. 1003	Missouri River Basin Project	Interior & Insular Affairs
	H.R. 6242	Registration of contractors of migrant laborers	Education & Labor
	H.R. 7073	Federal Home Loan Association's loan funds	Agriculture
	S. 1363	National wildlife refuge system	Commerce
	H.R. 10873	Amend the Labor-Management Reporting and Disclosure Act	Education & Labor
	H.R. 3607	Importation of refuse screenings	Agriculture
	S. 649	Amend Federal Water Pollution Control Act	Public Works
	H.R. 2155	Amend Civil Service Retirement Act	Post Office & Civil Service
	S. 1111	Water Resources Planning Act	Interior & Insular Affairs
89th	H.R. 8330	To amend the National Defense Education Act	Education & Labor
	S. 408	Authorized study to help provide financial assistance to future natural disaster victims	Banking & Currency
	H.R. 7372	To amend the Bank Holding Company Act	Banking & Currency
	H.R. 6183	For mid-decade census of population	Post Office & Civil Service
	H.R. 10263	Annuities of secretaries of federal judges	Post Office & Civil Service
	H.R. 10622	Federal sabbatical program to improve elementary and secondary schools	Education & Labor
	H.R. 10774	Amend Labor-Management Act	Education & Labor
	H.R. 11322	Improve educational opportunities through child development specialist	Education & Labor
	H.R. 6775	Steel Shipping Identification Act	Interstate & Foreign Commerce
	H.R. 14909	Naming of Veterans' Administration facilities	Veterans' Affairs
	H.R. 13286	CA-TV bill	Interstate & Foreign Commerce
	H.J.Res. 1030	Development of Pennsylvania Avenue as historic site	Interior & Insular Affairs

Congress	Bill Number	Title	Committee
	H.R. 4671	Colorado River Basin project	Interior & Insular Affairs
	S.J.Res. 186	Settlement of labor dispute between air carriers and employees	Labor & Public Welfare
	H.R. 11778	Welfare and Pension Disclosure Act	Education & Labor
	S. 936	Sleeping Bear National Lakeshore	Interior & Insular Affairs
	H.R. 16491	Interstate Taxation Act	Judiciary
	H.R. 11667	Coal Mine Assistance Act	Interior & Insular Affairs
	S. 1556	Federal Reserve Board delegation	Banking & Currency
	H.R. 17505	Civil government for trust territory of the Pacific islands	Interior & Insular Affairs
90th	H.J.Res. 396	Providing representation in Congress for the District of Columbia	Judiciary
	H.R. 13103	Bilingual Education Act	Education & Labor
	H.R. 15710	Extend to the District of Columbia commissioner and District of Columbia council exemption to the Hatch Act	House Administration
	H.R. 17748	Occupational safety bill	Education & Labor
	H.R. 16775	Increased participation in International Development Association	Banking & Currency
	H.J.Res. 1384	Relating to the administration of the National Park Service	Interior & Insular Affairs
	H.R. 2567	Construction industry and safety	Education & Labor
	H.R. 18663	Employment of necessary postal field personnel	Post Office & Civil Service
91st	H.R. 19413	Delegates from Guam and Virgin Islands	Interior & Insular Affairs
	H.R. 19163	Emergency Detention Act of 1950 amendments	Internal Security
	H.R. 18469	Amend National Science Foundation Act	Science & Astronautics
	H.R. 17555	Equal Employment Opportunities Enforcement Act of 1970	Education & Labor
	H.R. 7	Amend the Rural Electrification Act	Agriculture
	H.R. 2690	Marketing orders on pears	Agriculture
	H.R. 10019	Commission on Marihuana	Judiciary
	H.R. 16418	Subscription television	Interstate & Foreign Commerce
	H.R. 16538	Fire and Safety Act authorization	Science & Astronautics
92nd	H.R. 4874	Restriction on imports of filberts	Agriculture
	H.R. 10645	Congressional redistricting	Judiciary

(Continued on next page)

Table 6.1 (cont.)

Congress	Bill Number	Title	Committee
92nd (cont.)	J.Res. 253	Constitutional amendment to provide representation in Congress for the District of Columbia	Judiciary
	J.Res. 375	New York–New Jersey Compact	Judiciary
	H.Res. 933	Sense of the House in reaction against members convicted of certain crimes	Judiciary
	H.R. 11453	Legislative Activities Disclosure Act	Standards of Official Conduct
	H.R. 6292	Establishment of Department of Community Development	Government Operations
	H.R. 2374	State-conducted lotteries	Judiciary
	H.R. 14153	Mid-Decade Population Survey	Post Office & Civil Service
	H.R. 7211	National land policy, planning and management	Interior & Insular Affairs
	H.R. 11255	Age and service requirement for retirement	Post Office & Civil Service
93rd	H.R. 16742	Restrict travel to certain countries	Internal Security
	H.J.Res. 1300	Deficiency payment to wheat farmers	Agriculture
	H.R. 7202	Establish arbitration board to settle disputes between supervisory organizations and the U.S. Postal Service	Post Office & Civil Service
	H.R. 7762	Confidentiality of census data	Post Office & Civil Service
	H.R. 8023	Amend the Internal Security Act of 1950	Internal Security
	H.R. 9468	Authorize the Secretary of Agriculture to distribute seeds and plants for use in home gardens	Agriculture
	H.R. 12462	Amend the Freedom of Information Act	Government Operations
	H.R. 16994	Amend the Internal Revenue Code of 1954 to exclude from gross income $500 interest on savings	Ways & Means
	H.R. 17488	Windfall profits tax on oil	Ways & Means

Table 6.2 *Bills Denied Rules Committee Rules Which Did Not Reach Floor by Other Means*

Congress	Bill Number	Title	Committee
87th	H.R. 5741	Federal Coal Mine Safety Act	Education & Labor
	H.R. 10896	Adult basic education bill	Education & Labor
	S. 1126	Registration of contractors of migrant agricultural workers	Education & Labor
	H.R. 7306	School construction & teachers' salaries	Education & Labor
	H.R. 5028	Settlement of claims of successor organizations for return of vested heirless property	Education & Labor
	H.R. 7904	National Defense Education Act amendment	Education & Labor
	H.R. 7812	Farm labor contractor registration	Education & Labor
	H.R. 12201	Freight forwarders bill	Post Office & Civil Service
	H.R. 7215	Education assistance bill	Education & Labor
	H.R. 5978	Re terminal area motor carrier operations performed by or for common carriers by water in interstate commerce	Interstate & Foreign Commerce
88th	H.R. 3669	Quality stabilization bill	Interstate & Foreign Commerce
	H.R. 7194	Repeal juke box exemption of Copyright Act	Judiciary
	H.R. 9903	Amend the Interstate Commerce Act and the Federal Aviation Act to improve the national transportation system	Interstate & Foreign Commerce
	H.R. 904	Potato bill	Agriculture
	H.R. 5886	Establishment of concession policies in national park areas	Interior & Insular Affairs
	H.J.Res. 915	Smoking and health research bill	Agriculture
89th	H.R. 9339	Children's Summer School Lunch Program (passed under suspension)	Education & Labor
	H.R. 9020	Administration Expenses Act	Government Operations
	H.R. 12453	International Health Act of 1966	Interstate & Foreign Commerce
	H.R. 9713	Create a Freedom Commission & Freedom Academy	Un-American Activities
	H.Res. 670	Select committee to investigate Office of Economic Opportunity	Judiciary
	H.R. 11696	Federal Maritime Act	Merchant Marine & Fisheries
	H.Res. 826	Select committee to investigate Commissioner of Education	Ways & Means
	H.R. 10027	Common situs picketing	Education & Labor
	H.R. 2452	Classification Act benefits for county committee employees	Post Office & Civil Service
	H.R. 10329	Metric system (investigation & research)	Science & Astronautics

(Continued on next page)

Table 6.2 (cont.)

Congress	Bill Number	Title	Committee
90th	H.R. 10190	Supplemental financing of rural electrification and telephone programs	Agriculture
	H.R. 100	Common situs picketing bill	Education & Labor
	H.R. 12066	Rural Telephone Bank	Agriculture
	H.R. 13718	Federal savings institutions	Banking & Currency
	H.R. 150	To provide for the designation of certain Veterans' Administration facilities	Veterans' Affairs
	H.R. 12510	Establish a commission on government procurement	Government Operations
	H.R. 735	Create the Freedom Commission and the Freedom Academy	Un-American Activities
	H.R. 16014	Coverage of agricultural employees under the NLRA	Education & Labor
	H.R. 13016	Cost of living allowances for judicial employees	Judiciary
	H.R. 9382	Payment of travel expenses of applicants for government employment in manpower shortage positions	Government Operations
	H.R. 11190	Amendments to the Federal Aid in Wildlife Restoration Act	Merchant Marine & Fisheries
	H.R. 15030	Potato bill	Agriculture
	H.R. 11233	Election Reform Act of 1968	House Administration
	H.R. 13940	Amending Title V of the Merchant Marine Act of 1936	Merchant Marine & Fisheries
	H.R. 15626	Defense Facilities and Industrial Security Act of 1968	Un-American Activities
	H.Con.Res. 48	Establishment of an Atlantic Union Delegation	Foreign Affairs
91st	H.Res. 840	Committee to investigate educational quality	Judiciary
	H.Res. 142	Pay raise	Merchant Marine & Fisheries
	H.R. 18214	Consumer Protection Agency	Government Operations
	H.R. 15931	HEW appropriations	Appropriations
	H.R. 11542	National program of institutional grants	Science & Astronautics
	H.R. 13954	Depository facilities for Smithsonian	House Administration
92nd	H.R. 7287	Prohibit potato futures trading	Agriculture
	H.J.Res. 900	Create an Atlantic Union Delegation	Foreign Affairs
	H.R. 16704	Housing and urban development	Banking & Currency
	H.R. 13916	Busing moratorium	Judiciary
93rd	H.R. 5050	Amend the Securities and Exchange Act of 1934	Interstate & Foreign Commerce
	H.R. 13320	Amend Federal Civil Defense Act of 1950	Armed Services

Table 7.1 Voting Analyses Summary

	57-58 85th Eisenhower	59-60 86th Eisenhower	61-62 87th Kennedy	63-64 88th Kennedy	65-66 89th Johnson	67-68 90th Johnson	69-70 91st Nixon	71-72 92nd Nixon	1/73-9/73 93rd(1) Nixon	10/73-12/74 93rd(2) Nixon/Ford
Year / Congress / President										
Percent of decisive committee votes in agreement with leadership floor votes										
No. of Bills	6	7	5	19	11	9	12	11	21	26
Democrats	78.1	73.1	78.0	79.1	79.3	73.9	65.2	65.8	91.0	80.6
Republicans	78.2	85.8	60.2	77.6	78.8	57.4	83.6	65.8	81.2	59.3
Percent of members' final committee votes consistent with final floor votes										
No. of Bills	6	7	5	19	12	9	12	11	22	7[b]
Democrats										
c-1/f-1[a]	70.2	53.9	67.0	63.6	70.0	61.0	48.0	48.2	61.9	65.8
c-1/f-0	6.3	12.0	2.0	3.2	3.3	5.6	8.3	1.8	8.2	1.4
c-0/f-0	12.5	21.6	13.0	15.7	15.0	13.0	13.0	27.2	3.6	5.7
c-0/f-1	6.5	2.0	6.0	3.2	1.7	12.0	12.5	10.9	2.9	8.6
Republicans										
c-1/f-1	58.3	39.3	0	21.1	18.3	33.7	41.7	47.0	13.6	28.6
c-1/f-0	0	3.6	0	3.2	10.0	0	11.8	2.3	1.8	17.1
c-0/f-0	20.8	35.7	90.0	37.8	50.0	38.0	26.7	34.5	56.3	28.6
c-0/f-1	16.7	3.6	0	4.2	3.3	16.0	6.7	9.0	8.6	8.6
Rice Index of Cohesion[c]										
No. of Votes	11	11	16	46	30	22	28	27	34	82
Democrats	34.7	45.6	57.7	43.5	48.7	46.5	48.1	33.2	82.1	54.7
Republicans	57.8	66.7	94.0	76.6	80.0	62.2	78.1	71.2	86.0	71.5

[a] c = committee vote, f = floor vote; 1 = support, 0 = oppose.
[b] On consistency only, votes for the 1974 session are not included. 93rd(2) reflects only votes for 10/73-12/73.
[c] See chap. 7, n. 10.

Table 7.2   *Involvement of Rules Committee Members
with Funding Agencies (90th-92nd Congresses)*

Agency or Department	No. of High-Involvement States in House[a]	Ideal No. of High-Involvement States on Rules[b]	Actual No. of High-Involvement States Represented on Rules[c]	Actual No. of High-Involvement Rules Members, Based on District Outlays[d]
Housing & Urban Development	14	3.6	7	8
Veterans' Administration	13	3.4	9	7
Office of Economic Opportunity	12	3.1	9	7
Agriculture	13	3.4	8	6
Post Office	12	3.1	9	6
Railroad Retirement Board	14	3.6	9	5
Defense	17	4.4	9	5
Transportation	12	3.1	8	4
Labor	14	3.6	9	4
Commerce	9	2.3	6	3
Health, Education & Welfare	12	3.1	8	3
Agency for International Development	12	3.1	6	3
National Aeronautics & Space Administration	9	2.3	6	2
Interior	10	2.6	3	2
Civil Service Commission	13	3.4	7	2
Treasury	10	2.6	5	1
Atomic Energy Commission	14	3.6	5	1

(Column 4 annotated: upper portion "overrepresented," lower portion "underrepresented." Column 5 annotated: upper portion "overrepresented," lower portion "underrepresented.")

[a] High-involvement states are those states which received an average outlay of funds from an agency which was greater than the national average.

[b] Ideal no. of high-involvement states on Rules = X, where

$$\frac{\text{high-involvement states}}{\text{all states (50)}} = \frac{X}{\text{no. of states represented on Rules (13)}}$$

[c] Actual no. of high-involvement states represented on Rules is the number of states which received an average outlay of funds from an agency which was higher than the national average. Of the thirteen states represented on Rules, eight are big states with high-involvement status in at least half of the agency areas. This may have accounted for the overrepresentation of states for every agency on Rules.

[d] Actual no. of high-involvement members on Rules, based on district outlays, is the number of members whose districts received an average outlay of funds from an agency which was greater than the national district average for all members.

Table 8.1   *Party Makeup of House Membership (84th-94th Congresses)*

Congress	Total Democrats	Northern Democrats	Southern Democrats	Total Re-publicans	Total Con-servative Coalition
84th	231	120	111	203	314
85th	233	124	109	201	310
86th	282	171	111	152	263
87th	263	149	114	174	288
88th	259	154	105	176	281
89th	295	195	100	140	240
90th	248	156	92	187	279
91st	243	156	87	192	279
92nd	255	168	87	180	267
93rd	244	151	93	191	284
94th	291	199	92	144	236

Appendixes

Appendix A-1
Incumbent and Former Congressmen Interviewed
(1970-75)

Carl Albert	(D-Okla.)	Durward G. Hall	(R-Mo.)
John B. Anderson	(R-Ill.)	F. Edward Hébert	(D-La.)
William R. Anderson	(D-Tenn.)	Richard H. Ichord	(D-Mo.)
Leslie C. Arends	(R-Ill.)	Gillis W. Long	(D-La.)
Wayne N. Aspinall	(D-Colo.)	Trent Lott	(R-Miss.)
Page Belcher	(R-Okla.)	John McCormack	(D-Mass.)
Hale Boggs	(D-La.)	John J. McFall	(D-Calif.)
Richard Bolling	(D-Mo.)	Clem R. McSpadden	(D-Okla.)
Frank T. Bow	(R-Ohio)	Hervey Machen	(D-Md.)
John Brademas	(D-Ind.)	Ray J. Madden	(D-Ind.)
George E. Brown	(D-Calif.)	George H. Mahon	(D-Tex.)
John W. Byrnes	(R-Wis.)	William S. Mailliard	(R-Calif.)
Elford A. Cederberg	(R-Mich.)	David Martin	(R-Nebr.)
Shirley Chisholm	(D-N.Y.)	Abner J. Mikva	(D-Ill.)
Del Clawson	(R-Calif.)	F. Bradford Morse	(R-Mass.)
William M. Colmer	(D-Miss.)	Morgan F. Murphy	(D-Ill.)
E. de la Garza	(D-Tex.)	Thomas P. O'Neill, Jr.	(D-Mass.)
James J. Delaney	(D-N.Y.)	Thomas M. Pelly	(R-Wash.)
Dante B. Fascell	(D-Fla.)	Claude Pepper	(D-Fla.)
Gerald R. Ford	(R-Mich.)	Carl D. Perkins	(D-Ky.)
Edward A. Garmatz	(D-Md.)	W. R. Poage	(D-Tex.)

Albert H. Quie	(R-Minn.)	B. F. Sisk	(D-Calif.)
James H. Quillen	(R-Tenn.)	Howard W. Smith	(D-Va.)
Peter W. Rodino, Jr.	(D-N.J.)	William L. Springer	(R-Ill.)
Benjamin S. Rosenthal	(D-N.Y.)	Harley O. Staggers	(D-W.Va.)
John P. Saylor	(R-Pa.)	Joe D. Waggoner, Jr.	(D-La.)
Herman T. Schneebeli	(R-Pa.)	Jim Wright	(D-Tex.)
Fred Schwengel	(R-Iowa)	John Young	(D-Tex.)
George E. Shipley	(D-Ill.)		

Total number of congressmen interviewed	59
Democrats	40
Republicans	19
Southern Democrats	9
Democratic leaders	5
Republican leaders	2
Rules Committee members	17
Democratic Rules Committee members	13
Republican Rules Committee members	4
Committee chairmen	13
Subcommittee chairmen	6

Appendix A-2
Interview Questions

1. What in your view are the most important functions performed by the Rules Committee?
   a) Substantive control over legislation
   b) Setting the rules for debate on a bill
   c) Technical review and oversight over bills
   d) Protection of the leadership and other members by killing controversial bills
   e) Information clearinghouse
   f) Determining priorities in House consideration of bills (traffic cop)
   g) Purely procedural
   h) All listed
   i) Effective floor debate
   j) Arm of leadership and responsive to leadership
   k) Moderating effect on both parties

2. What criteria should be used to choose Rules Committee members?
   a) Loyalty to party platform
   b) Loyalty to House leadership
   c) Representative from safe district and reelection assured
   d) Equitable geographic distribution
   e) Enthusiasm to serve
   f) Loyalty to the President
   g) Proper balance of conservatives and liberals
   h) None
   i) Public trust
   j) Loyalty, ability, and integrity
   k) Independent judgment

l) Articulate and informed members
m) Personal conviction

3. Should individual members of the Rules Committee be bound by commitments to the following:

a) House leadership
b) Party platform or leadership
c) Legislative committee members
d) The President or his representative
e) Federal agencies involved
f) His district and state
g) Organizations and groups without whose support reelection may be doubtful
h) No commitment to anyone
i) What is best for the country
j) House membership
k) Majority members should follow house leadership
l) Bound by commitments they have made
m) Personal conviction

Appendix B
Rules of Procedure for the Committee on Rules, 94th Congress*

Rule 1 — Meetings

(a) The Committee on Rules shall meet at 10:30 a.m. on Tuesday of each week when the House is in session. Meetings and hearings shall be called to order and presided over by the Chairman or, in the absence of the Chairman, by the Ranking Majority Member of the Committee present as Acting Chairman.

(b) A minimum 48 hours' notice of regular meetings and hearings of the Committee shall be given to all members except that the Chairman, acting on behalf of the Committee, may schedule a meeting or hearing for the consideration of emergency and/or procedural measures or matters at any time. As much notice as possible will be given to all members when emergency meetings or hearings are called; provided, however, that an effort has been made to consult the Ranking Minority Member. In the event of his absence, an effort shall be made to consult the Member next in rank, and so on down the line until an effort has been made with respect to all Members of the Minority. Copies of bills and reports to be considered for a rule by the Committee are to be sent to Members of the Committee at least one day in advance of consideration by the Committee, except in cases of emergencies.

(c) Meetings, hearings, and executive sessions of the Committee shall be open to the public in accordance with clause 26 and clause 27 of Rule XI of the Rules of the House of Representatives.

(d) For the purpose of hearing testimony on requests for rules, seven Members of the Committee shall constitute a quorum.

(e) For the purpose of hearing and taking testimony on matters or

* Adopted February 3, 1975; amended May 8, 1975.

measures of original jurisdiction before the Committee, three Members of the Committee shall constitute a quorum.

(f) For the purpose of executive meetings, a majority of the Committee shall constitute a quorum.

(g) All measures or matters which have been scheduled for consideration by the Committee on which any Member of the House wishes to testify, and so requests, will be the subject of hearings, at which time all interested Members who are proponents or opponents will be provided a reasonable opportunity to testify.

(h) There shall be a transcript of regularly scheduled hearings and meetings of the Committee which may be printed if the Chairman decides it is appropriate, or if a majority of the members request it.

(i) A Tuesday meeting of the Committee may be dispensed with where, in the judgment of the Chairman, there is no need therefor, and additional meetings may be called by the Chairman, or by written request of a majority of the Committee duly filed with the Counsel of the Committee.

(j) The Committee may permit, by a majority vote on each separate occasion, the coverage of any open meeting or hearing, in whole or in part, by television broadcast, radio broadcast, and still photography under such requirements and limitations as set forth in the Rules of the House of Representatives.

(k) The five-minute rule in the interrogation of witnesses, until such time as each Member of the Committee who so desires has had an opportunity to question the witness, shall be followed.

(l) When a recommendation is made as to the kind of rule which should be granted, a copy of the language recommended shall be furnished to each member of the Committee at the beginning of the meeting where such language is to be considered or as soon thereafter as such recommendation becomes available.

Rule 2 — Voting

(a) No measure or recommendation shall be reported, deferred, or tabled by the Committee unless a majority of the Committee is actually present.

(b) A rollcall vote of the Members of the Committee may be had upon the request of any member.

(c) The result of each rollcall vote, including the names of Committee Members and how they voted on specific issues, shall be available for public inspection at the office of the Committee.

Rule 3 — Reporting

(a) Whenever the Committee authorizes the favorable reporting of a bill or resolution from the Committee, the Chairman or Acting Chairman shall report the same or designate some member of the Committee to report the same to the House, such report to include the totals of any record vote thereon.

Rule 4 — Committee Staffing

(a) The professional and clerical staffs of the Committee shall serve under the general supervision and direction of the Chairman, who shall establish and assign the duties and responsibilities of the members of the staffs and delegate such authority as the Chairman deems appropriate, with the exception of the Minority staff, who shall serve under the general supervision and direction of the Ranking Minority Member of the Committee.

(b) The appointment of staff members of the Committee shall be made as follows:

(1) each member of the Committee shall be authorized to appoint one (1) staff member;

(2) the Chairman of the Committee with concurrence of the majority party members shall be authorized to appoint the remaining staff members authorized under clause 6 of Rule XI of the Rules of the House of Representatives;

(3) the ranking minority party member of the Committee, with concurrence of the minority party members, shall be authorized to appoint the remaining minority staff members authorized under clause 6 of Rule XI of the Rules of the House of Representatives.

(c) Each staff member appointed under subsection (b) (1) shall be paid at a beginning rate of pay which shall not be less than $18,400, nor more than $24,600, per annum.

Rule 5 — Miscellaneous

(a) The Committee shall have prepared, maintained, printed, and published a calendar listing all matters formally before it. Information on this calendar shall include the number of the bill or resolution, a brief description of the measure's contents, including the legislative committee reporting it, and the name of the principal sponsoring Member.

(b) The staff shall prepare, maintain, and furnish to the Members of the Committee a list of all pending bills or resolutions from other committees concerning which a hearing request has been properly filed with the Committee. This list shall be distributed to the Members of the Committee on a regular weekly basis when the House is in session and shall include the number of the bill or resolution, the name of the legislative committee reporting it, the principal sponsoring Member, and the date upon which the request for a rule was filed, along with a brief analysis of the contents of the scheduled measures and a description of the rule requested by the reporting legislative committee, if so requested.

(c) For purpose of this rule, matters formally before the Committee include: bills or resolutions over which the Committee has original jurisdiction, and bills or resolutions from other committees concerning which the chairman or designated member of such committee has requested a hearing in writing and forwarded to the Committee on Rules a copy of such bill or resolution as reported, together with the final printed committee report.

(d) Executive meeting minutes shall be available to the Committee members but may not be released to any other person without the consent of the Committee, in compliance with Rule XI, clause 27(o).

(e) Upon adoption of the rules and procedures of the Committee at the opening of each Congress, the Chairman may have these rules and procedures printed in an early issue of the Congressional Record.

Appendix C
Rules Committee Members (1931-76)

Majority	*Minority*
72nd Congress 1931-32	
Edward W. Pou, N.C.	Fred S. Purnell, Ind.
William B. Bankhead, Ala.	Earl C. Michener, Mich.
John J. O'Connor, N.Y.	Harry C. Ransley, Pa.
Adolph J. Sabath, Ill.	Joseph W. Martin, Jr., Mass.
Daniel E. Garrett, Tex.	
Arthur H. Greenwood, Ind.	
E. E. Cox, Ga.	
Thomas S. McMillan, S.C.	
73rd Congress 1933-34	
1st Session	
Edward W. Pou, N.C.	Harry C. Ransley, Pa.
William B. Bankhead, Ala.	Joseph W. Martin, Jr., Mass.
John J. O'Connor, N.Y.	Carl E. Mapes, Mich.
Adolph J. Sabath, Ill.	Frederick R. Lehlbach, N.J.
Arthur H. Greenwood, Ind.	
E. E. Cox, Ga.	
William J. Driver, Ark.	
Howard W. Smith, Va.	
2nd Session	
William B. Bankhead, Ala.	Harry C. Ransley, Pa.
John J. O'Connor, N.Y.	Joseph W. Martin, Jr., Mass.
Adolph J. Sabath, Ill.	Carl E. Mapes, Mich.
Arthur H. Greenwood, Ind.	Frederick R. Lehlbach, N.J.
E. E. Cox, Ga.	

Majority	*Minority*
William J. Driver, Ark.	
Howard W. Smith, Va.	
J. Bayard Clark, N.C.	

74th Congress 1935-36

1st Session

Same as in the 73rd Congress, 2nd Session

2nd Session

John J. O'Connor, N.Y.	Harry C. Ransley, Pa.
Adolph J. Sabath, Ill.	Joseph W. Martin, Jr., Mass.
Arthur H. Greenwood, Ind.	Carl E. Mapes, Mich.
E. E. Cox, Ga.	Frederick R. Lehlbach, N.J.
William J. Driver, Ark.	
Howard W. Smith, Va.	
J. Bayard Clark, N.C.	
Martin Dies, Tex.	
Byron B. Harlan, Ohio	
Lawrence Lewis, Colo.	

75th Congress 1937-38

1st Session

John O'Connor, N.Y.	Joseph W. Martin, Jr., Mass.
Adolph J. Sabath, Ill.	Carl E. Mapes, Mich.
Arthur H. Greenwood, Ind.	————
E. E. Cox, Ga.	————
William J. Driver, Ark.	
Howard W. Smith, Va.	
J. Bayard Clark, N.C.	
Martin Dies, Tex.	
Byron B. Harlan, Ohio	
Lawrence Lewis, Colo.	

2nd Session

John O'Connor, N.Y.	Joseph W. Martin, Jr., Mass.
Adolph J. Sabath, Ill.	Carl E. Mapes, Mich.
Arthur H. Greenwood, Ind.	J. Will Taylor, Tenn.
E. E. Cox, Ga.	Donald H. McLean, N.J.
William J. Driver, Ark.	

Majority	*Minority*
Howard W. Smith, Va.	
J. Bayard Clark, N.C.	
Martin Dies, Tex.	
Byron B. Harlan, Ohio	
Lawrence Lewis, Colo.	

76th Congress 1939-40

1st Session

_____	Joseph W. Martin, Jr., Mass.
Adolph J. Sabath, Ill.	Carl E. Mapes, Mich.
E. E. Cox, Ga.	J. Will Taylor, Tenn.
Howard W. Smith, Va.	Donald H. McLean, N.J.
J. Bayard Clark, N.C.	
Martin Dies, Tex.	
Lawrence Lewis, Colo.	
_____	
_____	
_____	

2nd Session

Adolph J. Sabath, Ill.	Hamilton Fish, N.Y.
E. E. Cox, Ga.	Leo E. Allen, Ill.
Howard W. Smith, Va.	Earl C. Michener, Mich.
J. Bayard Clark, N.C.	Charles A. Halleck, Ind.
Martin Dies, Tex.	
Lawrence Lewis, Colo.	
John J. Delaney, N.Y.	
William M. Colmer, Miss.	
William L. Nelson, Mo.	
John J. Dempsey, N.Mex.	

77th Congress 1941-42

1st Session

Adolph J. Sabath, Ill.	Hamilton Fish, N.Y.
E. E. Cox, Ga.	Leo E. Allen, Ill.
Howard W. Smith, Va.	Earl C. Michener, Mich.
J. Bayard Clark, N.C.	Charles A. Halleck, Ind.
Martin Dies, Tex.	
Lawrence Lewis, Colo.	

Majority	*Minority*
John J. Delaney, N.Y.	
William M. Colmer, Miss.	
William L. Nelson, Mo.	

2nd Session

Adolph J. Sabath, Ill.	Hamilton Fish, N.Y.
E. E. Cox, Ga.	Leo E. Allen, Ill.
Howard W. Smith, Va.	Earl C. Michener, Mich.
J. Bayard Clark, N.C.	Charles A. Halleck, Ind.
Martin Dies, Tex.	
Lawrence Lewis, Colo.	
John J. Delaney, N.Y.	
William M. Colmer, Miss.	
William L. Nelson, Mo.	
Jack Nichols, Okla.	

78th Congress 1943-44

1st Session

Adolph J. Sabath, Ill.	Hamilton Fish, N.Y.
E. E. Cox, Ga.	Leo E. Allen, Ill.
Howard W. Smith, Va.	Earl C. Michener, Mich.
J. Bayard Clark, N.C.	Charles A. Halleck, Ind.
Martin Dies, Tex.	Clarence J. Brown, Ohio
Lawrence Lewis, Colo.	
John J. Delaney, N.Y.	
William M. Colmer, Miss.	
Jack Nichols, Okla.	

2nd Session

Adolph J. Sabath, Ill.	Hamilton Fish, N.Y.
E. E. Cox, Ga.	Leo E. Allen, Ill.
Howard W. Smith, Va.	Earl C. Michener, Mich.
J. Bayard Clark, N.C.	Charles A. Halleck, Ind.
Martin Dies, Tex.	Clarence J. Brown, Ohio
John J. Delaney, N.Y.	
William M. Colmer, Miss.	
Joe B. Bates, Ky.	
Roger C. Slaughter, Mo.	

Majority	*Minority*

79th Congress   1945-46

1st and 2nd Sessions

Adolph J. Sabath, Ill.	Leo E. Allen, Ill.
E. E. Cox, Ga.	Earl C. Michener, Mich.
Howard W. Smith, Va.	Charles A. Halleck, Ind.
J. Bayard Clark, N.C.	Clarence J. Brown, Ohio
John J. Delaney, N.Y.	
William M. Colmer, Miss.	
Joe B. Bates, Ky.	
Roger C. Slaughter, Mo.	

80th Congress   1947-48

1st and 2nd Sessions

Leo E. Allen, Ill.	Adolph J. Sabath, Ill.
Clarence J. Brown, Ohio	E. E. Cox, Ga.
James W. Wadsworth, N.Y.	Howard W. Smith, Va.
Forest A. Harness, Ind.	J. Bayard Clark, N.C.
J. Edgar Chenoweth, Colo.	
Ross Rizley, Okla.	
Christian A. Herter, Mass.	
Robert F. Rich, Pa.	

81st Congress   1949-50

1st and 2nd Sessions

Adolph J. Sabath, Ill.	Leo E. Allen, Ill.
E. E. Cox, Ga.	Clarence J. Brown, Ohio
Howard W. Smith, Va.	James W. Wadsworth, N.Y.
William M. Colmer, Miss.	Christian A. Herter, Mass.
Ray J. Madden, Ind.	
John E. Lyle, Jr., Tex.	
John McSweeney, Ohio	
James J. Delaney, N.Y.	

82nd Congress   1951-52

1st and 2nd Sessions

Adolph J. Sabath, Ill.	Leo E. Allen, Ill.
E. E. Cox, Ga.	Clarence J. Brown, Ohio
Howard W. Smith, Va.	Harris Ellsworth, Ore.

Majority	*Minority*
William M. Colmer, Miss.	Henry J. Latham, N.Y.
Ray J. Madden, Ind.	
John E. Lyle, Jr., Tex.	
James J. Delaney, N.Y.	
Hugh B. Mitchell, Wash.	

83rd Congress 1953-54

1st and 2nd Sessions

Leo E. Allen, Ill.	Howard W. Smith, Va.
Clarence J. Brown, Ohio	William M. Colmer, Miss.
Harris Ellsworth, Ore.	Ray J. Madden, Ind.
Henry J. Latham, N.Y.	John E. Lyle, Jr., Tex.
Hugh Scott, Pa.	
Donald W. Nicholson, Mass.	
J. Edgar Chenoweth, Colo.	
B. Carroll Reece, Tenn.	

84th Congress 1955-56

1st and 2nd Sessions

Howard W. Smith, Va.	Leo E. Allen, Ill.
William M. Colmer, Miss.	Clarence J. Brown, Ohio
Ray J. Madden, Ind.	Harris Ellsworth, Ore.
James J. Delaney, N.Y.	Henry J. Latham, N.Y.
James W. Trimble, Ark.	
Homer Thornberry, Tex.	
Richard Bolling, Mo.	
Thomas P. O'Neill, Jr., Mass.	

85th Congress 1957-58

1st and 2nd Sessions

Howard W. Smith, Va.	Leo E. Allen, Ill.
William M. Colmer, Miss.	Clarence J. Brown, Ohio
Ray J. Madden, Ind.	Henry J. Latham, N.Y.
James J. Delaney, N.Y.	Hugh Scott, Pa.
James W. Trimble, Ark.	
Homer Thornberry, Tex.	
Richard Bolling, Mo.	
Thomas P. O'Neill, Jr., Mass.	

| *Majority* | *Minority* |

86th Congress 1959-60

1st and 2nd Sessions

Howard W. Smith, Va.	Leo E. Allen, Ill.
William M. Colmer, Miss.	Clarence J. Brown, Ohio
Ray J. Madden, Ind.	B. Carroll Reece, Tenn.
James J. Delaney, N.Y.	Hamer Budge, Idaho
James W. Trimble, Ark.	
Homer Thornberry, Tex.	
Richard Bolling, Mo.	
Thomas P. O'Neill, Jr., Mass.	

87th Congress 1961-62

1st Session

From January 23 to February 6, 1961

Howard W. Smith, Va.	Clarence J. Brown, Ohio
William M. Colmer, Miss.	B. Carroll Reece, Tenn.
Ray J. Madden, Ind.	
James J. Delaney, N.Y.	
James W. Trimble, Ark.	
Homer Thornberry, Tex.	
Richard Bolling, Mo.	
Thomas P. O'Neill, Jr., Mass.	

On January 31, 1961, a resolution was adopted by the House for the Committee on Rules membership to consist of fifteen members during the 87th Congress.

On February 6, 1961, the following Democrats were appointed to the Committee on Rules:

Carl Elliott, Ala.
B. F. Sisk, Calif.

On February 13, 1961, the following Republicans were appointed to the Committee on Rules:

Katharine St. George, N.Y.
H. Allen Smith, Calif.
Elmer J. Hoffman, Ill.

On March 16, 1961, B. Carroll Reece passed away and on March 28, 1961, William H. Avery, Kan., was appointed in his place.

Majority	*Minority*

2nd Session

Howard W. Smith, Va.	Clarence J. Brown, Ohio
William M. Colmer, Miss.	Katharine St. George, N.Y.
Ray J. Madden, Ind.	H. Allen Smith, Calif.
James J. Delaney, N.Y.	Elmer J. Hoffman, Ill.
James W. Trimble, Ark.	William H. Avery, Kan.
Homer Thornberry, Tex.	
Richard Bolling, Mo.	
Thomas P. O'Neill, Jr., Mass.	
Carl Elliott, Ala.	
B. F. Sisk, Calif.	

88th Congress   1963-64

1st Session

From January 9 to December 9, 1963

Howard W. Smith, Va.	Clarence J. Brown, Ohio
William M. Colmer, Miss.	Katharine St. George, N.Y.
Ray J. Madden, Ind.	H. Allen Smith, Calif.
James J. Delaney, N.Y.	Elmer J. Hoffman, Ill.
James W. Trimble, Ark.	William H. Avery, Kan.
Homer Thornberry, Tex.	
Richard Bolling, Mo.	
Thomas P. O'Neill, Jr., Mass.	
Carl Elliott, Ala.	
B. F. Sisk, Calif.	

On December 10, 1963, Homer Thornberry resigned from the committee and John Young, Tex., was appointed to succeed him.

2nd Session

Howard W. Smith, Va.	Clarence J. Brown, Ohio
William M. Colmer, Miss.	Katharine St. George, N.Y.
Ray J. Madden, Ind.	H. Allen Smith, Calif.
James J. Delaney, N.Y.	Elmer J. Hoffman, Ill.
James W. Trimble, Ark.	William H. Avery, Kan.
Richard Bolling, Mo.	
Thomas P. O'Neill, Jr., Mass	
Carl Elliott, Ala.	
B. F. Sisk, Calif.	
John Young, Tex.	

On June 16, 1964, Elmer J. Hoffman resigned from the committee and John B. Anderson, Ill., was appointed to succeed him.

On June 24, 1964, William H. Avery resigned from the committee and Dave Martin, Nebr., was appointed to succeed him.

Majority	*Minority*

89th Congress 1965-66

1st Session

Howard W. Smith, Va.	Clarence J. Brown, Ohio
William M. Colmer, Miss.	(Died August 23, 1965)
Ray J. Madden, Ind.	H. Allen Smith, Calif.
James J. Delaney, N.Y.	John B. Anderson, Ill.
James W. Trimble, Ark.	Dave Martin, Nebr.
Richard Bolling, Mo.	James H. Quillen, Tenn.
Thomas P. O'Neill, Jr., Mass.	Delbert L. Latta, Ohio
B. F. Sisk, Calif.	(Appointed August 31, 1965)
John Young, Tex.	
Claude Pepper, Fla.	

2nd Session

Howard W. Smith, Va.	H. Allen Smith, Calif.
William M. Colmer, Miss.	John B. Anderson, Ill.
Ray J. Madden, Ind.	Dave Martin, Nebr.
James J. Delaney, N.Y.	James H. Quillen, Tenn.
James W. Trimble, Ark.	Delbert L. Latta, Ohio
Richard Bolling, Mo.	
Thomas P. O'Neill, Jr., Mass.	
B. F. Sisk, Calif.	
John Young, Tex.	
Claude Pepper, Fla.	

90th Congress 1967-68

1st and 2nd Sessions

William M. Colmer, Miss.	H. Allen Smith, Calif.
Ray J. Madden, Ind.	John B. Anderson, Ill.
James J. Delaney, N.Y.	Dave Martin, Nebr.
Richard Bolling, Mo.	James H. Quillen, Tenn.
Thomas P. O'Neill, Jr., Mass.	Delbert L. Latta, Ohio
B. F. Sisk, Calif.	
John Young, Tex.	

Majority	*Minority*
Claude Pepper, Fla.	
Spark M. Matsunaga, Hawaii	
William R. Anderson, Tenn.	

91st Congress 1969-70

1st and 2nd Sessions

Same as in the 90th Congress

92nd Congress 1971-72

1st and 2nd Sessions

Same as in the 90th Congress

93rd Congress 1973-74

1st and 2nd Sessions

Ray J. Madden, Ind.	Dave Martin, Nebr.
James J. Delaney, N.Y.	John B. Anderson, Ill.
Richard Bolling, Mo.	James H. Quillen, Tenn.
B. F. Sisk, Calif.	Delbert L. Latta, Ohio
John Young, Tex.	Del Clawson, Calif.
Claude Pepper, Fla.	
Spark M. Matsunaga, Hawaii	
Morgan F. Murphy, Ill.	
Gillis W. Long, La.	
Clem McSpadden, Okla.	

94th Congress 1975-76

1st and 2nd Sessions

Ray J. Madden, Ind.	James H. Quillen, Tenn.
James J. Delaney, N.Y.	John B. Anderson, Ill.
Richard Bolling, Mo.	Delbert L. Latta, Ohio
B. F. Sisk, Calif.	Del Clawson, Calif.
John Young, Tex.	Trent Lott, Miss.
Claude Pepper, Fla.	
Spark M. Matsunaga, Hawaii	
Morgan F. Murphy, Ill.	
Gillis W. Long, La.	
Joseph Moakley, Mass.	
Andrew Young, Ga.	

Bibliography

Academy of Political Science. *See* Mansfield, Harvey C.

Bailey, Stephen K. *Congress in the Seventies.* New York: St. Martin's Press, 1970.

Bibby, John, and Davidson, Roger. *On Capitol Hill: Studies in the Legislative Process.* New York: Holt, Rinehart and Winston, 1967.

Bolling, Richard. *House Out of Order.* New York: E. P. Dutton & Co., 1965.

———. "What the New Congress Needs Most: Concerning Choice of Chairmanships." *Harpers,* January, 1967, pp. 79-81.

———. *Power in the House: A History of the Leadership of the House of Representatives.* New York: E. P. Dutton & Co., 1968.

Bullock, Charles, III. "Apprenticeship and Committee Assignments in the House of Representatives." *Journal of Politics,* November, 1970, pp. 717-20.

———. "Committee Transfers in the U.S. House of Representatives." Paper prepared for the Midwest Political Science Association Annual Meeting, April 29–May 1, 1971, Chicago.

Carroll, Holbert N. *The House of Representatives and Foreign Affairs.* Revised edition. Boston: Little, Brown & Co., 1966.

Clapp, Charles L. *The Congressman: His Work As He Sees It.* Washington, D.C.: The Brookings Institution, 1963.

Clausen, Aage R. "Home State Influence on Congressional Behavior." Paper presented at the American Political Science Association Annual Meeting, September 8-12, 1970, Los Angeles.

———. *How Congressmen Decide: A Policy Focus.* New York: St. Martin's Press, 1973.

Davidson, Roger H. *The Role of the Congressman.* New York: Pegasus, 1969.

Davidson, Roger H.; Kovenock, David M.; and O'Leary, Michael K. *Congress in Crisis: Politics and Congressional Reform.* Belmont, Calif.: Wadsworth Publishing Co., 1966.

Dexter, Lewis A. *The Sociology and Politics of Congress.* Chicago: Rand McNally & Co., 1969.

Ehrenhalt, Alan. "House Rules Committee Regains Image of Independence." *Congressional Quarterly Weekly Report,* March 30, 1974, pp. 804-10.

Eidenberg, Eugene, and Morey, Roy D. *An Act of Congress: The Legislative Process and the Making of Education Policy.* New York: W. W. Norton & Co., 1969.

Fenno, Richard. *The Power of the Purse: Appropriations Politics in Congress.* Boston: Little, Brown & Co., 1966.

————. "Congressional Committees: A Comparative View." Paper presented at the American Political Science Association Annual Meeting, September 8-12, 1970, Los Angeles.

————. *Congressmen in Committees.* Boston: Little, Brown & Co., 1973.

Fox, Douglas M., and Clapp, Charles H. "The House Rules Committee's Agenda-Setting Function, 1961-1968." *The Journal of Politics,* May, 1970, pp. 440-44.

Froman, Lewis A. *The Congressional Process: Strategies, Rules, and Procedures.* Boston: Little, Brown & Co., 1967.

Galloway, George B. *Congress at the Crossroads.* New York: Thomas Y. Crowell, 1946.

Gawthrop, L. C. "Changing Membership Patterns in House Committees." *American Political Science Review,* June, 1966, pp. 366-73.

Goodwin, George, Jr. *The Little Legislatures: The Committees of Congress.* Amherst: University of Massachusetts Press, 1970.

Green, Mark J.; Fallows, James M.; and Zwick, David R. *Who Runs Congress?* New York: Grossman Publishers, 1972.

Harris, Joseph P. *Congress and the Legislative Process.* New York: McGraw-Hill Book Co., 1972.

Hechler, Kenneth W. *Insurgency: Personalities and Politics of the Taft Era.* 1940. Reprinted. New York: Russell & Russell Publishers, 1964.

Hinckley, Barbara. *The Seniority System in Congress.* Bloomington: Indiana University Press, 1971.

————. *Stability and Change in Congress*. New York: Harper & Row, Publishers, 1971.

House Republican Task Force on Congressional Reform and Minority Staffing. *We Propose: A Modern Congress*. New York: McGraw-Hill Book Co., 1966.

Huitt, Ralph K., and Peabody, Robert L. *Congress: Two Decades of Analysis*. New York: Harper & Row, Publishers, 1969.

Jewell, Malcolm E., and Patterson, Samuel C. *The Legislative Process in the United States*. 2nd edition. New York: Random House, 1973.

Jones, Charles O. *Party and Policy-Making: The House Republican Policy Committee*. New Brunswick, N.J.: Rutgers University Press, 1965.

————. *The Minority Party in Congress*. Boston: Little, Brown & Co., 1970.

Kingdon, John W. *Congressmen's Voting Decisions*. New York: Harper & Row, Publishers, 1973.

Kravitz, Walter. "A Short History of the Development of the House Committee on Rules." Mimeographed. Washington, D.C.: Legislative Reference Service, Library of Congress, 1969.

Lowi, Theodore J., and Ripley, Randall B., eds. *Legislative Politics U.S.A.* 3rd revised edition. Boston: Little, Brown & Co., 1973.

Manley, John. *The Politics of Finance: The House Committee on Ways and Means*. Boston: Little, Brown & Co., 1970.

Mansfield, Harvey C., ed. *Congress against the President*. Proceedings of the Academy of Political Science, vol. 32, no. 1. New York: Praeger Publishers, 1975.

Masters, Nicholas. "Committee Assignments in the House of Representatives." *American Political Science Review*, June, 1961, pp. 345-57.

Matthews, Donald R. *U.S. Senators and Their World*. New York: Random House, 1960.

Mayhew, David R. *Congress: The Electoral Connection*. New Haven: Yale University Press, 1974.

Miller, Clem. *Member of the House: Letters of a Congressman*. Edited by John W. Baker. New York: Charles Scribner's Sons, 1962.

Moley, Raymond. "Smith of Virginia," *Newsweek*, August 25, 1958, p. 80.

Oberdorfer, Don. "Judge Smith Moves with Deliberate Drag." *New York Times Magazine*, January 12, 1964, p. 13.

Orfield, Gary. *Congressional Power: Congress and Social Change.* New York: Harcourt Brace Jovanich, 1974.

Ornstein, Norman J., ed. *Congress in Change: Evolution and Reform.* New York: Praeger Publishers, 1975.

Peabody, Robert, and Polsby, Nelson, eds. *New Perspectives on the House of Representatives.* Chicago: Rand McNally & Co., 1963.

Peabody, Robert L.; Berry, Jeffrey M.; Frasure, William G.; and Goldman, Jerry. *To Enact a Law: Congress and Campaign Financing.* New York: Praeger Publishers, 1972.

Pettit, Lawrence K., and Keynes, Edward, eds. *The Legislative Process in the U.S. Senate.* Chicago: Rand McNally & Co., 1969.

Polsby, Nelson W. *Congress and the Presidency.* 2nd edition. Englewood Cliffs, N.J.: Prentice-Hall, 1971.

———, ed. *Congressional Behavior.* New York: Random House, 1970.

Pratt, R. L. "The Taming of the Shrew: Myth and Politics in the House Committee on Rules." B.A. thesis, Wesleyan University, 1969.

Preston, Nathaniel S., ed. *The Senate Institution.* New York: Van Nostrand Reinhold Co., 1969.

Redman, Eric. *The Dance of Legislation.* New York: Simon and Schuster, 1973.

Rieselbach, Leroy. *Congressional Politics.* New York: McGraw-Hill Book Co., 1972.

———. *Congressional Reform in the Seventies.* Morristown, N.J.: General Learning Press, forthcoming.

Ripley, Randall B. *Majority Party Leadership in Congress.* Boston: Little, Brown & Co., 1969.

———. *Power in the Senate.* New York: St. Martin's Press, 1969.

———. *Congress: Process and Policy.* New York: W. W. Norton & Co., 1975.

Ripley, Randall B., and Franklin, Grace A. *Congress, the Bureaucracy, and Public Policy.* Homewood, Ill.: Dorsey Press, 1976.

Robinson, James A. *House Rules Committee.* Indianapolis: Bobbs-Merrill Co., 1963.

Rohde, David, and Shepsle, Kenneth. "Democratic Committee Assignments in the House of Representatives: Strategic Aspects of a Social Choice Process." *American Political Science Review,* September, 1973, pp. 889-905.

Rundquist, Barry. "The House Seniority System and the Distribution of Prime Military Contracts." Paper delivered at the American

Political Science Association Annual Meeting, September 7-11, 1971, Chicago.

Saloma, John S. *Congress and the New Politics.* Boston: Little, Brown & Co., 1969.

Seligman, Lester G. "Recruitment in Politics." *Prod,* March, 1958, pp. 14-17.

Shannon, W. Wayne. *Party, Constituency and Congressional Voting: A Study of Legislative Behavior in the United States House of Representatives.* Baton Rouge: Louisiana State University Press, 1968.

Tacheron, Donald G., and Udall, Morris K., eds. *Job of the Congressman: An Introduction to Service in the House of Representatives.* 2nd edition. Indianapolis: Bobbs-Merrill Co., 1970.

Truman, David. *The Congressional Party.* New York: John Wiley & Sons, 1959.

————, ed. *The Congress and America's Future.* 2nd edition. Englewood Cliffs, N.J.: Prentice-Hall, 1973.

U.S. House of Representatives, Select Committee on Committees. *Hearings on Committee Organization in the House.* 93rd Congress, 1st session, 1973.

Van Hollen, Christopher. "The House Committee on Rules (1933-1951): Agent of Party and Agent of Opposition." Ph.D. dissertation, Johns Hopkins University, 1951.

Viorst, M. "Speaker vs. the Hard-Liners: House Rules Committee Vacancies." *Reporter,* October 24, 1963, pp. 43-44.

Vogler, David J. *The Third House: Conference Committees in the United States Congress.* Evanston: Northwestern University Press, 1971.

————. *The Politics of Congress.* Boston: Allyn and Bacon, 1973.

Weaver, Warren, Jr. *Both Your Houses: The Truth about Congress.* New York: Praeger Publishers, 1972.

Index